A 1999 HOMETOWN COLLECTION

America's Best Recipes

Oxmoor House®

©1999 by Oxmoor House, Inc.
Book Division of Southern Progress Corporation
P.O. Box 2463, Birmingham, Alabama 35201

ISBN: 0-8487-1832-1
ISSN: 0898-9982

Manufactured in the United States of America
First Printing 1999

Editor-in-Chief: Nancy Fitzpatrick Wyatt
Senior Foods Editor: Susan Payne Stabler
Senior Editor, Copy and Homes: Olivia Kindig Wells
Art Director: James Boone

America's Best Recipes: A 1999 Hometown Collection

Editor: Janice Krahn Hanby
Assistant Editor: Kelly Hooper Troiano
Copy Editor: Donna Baldone
Editorial Assistant: Allison Long
Director, Test Kitchens: Kathleen Royal Phillips
Assistant Director, Test Kitchens: Gayle Hays Sadler
Test Kitchens Staff: Julie Christopher, Natalie E. King,
    L. Victoria Knowles, Regan Miller, Rebecca Mohr,
    Jan A. Smith, Kate M. Wheeler, R.D.
Senior Photographer: Jim Bathie
Photographer: Brit Huckabay
Senior Photo Stylist: Kay E. Clarke
Photo Stylist: Virginia R. Cravens
Production and Distribution Director: Phillip Lee
Associate Production Manager: Theresa L. Beste
Production Assistant: Faye Porter Bonner

CONTRIBUTORS
Designer: Rita Yerby
Editorial Assistant: Shari K. Wimberley
Indexer: Mary Ann Laurens
Project Consultants: Meryle Evans, Jean W. Liles

Cover: Fiesta Cheesecake *(page 64)*

WE'RE HERE FOR YOU!
   We at Oxmoor House are dedicated to serving you with
reliable information that expands your imagination and
enriches your life. We welcome your comments and
suggestions. Please write to us at:
   Oxmoor House, Inc.
   Editor, *America's Best Recipes*
   2100 Lakeshore Drive
   Birmingham, AL 35209

To order additional publications, call 1-205-877-6560.

Contents

Introduction

If you love to cook and share good recipes, you'll love *America's Best Recipes–A 1999 Hometown Collection*. It's a one-of-a-kind cookbook of beloved family recipes found tucked away in fund-raising community cookbooks from all across the country. In this book you'll find the best of regional cuisine as well as cherished family fare gathered from coast to coast. After considerable recipe testing, only those recipes withstanding the scrutiny of our test kitchens staff are found in *America's Best Recipes.* Any minor changes from the originals were made to update can sizes and cooking techniques.

We've kept *America's Best Recipes* unpretentious and easy-to-use for beginner cooks, but the high quality and creativity of the recipes appeals to experienced cooks as well. Because everyone can relate to not having enough time to cook now and then, we've added a Quick and Easy Recipes chapter plus a special Helpful Appliances chapter. These two chapters give you everything you need to get a meal on the table in a hurry. You'll find:

• recipes that can be prepared and cooked in 45 minutes or less
• recipes that conveniently fit your schedule by using helpful appliances, such as the slow cooker, pressure cooker, and microwave oven. They save you time and even let you simmer dinner while you're away from home.

As a bonus, *America's Best Recipes* introduces you to wonderful charitable organizations across America. We invite you to find out more about these groups and their efforts to lend a helping hand to their communities. On page 320 you'll find addresses where you can contact the organizations to place an order for their cookbooks. Your purchase of their publications provides you with family-pleasing recipes as well as the satisfaction of knowing you've helped support the local communities and their charitable causes.

The Editors

Helpful Appliances

Chicky Kowloon, page 19

Helpful Appliances

Even the most organized cook can feel the time constraints of a hectic lifestyle. Fortunately, today's busy cook can choose from a number of helpful, timesaving kitchen appliances that include the slow cooker, pressure cooker, and microwave oven. This special chapter includes a wide range of recipes that depend on these appliances. But first, familiarize yourself with the basics about the appliances.

Slow Cooker

Time is on your side when you use an enclosed electric slow cooker. Made of thick stoneware, the slow cooker bowl or crock is surrounded by an heating system. The low temperature gently and safely simmers food for hours so that, even while you're away from home, you can cook a meal to enjoy later in the day.

TIPS

- Choose the right size slow cooker. They range from 1 to 6 quarts. Some have a convenient removable stoneware liner that's ovenproof and microwave-oven safe. The 1-quart slow cooker has no HIGH or LOW setting, just an ON/OFF switch. It's ideal for making a vegetable side dish or fondue. The 6-quart cooker is ideal for family meals.

- The convenient aspect of slow cookers is that you can match the recipe cooking time to your schedule. For all-day cooking, start on the HIGH setting for 1 hour (to shorten the time it takes to heat up everything), and then reduce to the LOW setting for the remainder of the cooking time. For part-of-the-day cooking, cook the whole time on HIGH. If you want to juggle times, remember that one hour on HIGH generally equals about 2 hours on LOW.

- Don't worry if the food cooks 30 minutes to 1 hour longer than intended—the low cooking temperatures give you a bit of a cushion.

- To ensure that large pieces of meat cook safely in your slow cooker, cut them into smaller pieces before adding them to the pot.

- Fill your slow cooker at least half full for best results. Reduce the recipe's cooking times if using smaller quantities. Always cook with the lid on the cooker, and avoid lifting the lid to peek.

- Allow the slow cooker insert to cool completely before washing it. Running cold water over the insert to cool it may cause it to crack.

- To convert a favorite conventionally prepared recipe to the slow cooker method, reduce the amount of liquid by half, unless you're preparing soup. Avoid recipes that contain dairy products because they can break down during extended cooking times.

Pressure Cooker

Pressure cookers have been used by American cooks since before World War II. They were instantly popular with cooks, but the popularity of pressure cookers dropped with the introduction of frozen dinners.

Today, pressure cookers are back in vogue because they can help you prepare good food fast. They cook foods up to 10 times faster than ordinary methods, and this preserves flavor and nutrients and tenderizes tough cuts of meat.

A pressure cooker has a locking cover and special features that allow steam under pressure to reach temperatures much higher than the boiling point of water. When used according to the manufacturer's directions, a pressure cooker is a safe, convenient, and timesaving way to cook. The recipes in this chapter were tested in a 6-quart pressure cooker.

TIPS
- Check the air vent/cover lock to be sure it moves freely before use. Hold the cover up to a light and look through the vent pipe to make sure the vent is open.

- Never fill the pressure cooker more than one-half to two-thirds full, depending on which type of food you're cooking. (Be sure to consult your manual.)

- Do not pressure-cook applesauce, cranberries, rhubarb, pearl barley, oatmeal or other cereals, split peas, soup mixes containing dried vegetables, or pasta. These food tend to foam and sputter, and may clog the vent.

- Cooking time begins when the pressure regulator begins to rock gently. Adjust the heat as necessary to maintain a slow, steady rocking motion, which indicates that the proper cooking pressure is being maintained. If the pressure regulator is allowed to rock vigorously, excess steam will escape, liquid will evaporate, and food may scorch.

- Cool your dish according to manual directions. In general, for foods that might easily overcook, set the pot in the kitchen sink under cold running water until the pressure drops completely for a "quick release." For food that's dense, the pressure is usually allowed to drop on its own for a "natural release."

- Do not open the cooker until internal pressure is completely reduced, air vent/cover lock has dropped, and no steam escaped when the pressure regulator is removed.

- After each use, wash all parts of your pressure pan. Make sure the vent isn't clogged. When storing the cooker, turn the cover upside down over the pan. Do not fasten the lid to the pan.

Microwave Ovens

Microwave ovens convert electricity to electromagnetic waves which cook the food significantly faster than a conventional oven. Microwave ovens vary significantly in wattage (power output). The higher the oven wattage, the quicker the food cooks. We tested our recipes with 700-watt ovens. With new models on the market, wattage can exceed 1000 watts. Check your manufacturer's direction manual, because if your oven is higher or lower than 700 watts, you may need to adjust the cooking time.

Here are helpful pointers for making the most of your microwave.

TIPS
- When cooking foods that might tend to spatter or dry out, cover containers with microwave-safe plastic wrap. When covering with plastic wrap, vent it by turning back one corner to allow excess steam to escape. When removing plastic wrap, lift it away from you to avoid the escaping steam.

- When trapping moisture is not your goal, loosely cover containers with a sheet of wax paper.

- Because microwave energy tends to penetrate the edges of food first, stirring food or rotating the cooking dish is sometimes recommended in recipes.

- Always test food for doneness after the minimum cooking time given in a recipe has elapsed, using the doneness test specified in the recipe.

Micro Caponata

This pretty microwave version of caponata stars eggplant and olive oil. Dust the mixture with freshly grated Parmesan cheese, and serve it as an appetizer with assorted crackers. For the best flavor serve the caponata at room temperature. You can store it in the refrigerator for one week or freeze it up to one month.

¼ cup olive oil
1 large onion, chopped (about 1½ cups)
1 large celery stalk, cut into ¼-inch pieces (about ½ cup)
¾ pound eggplant, peeled and cut into ¼-inch cubes (about 3½ cups)
1 cup cherry tomatoes, quartered
1 (8-ounce) can tomato sauce
½ cup pitted ripe olives, quartered

½ cup pimiento-stuffed olives
¼ cup sugar
¼ cup tomato paste
¼ cup red wine vinegar
1½ tablespoons capers, drained
1½ teaspoons salt
1 teaspoon dried basil
¾ teaspoon black pepper
¼ teaspoon ground red pepper

Combine oil and onion in a large glass bowl. Cover tightly with heavy-duty plastic wrap, and fold back a small corner of wrap to allow steam to escape. Microwave at HIGH 6 minutes, stirring every 2 minutes.

Add celery; cover and vent. Microwave at HIGH 6 minutes, stirring every 2 minutes.

Add eggplant and remaining 12 ingredients to bowl; cover and vent. Microwave at HIGH 10 minutes, stirring every 3 minutes. Remove from microwave oven; let stand, covered, until cool, stirring occasionally. Serve caponata at room temperature with assorted crackers. Yield: 2¾ cups.

Food Fabulous Food
The Women's Board to Cooper Hospital/
University Medical Center
Camden, New Jersey

Almond-Raspberry Brie

MICROWAVE

1 (12-ounce) wedge Brie
2 tablespoons seedless
 raspberry jam
1 tablespoon Chambord or
 other raspberry-flavored
 liqueur

3 tablespoons sliced almonds,
 toasted
1½ teaspoons brown sugar
1 tablespoon honey

Cut Brie in half horizontally; place bottom half on a microwave-safe serving plate.

Combine jam and liqueur; spoon over bottom half of cheese. Place top half of cheese over jam mixture. (Filling will drip over sides.) Sprinkle with almonds and sugar; drizzle with honey.

Microwave at HIGH 1 minute or just until soft. Serve immediately with gingersnaps. Yield: 6 appetizer servings.

A Capital Affair
The Junior League of Harrisburg, Pennsylvania

Italian Roast Beef

SLOW COOKER

Here's the beef–cooked to tender perfection in beer and seasoned with Italian spices. Toast some big buns, and top with sliced beef and juices.

1 (4-pound) boneless chuck
 roast
1 (10½-ounce) can French
 onion soup
⅔ cup beer

1 teaspoon salt
1 teaspoon black pepper
1 teaspoon garlic salt
1 teaspoon dried oregano
½ teaspoon ground red pepper

Slice roast in half to ensure even cooking; place in a 6-quart electric slow cooker. Combine soup and remaining 6 ingredients; pour over roast. Cover and cook on HIGH setting 1 hour; reduce to LOW setting 7 hours. Remove roast from slow cooker; slice thinly. Skim fat from juices; serve with roast. Yield: 8 servings.   Oahe FCE Club

Fun Cookin' Everyday
North Dakota Association for Family & Community Education
Grand Forks, North Dakota

Slow-Cooker Sauerbraten

The twang of white vinegar is softened by the spicy sweetness of crumbled gingersnaps in this classic German specialty. Serve the tender marinated beef and sauce over spaetzle (tiny noodles or dumplings) for authenticity.

1 (3- to 4-pound) rump roast
1 cup water
1 cup white vinegar
1 medium onion, sliced
1 lemon, sliced
10 whole cloves

6 peppercorns
3 bay leaves
2 tablespoons salt
2 tablespoons sugar
15 gingersnaps, crumbled (we tested with Nabisco)

Place roast in a deep glass bowl. Combine water and next 8 ingredients. Pour mixture over meat; cover and marinate in refrigerator 24 to 36 hours, turning meat occasionally.

Remove meat from marinade, reserving 1½ cups marinade; discard remaining marinade. Slice roast in half to ensure even cooking; place in a 5-quart electric slow cooker, and pour reserved marinade over meat. Cover and cook on HIGH setting 1 hour; reduce to LOW setting 7 to 8 hours or until roast is tender.

Remove meat from slow cooker; set aside, and keep warm. Pour liquid through a wire-mesh strainer into a bowl, discarding solids; return liquid to slow cooker. Add crumbled gingersnaps; cover and cook on HIGH setting 12 to 15 minutes. Serve meat with gravy. Yield: 6 servings.

Nancy Freauff

Tasty Temptations
Our Lady of the Mountains Church
Sierra Vista, Arizona

Hungarian Goulash

SLOW COOKER

Here's a timesaving tip you'll use again and again. To quickly chop a can of whole tomatoes, use kitchen shears to snip the tomatoes while they are still in the can.

2 pounds round steak (¾ inch thick), cut into ½-inch pieces
1 cup chopped onion (about 1 small)
1 clove garlic, minced
2 tablespoons all-purpose flour
1 tablespoon paprika
1 teaspoon salt
½ teaspoon pepper
¼ teaspoon dried thyme
1 (28-ounce) can whole tomatoes, undrained and coarsely chopped
1 bay leaf
1 (8-ounce) carton sour cream
Hot buttered noodles or rice

Combine first 3 ingredients in a 5-quart electric slow cooker, stirring well. Combine flour and next 4 ingredients in a small bowl, stirring well; add to meat mixture, tossing well to coat. Add tomatoes and bay leaf to meat mixture; stir well. Cover and cook on HIGH setting 1 hour; reduce to LOW setting 5½ hours. Stir in sour cream. Cover and cook on LOW setting 30 additional minutes. Serve over noodles or rice. Yield: 8 servings.   Sue Scott

150 Years of Good Eating
St. George Evangelical Lutheran Church
Brighton, Michigan

Traveling Swiss Steak

PRESSURE COOKER

2 (1-pound) round steaks (½ inch thick), cut into serving-size pieces
1 clove garlic, cut in half
¼ cup all-purpose flour
2 tablespoons paprika
1 teaspoon salt
¼ teaspoon pepper
3 tablespoons vegetable oil
1½ cups water
1 small onion, sliced (about ¼ cup)
1 (3-ounce) can sliced mushrooms, drained
½ cup sour cream

Rub both sides of meat with garlic. Combine flour and next 3 ingredients; stir well. Sprinkle flour mixture evenly over both sides of steak, and pound into medaillons, using a meat mallet or rolling pin. Brown meat, in batches, in hot oil in a 6-quart pressure cooker over medium-high heat.

Add water, onion, and mushrooms. Close lid securely. Bring to high pressure over high heat, according to manufacturer's directions. Reduce heat to medium or level needed to maintain high pressure; cook 15 minutes. Remove from heat; let pressure drop without disturbing.

Remove lid so that steam escapes away from you. Remove steak to a serving platter. Stir sour cream into liquid in pressure cooker; cook 5 minutes over medium-high heat, stirring constantly. Serve meat with gravy. Yield: 8 servings.   Mary Farrell

Treasured Recipes
Chaparral Home Extension
Chaparral, New Mexico

Slow-Cooked Pepper Steak   SLOW COOKER

2 pounds top round steak
  (1 inch thick), trimmed
2 tablespoons vegetable oil
1 (14½-ounce) can peeled
  tomato wedges, undrained
  (we tested with Delmonte
  Fresh Cut Fancy Tomato
  Wedges)
2 large green peppers, cut into
  1-inch strips
1 cup chopped onion
¼ cup soy sauce
1 clove garlic, minced
1 teaspoon sugar
1 teaspoon salt
¼ teaspoon black pepper
¼ teaspoon ground ginger
1 tablespoon cornstarch
½ cup cold water
Hot cooked noodles or rice

Cut steak into 3-inch pieces; brown in hot oil in a large skillet over medium-high heat. Transfer steak to a 4-quart electric slow cooker. Add tomatoes and pepper strips.

Combine onion and next 6 ingredients; pour over mixture in slow cooker. Cover and cook on HIGH setting 7 hours.

Combine cornstarch and water, stirring until smooth. Stir into mixture in slow cooker; cook, uncovered, on HIGH setting 10 to 15 minutes or until mixture is thickened. Serve over noodles or rice. Yield: 6 servings.   Pat Streeter

25 Years of Food, Fun & Friendship
Clifton Community Woman's Club
Clifton, Virginia

Ribs, Slow-Cooker Easy

SLOW COOKER

You'll need to degrease the flavorful juices after cooking the beef short ribs. Then lavish juices over mashed potatoes or rice to capture the home-cooked goodness.

3½ pounds lean beef short ribs
1 (8-ounce) can tomato sauce
½ cup finely chopped celery
¼ cup finely chopped onion
2 tablespoons brown sugar
½ teaspoon minced garlic

⅛ teaspoon ground red pepper
3 tablespoons Worcestershire sauce
2 tablespoons lemon juice
2 tablespoons prepared mustard

Place ribs in a 4-quart electric slow cooker. Combine tomato sauce and remaining 8 ingredients in a small bowl; stir well. Pour over ribs. Cover and cook on HIGH setting 1 hour; reduce to LOW setting 7 to 8 hours. Yield: 6 servings.   Claudette Landry

Nun Better: Tastes and Tales from Around a Cajun Table
St. Cecilia School
Broussard, Louisiana

Spaghetti Sauce

SLOW COOKER

1½ pounds ground beef
2 (15-ounce) cans tomato sauce
2 (15-ounce) cans whole tomatoes, undrained and coarsely chopped
2 (6-ounce) cans tomato paste
1 (8-ounce package) sliced fresh mushrooms
1 medium onion, chopped
1 medium-size green pepper, chopped

1 cup water
2 tablespoons brown sugar
2 teaspoons dried basil
1 teaspoon oregano
1 beef-flavored bouillon cube
¼ teaspoon salt
¼ teaspoon black pepper
2 cloves garlic, crushed
Dash of ground red pepper
Hot cooked pasta
Garnish: fresh basil sprig

Brown ground beef in a large nonstick skillet, stirring until it crumbles; drain beef, and place in a 5-quart electric slow cooker. Add tomato sauce and next 14 ingredients to slow cooker. Cover and cook on

HIGH setting 1 hour; reduce to LOW setting 7 hours. Serve over pasta. Garnish, if desired. Yield: 11 cups.   Susie Gerard

Recipes & Remembrances
Women of Opportunity Presbyterian Church
Spokane, Washington

One-Pot Dinner   SLOW COOKER

A bevy of beans and ground beef compose this one-stop dinner dish. A tossed green salad and crusty rolls would add to the nourishment nicely.

1 pound ground beef
1 pound bacon, diced
1 medium onion, chopped
2 (15-ounce) cans pork and beans
1 (16-ounce) can kidney beans, drained
1 (15-ounce) can butter beans, drained

¾ cup ketchup
¼ cup firmly packed brown sugar
3 tablespoons white vinegar
1 tablespoon liquid smoke
1 teaspoon salt
Dash of pepper

Brown ground beef in a large nonstick skillet, stirring until it crumbles. Drain beef, and place in a 4-quart electric slow cooker. Combine bacon and onion in skillet; cook until bacon is crisp. Remove bacon and onion, and place in slow cooker. Add pork and beans and remaining 8 ingredients to slow cooker; cover and cook on HIGH setting 5 hours. Yield: 6 servings.   Barbara Jenkins

Favorite Recipes
Tillamook County Dairy Women
Tillamook, Oregon

Barbecue for Sandwiches

1½ pounds beef stew meat
1½ pounds lean cubed pork
1 medium-size green pepper, chopped
1 small onion, chopped (about 1 cup)
1 (6-ounce) can tomato paste
½ cup firmly packed brown sugar
¼ cup white vinegar
1 tablespoon chili powder
2 teaspoons salt
1 teaspoon dry mustard
2 teaspoons Worcestershire sauce

Combine all ingredients in a 5-quart electric slow cooker. Cover and cook on HIGH setting 8 hours. Shred meat before serving. Yield: 6 servings.

Isabelle White

7 Alarm Cuisine
East Mountain Volunteer Fire Department
Gladewater, Texas

Italian Pork Chops

4 (1-inch-thick) center-cut pork loin chops
1 (8-ounce) package sliced fresh mushrooms
1 medium onion, thinly sliced
1 clove garlic, minced
1 (8-ounce) can tomato sauce
1 (6-ounce) can tomato paste
¾ cup water
¼ cup dry sherry
1 tablespoon lemon juice
½ teaspoon dried parsley flakes
¼ teaspoon dried oregano
¼ teaspoon dried basil
2 medium-size green peppers, cut into very thin strips
Hot cooked rice or egg noodles

Brown chops in a large nonstick skillet over medium-high heat. Drain on paper towels; set aside.

Place mushrooms, onion, and garlic in a 4-quart electric slow cooker. Arrange chops on top of vegetables. Combine tomato sauce and next 7 ingredients in a medium bowl. Stir well, and pour tomato mixture over chops. Cover and cook on HIGH setting 1 hour; reduce to LOW setting 7 hours.

Add green pepper strips to slow cooker; cover and cook on HIGH setting 30 minutes. Serve chops with rice or egg noodles. Yield: 4 servings.   Janeen Ashbrook Huppert

Morrisonville's 125th Anniversary Cookbook
Morrisonville Historical Society & Museum
Morrisonville, Illinois

Venison Swiss Steak   SLOW COOKER

Fines herbes, a mixture of chervil, chives, parsley, and tarragon, add complex flavor notes to this venison dish.

3 slices bacon
2 pounds venison round steak
½ teaspoon salt
¼ teaspoon pepper
¼ teaspoon paprika
1 tablespoon olive oil
1 medium onion, sliced
1 (14½-ounce) can diced
    tomatoes, undrained

1 (1-ounce) envelope onion
    soup mix
½ cup dry red wine
¼ teaspoon fines herbes
2 tablespoons water
1 tablespoon cornstarch

Cook bacon in a large skillet until crisp; remove bacon, reserving drippings in skillet. Reserve bacon for another use. Set skillet aside.

Pound steak to ½-inch thickness, using a meat mallet. Cut into 4 pieces; sprinkle salt, pepper, and paprika over both sides. Cook, in batches, in reserved bacon drippings in skillet over medium-high heat until browned on both sides. Remove to a 4-quart electric slow cooker.

Add 1 tablespoon oil to skillet; add onion. Cook over medium-high heat, stirring constantly, 5 minutes or until tender. Add tomatoes, soup mix, wine, and fines herbes. Bring to a boil; pour over steaks.

Cover and cook on LOW setting 8 hours or until meat is tender. Remove steaks to a serving platter, reserving tomato mixture in slow cooker. Combine water and cornstarch; stir until blended. Stir into tomato mixture. Cook on HIGH setting, uncovered, until slightly thickened, stirring often. Pour tomato mixture over steaks. Yield: 4 servings.

Cheyenne Frontier Days "Daddy of 'em All" Cookbook
Chuckwagon Gourmet
Cheyenne, Wyoming

Quick Mediterranean Fish

MICROWAVE

1 medium onion, sliced
1 clove garlic, crushed
2 tablespoons olive oil
1 (14½-ounce) can Italian-style stewed tomatoes, undrained
3 to 4 tablespoons medium-flavor green chile pepper salsa

¼ teaspoon ground cinnamon
1½ pounds red snapper, halibut, sea bass, or cod
12 pimiento-stuffed olives, cut in half crosswise

Combine first 3 ingredients in a 1½-quart microwaveable casserole. Cover with heavy-duty plastic wrap; fold back a small corner of wrap to allow steam to escape. Microwave at HIGH 3 minutes; drain liquid. Add tomatoes, salsa, and cinnamon; place fish over tomato mixture, and top with olives. Cover and vent; microwave at HIGH 6 minutes or until fish flakes easily when tested with a fork. Yield: 4 servings.

Carolina Sunshine, Then & Now
The Charity League of Charlotte, North Carolina

Cranberry Chicken

SLOW COOKER

Serve this sweet-and-sour chicken thigh combo over rice or noodles to soak up the sassy sauce.

1 small onion, thinly sliced
1 cup fresh or frozen cranberries
12 skinned and boned chicken thighs
¼ cup ketchup
2 tablespoons firmly packed brown sugar

1 teaspoon dry mustard
½ teaspoon salt
2 teaspoons cider vinegar
1½ tablespoons cornstarch
2 tablespoons cold water

Combine onion and cranberries in a 4-quart electric slow cooker. Arrange chicken on top of cranberry mixture.

Combine ketchup and next 4 ingredients; pour over chicken. Cover and cook on HIGH setting 1 hour; reduce to LOW setting 6 hours or until chicken is very tender. Transfer chicken to a serving platter, and keep warm.

Combine cornstarch and water, stirring until smooth. Stir into mixture in slow cooker; cook, uncovered, on HIGH setting 10 to 15 minutes or until mixture is thickened. Pour over chicken. Yield: 6 servings.

Home Cooking
Bison American Lutheran Church
Bison, South Dakota

Chicky Kowloon

SLOW COOKER

3½ pounds chicken breast halves and thighs, skinned
½ teaspoon salt
¼ teaspoon pepper
1 cup chicken broth
1 clove garlic, minced
¼ teaspoon ground ginger
1 (8½-ounce) can sliced pineapple in heavy syrup, undrained

1 (4-ounce) can sliced water chestnuts, drained
4 green onions, diagonally sliced
¼ cup soy sauce
1 tablespoon white vinegar
¼ cup cornstarch
Chow mein noodles
Hot cooked rice

Sprinkle chicken with salt and pepper; place in a 5-quart electric slow cooker.

Combine chicken broth, garlic, and ginger, stirring well. Drain pineapple, reserving syrup. Add syrup to broth mixture, stirring well; cut pineapple slices into fourths. Arrange pineapple and water chestnuts over chicken. Pour broth mixture over chicken. Cover and cook on HIGH setting 1 hour; reduce to LOW setting 6 to 7 hours.

Add green onions to mixture in slow cooker. Combine soy sauce and vinegar; add cornstarch, stirring until smooth. Stir into broth mixture, gently moving chicken pieces. Cover and cook on HIGH setting 10 minutes or until slightly thickened. Serve with chow mein noodles over rice. Yield: 6 servings.   Pat Warner

Howey Cook
Howey-in-the-Hills Garden and Civic Club
Howey-in-the-Hills, Florida

Vegetable Turkey Pie

MICROWAVE

Convenience products abound in this quick and easy turkey pie. If time allows, make your own mashed potatoes to propel the dish into out-of-the-ordinary territory.

2 cups frozen mixed vegetables
2 tablespoons water
⅓ cup ketchup
1 teaspoon prepared mustard
1 pound ground turkey
1 large egg, beaten
½ cup Italian-seasoned breadcrumbs
½ cup fat-free milk
¼ teaspoon salt
Dash of pepper
2⅔ cups instant mashed potatoes (we tested with Idahoan)
3 (¾-ounce) slices process American cheese, cut into triangles

Combine vegetables and water in a 1-quart microwaveable casserole. Cover tightly with heavy-duty plastic wrap; fold back a small corner of wrap to allow steam to escape. Microwave at HIGH 4 minutes or until crisp-tender; set aside.

Combine ketchup and mustard; set aside. Combine turkey and next 5 ingredients, stirring well. Press turkey mixture in bottom and up sides of an ungreased 9-inch pieplate. Cover loosely with wax paper; microwave at HIGH 6 minutes or until thoroughly cooked, turning once. Drain liquid. Spread with ketchup mixture.

Prepare potatoes according to package directions. Spread potatoes over turkey mixture; top with vegetables. Arrange cheese over vegetables. Microwave, uncovered, at HIGH 1 to 2 minutes or until cheese melts. Yield: 6 servings.

Brunetta S. Pfaender

Under the Canopy
The GFWC Tallahassee Junior Woman's Club
Tallahassee, Florida

Steak Soup

1½ pounds round steak, cut
  into ½-inch cubes
½ cup margarine, melted
1 cup all-purpose flour
6 cups water, divided
1 (14½-ounce) can stewed
  tomatoes, undrained
1 (10-ounce) package frozen
  mixed vegetables
3 cups peeled, diced baking
  potato

1 cup diced carrot
1 cup diced celery
¼ cup beef-flavored bouillon
  granules
1 (1-ounce) package onion soup
  mix
1 teaspoon sugar
¼ teaspoon salt
¼ teaspoon pepper

Brown beef in margarine in a large Dutch oven over medium-high heat; place in a 5-quart electric slow cooker. Combine flour and 3 cups water, stirring until smooth. Pour over beef in slow cooker. Add remaining 3 cups water, tomatoes, and remaining ingredients to slow cooker. Cook on HIGH setting 1 hour; reduce to LOW setting 7 hours. Yield: 16 cups.

Rhonda Myers

United Methodist Church Cookbook
Cairo United Methodist Church Women
Cairo, Nebraska

Hunter's Stew

SLOW COOKER

Pair this hearty stew with rye or pumpernickel bread and a robust ale.

1 pound Polish sausage, diagonally sliced into 1-inch pieces
1 (7-ounce) can sliced mushrooms, undrained
1 large cooking apple, peeled, cored, and sliced
2 (14.5-ounce cans) sauerkraut, rinsed and drained
1 medium onion, chopped
1 (14½-ounce) can diced tomatoes, undrained
3 strips bacon, cooked and crumbled

Place all ingredients in a 4-quart electric slow cooker, layering in order listed. Cook on HIGH setting 1 hour; reduce to LOW setting 7 hours. Yield: 8 cups.

Love for Others
Our Shepherd Lutheran Church
Birmingham, Michigan

Wild Game Stew

SLOW COOKER

If you're not a hunter, you can substitute beef or lamb for the venison in this man-pleaser of a stew. Serve bowlfuls with French or sourdough bread and a spirited red wine to suit.

2 pounds venison round roast, cut into 1-inch cubes
¼ cup all-purpose flour
1½ teaspoons salt
½ teaspoon pepper
2 baking potatoes, peeled, if desired, and diced
2 carrots, scraped and sliced
1 medium onion, chopped
1 stalk celery, chopped
1 clove garlic, minced
1 teaspoon paprika
1 bay leaf
1 cup beef broth
½ cup dry red wine
¼ cup brandy
1 teaspoon Worcestershire sauce
2 teaspoons seasoning and browning sauce (optional)

Place meat in a 4-quart electric slow cooker. Combine flour, salt, and pepper. Add to meat; stirring well. Add potato, next 10 ingredients, and seasoning and browning sauce, if desired; stirring well. Cover and cook on HIGH setting 1 hour; reduce to LOW setting 7 hours. Remove and discard bay leaf before serving. Yield: 6 servings.

Here, There & Everywhere
Volunteers in Overseas Cooperative Assistance
Washington, DC

Venison Chili

2 pounds ground venison or beef
1 medium onion, chopped
2 teaspoons chili powder
1 tablespoon Worcestershire sauce
1 (28-ounce) can whole tomatoes, undrained and coarsely chopped

1 (15-ounce) can tomato sauce
1 (16-ounce) can pinto beans, drained
1 (7-ounce) can mushroom pieces, drained
2 jalapeño peppers, sliced
1 teaspoon ground cumin

Cook first 4 ingredients in a large nonstick skillet over medium-high heat, stirring until meat is browned and crumbles. Transfer meat mixture to a 4-quart electric slow cooker; add tomatoes and remaining ingredients, stirring well. Cover and cook on HIGH setting 1 hour; reduce to LOW setting 3 hours. Yield: 12 cups.   Todd Sisk

Mounds of Cooking
Parkin Archeological Support Team
Parkin, Arkansas

Patty's Chili

2½ pounds beef chuck roast
2½ pounds pork rump roast
3 tablespoons vegetable oil, divided
1 medium onion, finely chopped
4 cloves garlic, minced
1 (28-ounce) can whole tomatoes, undrained and chopped

1 (46-ounce) can tomato juice
1 (15-ounce) can pinto beans, drained
1 (4.5-ounce) can chopped green chiles, undrained
¼ cup chili powder
2 tablespoons ground cumin
1½ teaspoons salt
1 teaspoon sugar
½ teaspoon pepper

Trim excess fat from meat; cut meat into bite-size pieces. Cook half of meat in 1 tablespoon oil in a large skillet over medium-high heat 10 minutes or until browned. Transfer meat to a 5-quart electric slow cooker. Repeat procedure with remaining half of meat, using an additional 1 tablespoon oil.

Cook onion and garlic in remaining 1 tablespoon oil in skillet over medium-high heat, stirring constantly, until tender. Add tomatoes to skillet, deglazing skillet by scraping particles that cling to bottom. Add tomato mixture, tomato juice, and remaining ingredients to slow cooker; stir well. Cover and cook on HIGH setting 1 hour; reduce to LOW setting 7 hours. Yield: 16 cups.   Patty O'Brien

The Phoenix Zoo Auxiliary Cookbook
Phoenix Zoo Auxiliary
Phoenix, Arizona

911 Chili

Don't let the title make you think that this chili is in the danger zone as far as being hot and fiery—it's really on the tame side. The catchy designation comes courtesy of the contributor who happens to be a paramedic.

2 pounds ground round
2 cups water
2 (6-ounce) cans no-salt-added
   tomato paste
1 large onion, finely chopped
1 clove garlic, minced
2 large bay leaves
3 tablespoons chili powder
1 tablespoon ground cumin
2 teaspoons ground allspice
1½ teaspoons ground
   cinnamon

1 teaspoon salt
1 teaspoon black pepper
¼ teaspoon ground red pepper
1 teaspoon white wine vinegar
1 teaspoon Worcestershire
   sauce
Hot cooked spaghetti
Shredded Cheddar cheese
Chopped onion
Oyster crackers

Combine beef and water in a 4-quart pressure cooker; stir until thoroughly blended. Add tomato paste and next 12 ingredients, stirring well. Close lid securely; place pressure regulator on vent pipe, and cook over high heat until pressure regulator rocks quickly back and forth. Reduce heat to medium or until pressure regulator rocks slowly, and cook 15 minutes. Remove from heat.

Run cold water over pressure cooker to reduce pressure instantly. Remove lid so that steam escapes away from you.

Remove and discard bay leaves. Stir chili well. Serve over hot spaghetti, and top with cheese, onion, and oyster crackers. Yield: 5 cups.

Mark O'Keefe

Souvenirs of Mount Dora, Florida
GFWC Mount Dora Area Junior Woman's Club
Mount Dora, Florida

Mexican Lasagna

1 medium onion, chopped (about 1½ cups)
1 medium-size green pepper, chopped (about 1¼ cups)
2 cloves garlic, minced
1½ teaspoons olive oil
1 teaspoon ground cumin
Dash of ground red pepper
1 (16-ounce) can pinto beans, drained
1 (8-ounce) can tomato sauce
1 cup frozen whole kernel corn
6 (6-inch) corn tortillas
1 cup 1% low-fat cottage cheese
1 cup (4 ounces) shredded Cheddar cheese

Cook first 3 ingredients in oil in a large skillet over medium-high heat, stirring constantly, until vegetables are tender. Stir in cumin and red pepper; cook 1 minute. Remove from heat; stir in beans, tomato sauce, and corn.

Place 3 tortillas in bottom of a lightly greased 11- x 7- x 1½-inch baking dish. Spread half of bean mixture over tortillas. Spread half of cottage cheese over bean mixture; sprinkle with half of Cheddar cheese. Layer remaining 3 tortillas over cheese. Repeat layers with remaining bean mixture, cottage cheese, and Cheddar cheese.

Microwave, uncovered, at HIGH 12 minutes or until thoroughly heated, turning one-quarter turn after 6 minutes. Let stand 5 minutes before serving. Yield: 6 servings.

Marla Knutsen

Literally Delicious!
California Literacy, Inc.
San Gabriel, California

Baked Beans

2 pounds ground chuck
1 large onion, chopped
3 (16-ounce) cans pork and
beans
1 (12-ounce) jar chili sauce
1 (8-ounce) can crushed
pineapple, drained

1 cup firmly packed brown
sugar
1 tablespoon dry mustard
1 tablespoon Worcestershire
sauce
6 slices bacon, cooked and
crumbled

Brown meat and onion in a large skillet, stirring until meat crumbles and onion is tender; drain.

Combine meat mixture, pork and beans, and remaining ingredients in a 4-quart electric slow cooker, stirring well. Cover and cook on HIGH setting 3½ hours. Yield: 10 servings.   Hope Weatherly

Carolina Cuisine: Nothin' Could Be Finer
The Junior Charity League of Marlboro County
Bennettsville, South Carolina

Golden Grated Carrots

1 pound carrots, scraped and
shredded
2 tablespoons dry white wine
1 tablespoon butter or
margarine

1 tablespoon honey
2 teaspoons lemon juice
⅓ cup golden raisins
1½ teaspoons brown sugar
1 teaspoon curry powder

Place carrot in a lightly greased 1½-quart baking dish. Add wine and next 3 ingredients, stirring well. Cover tightly with heavy-duty plastic wrap; fold back a small corner of wrap to allow steam to escape. Microwave at HIGH 5 to 6 minutes or until carrot is crisp-tender. Uncover and stir in raisins, brown sugar, and curry powder. Cover and microwave at HIGH 1 to 2 minutes or until thoroughly heated. Let stand, covered, 2 minutes. Uncover and stir; serve immediately. Yield: 5 servings.

O Taste & Sing
St. Stephen's Episcopal Church Choir
Richmond, Virginia

Corn

Five basic ingredients and no stirring on the front end make this potluck pleaser a breeze to make.

2 (1 pound, 12 ounce) bags
  frozen whole kernel corn
½ cup butter or margarine
1 (8-ounce) package cream
  cheese

¼ cup plus 2 tablespoons water
2 tablespoons sugar

    Place all ingredients in a 4-quart electric slow cooker (do not stir). Cover and cook on LOW setting 4 hours. Stir well before serving. Yield: 8 cups.

Cathy De Witt

Home Cooking
Sunshine City Library
Prairie View, Kansas

Delicious Potatoes

We tested this cheesy potato side dish with cream of potato soup, but it would be just as delicious using cream of celery or mushroom soup. Use whichever you prefer.

1 (26-ounce) package frozen
  country-style shredded
  potatoes
1 (10¾-ounce) can cream of
  potato soup
1⅓ cups milk
1 tablespoon butter or
  margarine

½ teaspoon salt
¾ teaspoon pepper
1 teaspoon grated onion
1 cup (4 ounces) shredded
  Cheddar cheese

    Combine first 7 ingredients in a 5-quart electric slow cooker. Cover and cook on LOW setting 7½ hours. Stir in cheese, and cook 30 additional minutes. Yield: 8 servings.

Hilda Kruse

A Taste of Greene
Playground Committee
Greene, Iowa

German Potato Salad

Tantalizingly top this classic warm potato salad with slices of hard-cooked eggs before serving.

4 medium onions, thinly sliced
4½ pounds medium-size red
    potatoes, cooked and peeled
    (about 20)
½ cup plus 2 tablespoons
    all-purpose flour
½ cup plus 2 tablespoons sugar
1 tablespoon plus 2 teaspoons
    salt

1 tablespoon plus 2 teaspoons
    dry mustard
2½ teaspoons celery seeds
1¼ teaspoons pepper
2¾ cups water
1⅔ cups cider vinegar
4 slices bacon, cooked and
    crumbled

Place onion in bottom of a 4-quart electric slow cooker. Cut potatoes into quarters; place on top of onion.

Combine flour and next 5 ingredients in a large saucepan; stir well with a wire whisk. Combine water and vinegar; gradually add to flour mixture, stirring well. Cook over medium-high heat, stirring constantly, until slightly thickened; pour over vegetables.

Cover and cook on LOW setting 5 hours. Sprinkle with bacon, and serve warm. Yield: 15 servings.

Betty Ruete

Savoring Cape Cod
Massachusetts Audubon Society/Wellfleet Bay Wildlife Sanctuary
South Wellfleet, Massachusetts

Overnight Cornbread Casserole MICROWAVE

2 cups frozen mixed vegetables,
   slightly thawed
1½ cups cubed cooked ham
1 (8-ounce) package cornbread
   stuffing mix (we tested with
   Pepperidge Farm)
2 cups milk

3 large eggs, lightly beaten
¼ teaspoon salt
¼ teaspoon freshly ground
   pepper
½ cup (2 ounces) shredded
   Cheddar cheese

Combine first 3 ingredients in a large bowl; pour mixture into a greased 11- x 7- x 1½-inch baking dish. Combine milk and next 3 ingredients in a bowl, stirring well; pour over cornbread mixture. Cover and chill at least 5 hours.

Uncover casserole, and cover loosely with a sheet of wax paper. Microwave at HIGH 7 minutes. Give dish a quarter-turn, and microwave at MEDIUM HIGH (70% power) 10 minutes or until done. Let casserole stand, covered, 10 minutes before serving. Yield: 6 servings.
Veronica Kessler

Let's Get Cooking
Monvale Health Resources Auxiliary
Monongahela, Pennsylvania

Creole Spanish Rice MICROWAVE

½ cup onion, chopped
2 tablespoons butter or
   margarine
⅓ cup green pepper, chopped
2 green onions, chopped
½ pound smoked or hot link
   sausage, sliced
1 (11.5-ounce) can vegetable
   juice

1 cup water
1 cup long-grain rice, uncooked
1 bay leaf
1 teaspoon dried parsley flakes
½ teaspoon salt
¼ teaspoon ground red pepper
Dash of garlic powder
Dash of Worcestershire sauce

Place onion and butter in a 2-quart microwaveable casserole; microwave, uncovered, at HIGH 3 minutes. Add green pepper and green onions; microwave, uncovered, at HIGH 3 minutes. Add sausage, vegetable juice, and water, stirring well. Microwave, uncovered, at HIGH 3 minutes. Stir in rice and remaining ingredients.

Cover and microwave at MEDIUM (50% power) 25 minutes. Let stand, covered, 10 minutes before serving. Remove and discard bay leaf. Yield: 4 servings.   John A. Broussard, Sr.

Somethin' to Smile About
St. Martin, Iberia, Lafayette Community Action Agency
Lafayette, Louisiana

Apple Butter

SLOW COOKER

2 quarts unsweetened
  applesauce
3½ cups sugar
⅔ cup firmly packed brown
  sugar

2⅔ tablespoons vinegar
2⅔ tablespoons lemon juice
1 teaspoon ground cinnamon
1 teaspoon ground allspice
1 teaspoon ground cloves

Combine all ingredients in a 4-quart electric slow cooker; cover and cook mixture on HIGH setting 2½ hours, stirring occasionally. Remove lid, and continue cooking, reducing heat to LOW setting if mixture begins to bubble up, 4½ hours or until mixture becomes very thick.

Immediately pack hot apple mixture into hot jars, filling to ¼ inch from top. Remove air bubbles; wipe jar rims. Cover at once with metal lids, and screw on bands.

Process in boiling water bath 20 minutes for pints; process 25 minutes for quarts. Yield: 10 cups.   Mary L. Traylor

Green Thumbs in the Kitchen
Green Thumb, Inc.
Arlington, Virginia

Citrus-Spiked Cranberry Sauce MICROWAVE

Easy! This microwave cranberry sauce goes from kitchen to table in about 15 minutes.

1 pound fresh or frozen
   cranberries, thawed
1 to 1½ cups sugar
1 tablespoon grated orange
   rind

1 cup orange juice
Dash of salt

Combine ingredients in a 2-quart microwaveable casserole. Cover with heavy-duty plastic wrap; fold back a small corner of wrap to allow steam to escape. Microwave at HIGH 10 to 15 minutes; stir every 5 minutes, until cranberry skins pop. Let stand, covered, 5 minutes. Stir. Serve warm or chilled. Yield: 2¾ cups.   Marilyn S. Short

Cooking in Harmony: Opus II
Brevard Music Center, Inc.
Brevard, North Carolina

Bread and Butter Pickles MICROWAVE

1 cup sugar
½ cup white vinegar (5%
   acidity)
1 teaspoon salt
½ teaspoon celery seeds
½ teaspoon mustard seeds

½ teaspoon ground turmeric
3 medium pickling cucumbers,
   cut into ¼-inch slices (about
   3 cups)
3 small onions, thinly sliced
   (about 2 cups)

Combine first 6 ingredients in a large microwaveable bowl, stirring well. Add cucumber and onion; stir well.

Microwave at HIGH 8 minutes, stirring every 2 minutes. Pack mixture evenly into hot, sterilized jars, filling to ½ inch from top. Cover with metal lids, and screw on bands. Let cool completely. Store in refrigerator. Yield: 2 pints.   Alberta S. Coots

Crossroads Cookbook
New Albany-Plain Township Historical Society
New Albany, Ohio

Bread Pudding

Supereasy and simply divine. If desired, add a bourbon or vanilla sauce to complement.

4 cups French bread cubes	**2 cups milk**
½ cup raisins	**¼ cup butter or margarine**
½ cup firmly packed brown sugar	**2 large eggs, beaten**

Place bread cubes in a greased 1½-quart round baking dish. Sprinkle with raisins and brown sugar.

Combine milk and butter in a 1-quart measuring cup; microwave at HIGH 4 minutes or until butter melts, stirring after 2 minutes. Gradually stir about one-fourth of hot milk mixture into eggs; add to remaining hot mixture, stirring constantly. Pour egg mixture over bread mixture. Microwave at HIGH 10 minutes or until set. Let stand 5 minutes before serving. Yield: 6 servings.

Recollections & Recipes
Deer Lake Writers' Workshop
Nashville, Tennessee

Lemon Pie

Ten minutes is all it takes to make this tangy lemon pie. We put the tart filling in a pastry shell, but you can also use a 9-inch graham cracker crust.

1¾ cups water, divided
1 cup sugar
¼ cup cornstarch
¼ teaspoon salt
3 egg yolks, lightly beaten

2 tablespoons butter
⅓ cup lemon juice
1 baked 9-inch pastry shell
Whipped cream

Combine ¼ cup water, sugar, cornstarch, and salt in a 1½-quart baking dish; set aside. Microwave remaining 1½ cups water at HIGH 2 to 3 minutes or until boiling. Stir boiling water into sugar mixture. Microwave at HIGH 4 to 6 minutes or until very thick, stirring every 2 minutes.

Gradually stir about one-fourth of hot sugar mixture into beaten egg yolks; add to remaining hot mixture, stirring constantly. Microwave at HIGH 1 minute. Stir in butter and lemon juice. Let mixture cool slightly; pour into pastry shell. Spread whipped cream over filling. Chill. Yield: one 9-inch pie.   Jean Butzer

Sampler Cookbook
Clarence Log Cabin Quilters
Clarence, New York

Quick & Easy Recipes

Quick and Easy Pie, page 52

Cheesy Almond Spread

1 (8-ounce) package cream
   cheese, softened
1½ cups (6 ounces) shredded
   Swiss cheese
⅓ cup sliced almonds
⅓ cup mayonnaise or salad
   dressing

2 tablespoons chopped green
   onions
¼ teaspoon ground nutmeg
⅛ teaspoon pepper
Garnish: toasted almond slices

Combine first 7 ingredients, stirring well. Spread mixture into a 9-inch pieplate. Bake, uncovered, at 350° for 15 minutes or until heated. Garnish, if desired. Serve with crackers. Yield: 2 cups.   Judy Cross

Party Pleasers
GFWC Philomathic Club
Duncan, Oklahoma

Peppy Pimiento Cheese

This sassy cheese blend is really two recipes in one. Serve it chilled as a light sandwich spread or warm as a cheese sauce for pasta or a dipping sauce for fresh vegetables, breadsticks, and crackers. For a thicker spread, drain the pimientos.

1 (16-ounce) loaf process
   cheese spread, cubed (we
   tested with Velveeta)
⅓ cup milk
1 (8-ounce) jar diced pimiento,
   undrained

1 large egg, beaten
3 tablespoons sugar
2 tablespoons white vinegar
⅛ teaspoon hot sauce
1 cup mayonnaise

Combine cheese and milk in a large saucepan. Cook over low heat until cheese melts, stirring often. Whisk in pimiento and next 4 ingredients; cook over low heat, stirring constantly, 15 minutes or until mixture thickens slightly. Remove from heat; stir in mayonnaise. Let cool. Cover and chill. Store in refrigerator. Yield: 4 cups.   Lois Gulledge

Recollections and Recipes
Deer Lake Writers' Workshop
Nashville, Tennessee

Orange Fizz

A generous dose of vodka or gin gives this citrus refresher a mighty punch. If you prefer a milder medley, just decrease the amount of alcohol accordingly. Create a child-friendly version by replacing the alcohol with sparkling water.

1½ cups orange juice
2 cups orange sherbet

1 cup vodka or gin
Garnish: fresh orange slices

Combine first 3 ingredients in container of an electric blender; process until smooth, stopping once to scrape down sides. Pour into stemmed glasses; garnish, if desired. Yield: 4 cups. Yolanda Williams

Literally Delicious!
California Literacy, Inc.
San Gabriel, California

Cheese-Garlic Biscuits

Pump up the personality of these easy drop biscuits by using a sharp Cheddar cheese instead of mild Cheddar.

2 cups biscuit and baking mix
 (we tested with Bisquick)
⅔ cup milk
½ cup (2 ounces) shredded
 sharp Cheddar cheese

¼ cup butter or margarine,
 melted
¼ teaspoon garlic powder

Combine first 3 ingredients in a medium bowl; beat with a wooden spoon until blended.

Drop dough by heaping tablespoonfuls onto an ungreased baking sheet. Bake at 350° for 12 to 13 minutes or until golden.

Combine butter and garlic powder; brush over tops of biscuits. Serve immediately. Yield: 10 biscuits.   Marge Wolf

Note Worthy Recipes
Wilson Presbyterian Church
Clairton, Pennsylvania

Italian Biscuit Flat Bread

Treat your hungry after-school crowd to these pizzalike flat breads. They're also the perfect accompaniment with bowlfuls of creamy tomato soup.

⅓ cup thinly sliced green onions
⅓ cup grated Parmesan cheese
⅓ cup mayonnaise
1 clove garlic, minced, or ⅛ teaspoon garlic powder
¼ teaspoon dried basil
¼ teaspoon dried oregano
1 (12-ounce) can refrigerated flaky biscuits (we tested with Hungry Jack)

Combine first 6 ingredients in a small bowl; stir well.

Press each biscuit into a 4-inch circle on an ungreased baking sheet. Spread about 1 tablespoon cheese mixture evenly on circles, leaving a ¼-inch border.

Bake at 400° for 8 to 10 minutes or until golden. Yield: 10 flat breads.
Jean McLain

A Taste of Gem Valley Country Living
North Gem Valley Development Corporation
Bancroft, Idaho

Breadsticks

½ (32-ounce) package frozen bread dough, thawed
1 cup grated Parmesan cheese
1½ teaspoons dried Italian seasoning
½ cup butter, melted

Divide bread dough into 8 portions; divide each portion into 4 pieces. Roll each piece into a 4-inch strip.

Combine cheese and Italian seasoning; dip strips in melted butter, and roll strips in cheese mixture. Place strips on greased baking sheets. Bake at 450° for 6 to 7 minutes or until lightly browned. Yield: 32 breadsticks.
Melinda Ross

Home Cooking
Sunshine City Library
Prairie View, Kansas

Grilled Porterhouse Steaks

¼ cup olive oil
2 tablespoons minced fresh basil
4 cloves garlic, crushed

2 (2-pound) porterhouse steaks
1 tablespoon seasoned salt
1 tablespoon freshly ground pepper

Combine first 3 ingredients in a small bowl. Rub oil mixture on both sides of steaks; sprinkle with seasoned salt and pepper. Grill, covered, over medium-hot coals (350° to 400°) 10 minutes on each side or to desired degree of doneness. Yield: 4 servings.   Paul Kirk

The Kansas City Barbeque Society Cookbook
Kansas City Barbeque Society
Kansas City, Missouri

Salisbury Steak

Serve these savory patties with plenty of mashed potatoes or hot cooked rice to soak up every bit of the mushroom gravy. These patties are comfort food at its best!

1 (10¾-ounce) can beefy mushroom soup, divided
1½ pounds ground chuck
1 large egg, beaten
½ cup fine, dry breadcrumbs (store-bought)

¼ cup finely chopped onion
⅛ teaspoon pepper
¼ cup water

Combine ¼ cup soup, ground chuck, and next 4 ingredients, mixing well. Divide meat mixture evenly into 6 portions. Shape each portion into a ½-inch-thick patty.

Cook patties in a large nonstick skillet over medium-high heat 3 to 4 minutes on each side or until browned.

Combine remaining soup and water, stirring well. Pour soup mixture over patties; cover, reduce heat, and simmer 20 minutes. Serve immediately. Yield: 6 servings.

Stepping Back to Old Butler
Butler Ruritan Club
Butler, Tennessee

Taco Casserole

1 pound ground beef
½ cup chopped onion
1 (1¼-ounce) package taco
   seasoning mix
1 (15½-ounce) can chili hot
   beans, undrained

1 (8-ounce) can tomato sauce
2 cups (8 ounces) shredded
   Colby cheese
1 (9-ounce) package nacho
   cheese-flavored tortilla chips,
   crushed

Brown ground beef and onion in a large skillet, stirring until beef crumbles and onion is tender; drain.

Return meat mixture to skillet; stir in taco seasoning, chili beans, and tomato sauce. Layer half each of meat mixture, shredded cheese, and tortilla chips in a lightly greased 13- x 9- x 2-inch baking dish. Repeat procedure with remaining meat mixture, shredded cheese, and tortilla chips.

Bake, uncovered, at 350° for 25 minutes or until thoroughly heated. Yield: 6 servings.

Cindy Skuce

Food for the Soul
Campground Church Ladies
Fosterville, Tennessee

Pork Chops Supreme

6 (1-inch-thick) boneless center-
   cut loin pork chops
½ teaspoon salt
½ teaspoon pepper
2 teaspoons vegetable oil

14 pitted dried prunes
3 small onions, thinly sliced
½ cup water
2 tablespoons brown sugar
2 tablespoons cider vinegar

Sprinkle pork chops with salt and pepper. Cook pork chops in hot oil in a large skillet over medium-high heat 5 minutes on each side or until browned. Drain.

Add prunes and remaining ingredients to skillet. Cover, reduce heat to medium, and simmer 30 minutes or until meat is tender. Yield: 6 servings.

Ginger Schlipf

Blue Stocking Club Forget-Me-Not Recipes
Blue Stocking Club
Bristol, Tennessee

Foil-Baked Fish

4 (4-ounce) orange roughy, flounder, or sole fillets
4 green onions, thinly sliced
½ cup diced green pepper
¼ cup peeled and diced cucumber
1 tablespoon minced fresh ginger
1 tablespoon soy sauce
1 teaspoon olive oil

Cut four 15-inch squares of aluminum foil; place 1 fillet in center of each square.

Combine green onions and next 3 ingredients; sprinkle over fillets. Combine soy sauce and oil; drizzle over fillets. Fold foil over fillets; seal tightly. Bake at 450° for 10 to 12 minutes or until fish flakes easily when tested with a fork. Yield: 4 servings.   Ginny Prevost

McClellanville Coast Seafood Cookbook
McClellanville Arts Council
McClellanville, South Carolina

Flounder au Gratin

If you're cooking for two, this recipe can be cut in half. Place the fillets in a smaller baking dish before covering with the crumb mixture.

2½ pounds (½-inch-thick) flounder fillets
3 tablespoons lemon juice
¼ cup fine, dry breadcrumbs (store-bought)
¼ cup grated Parmesan cheese
3 tablespoons butter or margarine, cut into small pieces

Arrange flounder in a buttered 13- x 9- x 2-inch baking dish; drizzle with lemon juice.

Combine breadcrumbs and cheese in a small bowl. Sprinkle breadcrumb mixture over flounder; dot with butter. Bake, uncovered, at 375° for 30 minutes or until fish flakes easily when tested with a fork. Serve immediately with a slotted spatula. Yield: 4 servings.

Flavor of Nashville
Home Economists in Home and Community
Nashville, Tennessee

Shrimp Manale

Serve these simply broiled shrimp with lots of crusty French bread. You'll need it to soak up the glorious garlic-butter sauce.

3 pounds unpeeled medium-size fresh shrimp
1 cup butter, melted

½ cup dry white wine
6 cloves garlic, crushed

Place shrimp in broiler pan. Combine butter, wine, and garlic; pour over shrimp. Broil 5 inches from heat (with electric oven door partially opened) 21 minutes or until shrimp turn pink. Yield: 6 servings.   Gina Banister

Texas Sampler
The Junior League of Richardson, Texas

Grilled Honey-Mustard Chicken with Toasted Almonds

¼ cup Dijon mustard
3 tablespoons honey
1 tablespoon lemon juice
1 clove garlic, minced

8 skinned and boned chicken breast halves
¼ cup sliced almonds, toasted

Combine first 4 ingredients in a small bowl, stirring well.
Grill chicken, covered, over medium-hot coals (350° to 400°) 15 minutes or until done, turning often and brushing with mustard mixture. Remove chicken to a serving platter. Sprinkle with almonds, and serve immediately. Yield: 8 servings.   Evelyn Schwanz

Kenwood Lutheran Church Cookbook
Kenwood Women of the Evangelical Lutheran Church in America
Duluth, Minnesota

Orange-Basil Chicken

Vegetable cooking spray
1 teaspoon olive oil
4 skinned and boned chicken
  breast halves
1 cup orange juice
1 tablespoon chopped fresh
  basil

¼ teaspoon freshly ground
  pepper
1 clove garlic, minced
2 teaspoons cornstarch
1 tablespoon water

Coat a large nonstick skillet with cooking spray; add oil, and place over medium-high heat until hot. Add chicken, and cook 2 minutes on each side or until browned. Add orange juice and next 3 ingredients; bring mixture to a boil. Cover, reduce heat, and simmer 15 minutes or until chicken is done. Remove chicken from skillet; set aside, and keep warm.

Bring orange juice mixture to a boil; cook, uncovered, 5 minutes or until mixture is reduced to about ¾ cup. Combine cornstarch and water, stirring well; add to orange juice mixture. Cook over medium heat until mixture thickens, stirring constantly. Spoon sauce over chicken, and serve immediately. Yield: 4 servings.

Swap Around Recipes
Delmarva Square Dance Federation
Salisbury, Maryland

Chicken and Stuffing Casserole

Five ingredients are all it takes to make this hearty, family-pleasing casserole. If you're watching your sodium intake, choose reduced-sodium versions of the stuffing mix, soup, and broth.

1 (8-ounce) package seasoned stuffing mix (we tested with Pepperidge Farms Herb Seasoned Stuffing Mix), divided

3 cups coarsely chopped cooked chicken

2 (10¾-ounce) cans cream of celery, chicken, or mushroom soup

1 (14½-ounce) can chicken broth or 1¾ cups water

½ cup butter or margarine, melted

Sprinkle ¾ cup stuffing mix in a greased 13- x 9- x 2-inch pan; top with chicken. Combine soup, broth, and butter, stirring with a wire whisk until blended; pour over chicken. Sprinkle remaining stuffing mix over soup mixture. Bake, uncovered, at 350° for 35 minutes or until hot and bubbly. Yield: 6 servings.

Our Lady of Fatima and Immaculate Conception Parish Cookbook
Our Lady of Fatima
New London, New Hampshire

Chicken Livers in Sour Cream

½ cup butter

1½ cups sliced fresh mushrooms

1 large onion, sliced or chopped

1 pound chicken livers

1 (8-ounce) carton sour cream

⅓ cup dry sherry

¼ teaspoon salt

⅛ teaspoon pepper

Melt butter in a large skillet over low heat. Add mushrooms and onion; cook over medium-high heat, stirring constantly, until vegetables are tender. Add livers, and cook 1 minute. Cover, reduce heat to low, and cook 15 minutes. Stir in sour cream and remaining 3 ingredients, and cook until thoroughly heated. Serve immediately over rice or puff pastry shells. Yield: 4 servings.   Jan Mayer

Quad City Cookin'
Queen of Heaven Circle of OLV Ladies Council
Davenport, Iowa

Prosciutto with Angel Hair

2 (9-ounce) packages
   refrigerated angel hair pasta
¼ cup butter
¼ pound prosciutto, cut into
   very thin strips
1 cup whipping cream
1 tablespoon chopped fresh
   parsley

1 cup freshly grated Parmesan
   cheese, divided
1 tablespoon grated lemon rind
2 tablespoons fresh lemon
   juice
¼ teaspoon salt
¼ teaspoon pepper

Prepare pasta according to package directions; drain. Return pasta to pan, and keep warm.

Melt butter in a skillet over medium heat. Add prosciutto, cream, and parsley; cook until heated. Stir in ⅓ cup cheese, lemon rind, and remaining 3 ingredients. Pour sauce over pasta; toss. Sprinkle with remaining ⅔ cup cheese. Serve immediately. Yield: 6 servings.

Cheyenne Frontier Days "Daddy of 'em All" Cookbook
Chuckwagon Gourmet
Cheyenne, Wyoming

Linguine with White River Clam Sauce

Top this classic dish with a generous sprinkling of Parmesan cheese.

12 ounces dried linguine,
   uncooked
2 (6½-ounce) cans chopped
   clams, undrained
1 tablespoon minced garlic

2 tablespoons olive oil
½ cup chopped fresh parsley
¼ cup dry white wine
2 teaspoons chopped fresh basil
   or 1 teaspoon dried basil

Cook pasta according to package directions. Meanwhile, drain clams, reserving juice; set aside.

Cook garlic in oil in a medium skillet over medium-high heat 1 minute, stirring constantly. Add clam juice and parsley, and simmer, uncovered, 3 minutes. Add clams, wine, and basil; simmer, uncovered, 5 minutes. Drain pasta. Pour clam sauce over pasta, and toss. Yield: 4 servings.

Colorado Collage
The Junior League of Denver, Colorado

Baked Orzo

Green chiles stud this rich cheese, sour cream, and orzo concoction and balance the flavors. Give your pepper mill a twist to add flecks of freshly ground pepper to this layered dish.

1 cup orzo, uncooked
1 cup (4 ounces) diced
  Monterey Jack cheese
1 (4.5-ounce) can chopped
  green chiles, undrained

1 (8-ounce) carton sour cream
½ cup freshly grated Parmesan
  cheese
2 tablespoons butter, cut into
  small pieces

Cook orzo according to package directions; drain. Combine orzo, Monterey Jack cheese, and chiles; place in a buttered 1½-quart baking dish. Spread sour cream over orzo mixture; sprinkle with Parmesan cheese, and dot with butter. Bake, uncovered, at 450° for 15 minutes or until cheeses melt and mixture is thoroughly heated. Yield: 6 servings.   Judy A. Gordon

St. Andrew's Foods for the Multitudes and Smaller Groups
St Andrew's Episcopal Church
Cripple Creek, Colorado

Lemon Vermicelli

A spritz of fresh lemon juice heightens the flavor of this buttery, creamy pasta side dish.

⅓ cup whipping cream
3 tablespoons butter
1 (7-ounce) package dried
  vermicelli

¼ cup fresh lemon juice
⅓ cup freshly grated Parmesan
  cheese

Combine cream and butter in a small saucepan; cook over medium-low heat until butter melts. Set aside, and keep warm.

Cook vermicelli according to package directions; drain. Place in a bowl, and toss with lemon juice; let stand 1 minute. Add cheese and warm cream mixture; toss. Serve immediately. Yield: 4 servings.

Project Open Hand Cookbook
Project Open Hand Atlanta, Georgia

Spicy Couscous

1 cup chicken broth
¼ cup sliced green onions
1 (4.5-ounce) can chopped
   green chiles, undrained

⅔ cup couscous, uncooked

Combine first 3 ingredients in a medium saucepan; bring to a boil. Remove from heat, and stir in couscous. Cover and let stand 5 minutes. Fluff with a fork before serving. Yield: 4 servings.

Beneath the Palms
The Brownsville Junior Service League
Brownsville, Texas

Sautéed Carrots and Zucchini

The fresh taste and simplicity of this vegetable dish make it a perfect companion for broiled fish and chicken.

2 tablespoons butter or
   margarine
1 pound carrots, thinly sliced
¼ cup chopped green onions
   (white part only)
1 pound zucchini, thinly sliced

¼ teaspoon salt
¼ teaspoon freshly ground
   pepper
3 tablespoons chopped fresh
   basil or 1 teaspoon dried
   basil

Melt butter in a large skillet over medium-high heat. Add carrot; cook, uncovered, 4 minutes, stirring often. Add green onions, and cook 1 additional minute. Add zucchini; cook 2 additional minutes, stirring occasionally. Stir in salt and pepper; cover, reduce heat to medium-low, and cook 4 minutes or until crisp-tender. Sprinkle with basil. Yield: 6 servings.

The Cumberland Cougars Are Cooking Now
Cumberland Elementary School P.T.A.
Lansing, Michigan

Roast Potato Duo

2 large baking potatoes (about 1½ pounds), cut lengthwise into 6 wedges
2 medium-size sweet potatoes (about 1½ pounds), cut lengthwise into 6 wedges
1 tablespoon olive oil
Vegetable cooking spray
½ teaspoon salt
¾ teaspoon dried rosemary

Place potato wedges in a large heavy-duty, zip-top plastic bag. Add oil; seal bag, and shake to coat. Place potatoes in a 15- x 10- x 1-inch jellyroll pan coated with cooking spray. Sprinkle with salt and rosemary. Bake, uncovered, at 450° for 30 minutes or until tender and lightly browned, stirring twice. Yield: 4 servings.

Classic Favorites
P.E.O., Chapter SB
Moraga, California

Tomato Pie

Fresh, ripe tomatoes make this dish a summer standout.

½ (15-ounce) package refrigerated piecrusts
2 large tomatoes, sliced
½ teaspoon dried basil
½ teaspoon dried chives
½ teaspoon pepper
½ cup mayonnaise
1 cup (4 ounces) shredded sharp Cheddar cheese

Fit piecrust into a 9-inch pieplate according to package directions; fold edges under, and crimp. Prick bottom and sides of crust with a fork. Bake at 450° for 9 minutes. Reduce oven temperature to 350°.

Arrange tomato slices in crust. Combine basil, chives, and pepper; sprinkle over tomato. Spread with mayonnaise; sprinkle with cheese.

Bake, uncovered, 20 minutes or until cheese melts and pie is thoroughly heated. Let stand 10 minutes before serving. Serve warm or let cool on a wire rack. Yield: 6 servings.

Claire S. Raneri

Katonah Cooks!
Katonah Village Improvement Society, Katonah Village Library
Katonah, New York

Chocolate Cherry Cake

Dessert can't be much easier than this double-chocolate cake made from staples and a couple of convenience products.

2 large eggs, lightly beaten
1 (21-ounce) can cherry pie
    filling
1 (18.5-ounce) package
    chocolate fudge cake mix (we
    tested with Duncan Hines)

1 teaspoon almond extract
1 cup sugar
½ cup milk
⅓ cup butter or margarine
1 cup (6 ounces) semisweet
    chocolate morsels

Combine first 4 ingredients; pour into a lightly greased 13- x 9- x 2-inch pan. Bake at 375° for 30 to 35 minutes or until a wooden pick inserted in center comes out clean. Cool in pan on a wire rack.

Combine sugar, milk, and butter in a saucepan; bring to a boil over medium heat, stirring often. Boil 3 minutes, stirring occasionally. Remove from heat.

Add chocolate morsels, stirring until chocolate melts. Pour chocolate mixture over cake, spreading to edges of pan. Let stand until chocolate mixture is set. Yield: 15 servings.   Elsie M. Snyder

Memorial Hospital Associates Favorites
Memorial Hospital Activities Committee
York, Pennsylvania

Easy 3-Step Blueberry-Swirl Cheesecake

Making a cheesecake just doesn't get any easier. A ready-made crust and canned pie filling take care of most of the fuss.

2 (8-ounce) packages cream
   cheese, softened
½ cup sugar
2 large eggs

¼ teaspoon vanilla extract
1 (9-inch) graham cracker crust
1 (21-ounce) can blueberry pie
   filling, divided

Beat cream cheese at medium speed of an electric mixer until creamy; gradually add sugar, beating well. Add eggs, one at a time, beating after each addition. Stir in vanilla.

Pour cream cheese mixture into graham cracker crust; spoon ⅔ cup blueberry pie filling over top of cream cheese mixture. Swirl gently with a knife to create a marbled effect. Cover remaining pie filling, and store in refrigerator.

Bake cheesecake at 350° for 40 minutes or until center is set. Let cool completely in pan on a wire rack. Cover and chill 8 hours.

Spread reserved pie filling on top of cheesecake before serving. Yield: 8 servings.

Agnes Burns

Let's Get Cooking
Monvale Health Resources Auxiliary
Monongahela, Pennsylvania

Lemon Glacier Bars

1 (18.25-ounce) package lemon
   cake mix (we tested with
   Duncan Hines)
1 large egg
⅓ cup vegetable oil

1 (8-ounce) package cream
   cheese, softened
⅓ cup sugar
1 large egg
1 teaspoon lemon juice

Combine cake mix, 1 egg, and oil in a large mixing bowl; beat at medium speed of an electric mixer until crumbly. Reserve 1 cup cake mixture for topping. Press remaining cake mixture into an ungreased 13- x 9- x 2-inch pan. Bake at 350° for 12 minutes or until lightly browned.

Meanwhile, beat cream cheese at medium speed until creamy; add sugar, 1 egg, and lemon juice, beating until smooth. Pour cream cheese mixture over baked crust; sprinkle with reserved cake mixture. Bake, uncovered, at 350° for 15 to 18 minutes or until lightly browned. Let cool slightly; cover and chill. Yield: 15 bars.   Judy Hoover

Canton McKinley Bulldogs Pup's Pantry
McKinley Booster Club
Canton, Ohio

Speedy Little Devils

1 (18.25-ounce) package devil's food cake mix
½ cup butter or margarine, melted

½ cup creamy peanut butter
1 (7-ounce) jar marshmallow cream

Combine cake mix and butter, stirring well (mixture will be crumbly). Set aside 1½ cups cake mixture. Press remaining cake mixture in bottom of a greased 13- x 9- x 2-inch pan.

Combine peanut butter and marshmallow cream in a bowl, stirring until blended. Dollop peanut butter mixture evenly over mixture in pan; spread evenly, using back of a spoon. Sprinkle reserved 1½ cups cake mixture over peanut butter mixture. Bake, uncovered, at 350°for 20 minutes. Let cool in pan on a wire rack. Cut into bars. Yield: 3 dozen.   Joseph Moellers

A Taste of Greene
Playground Committee
Greene, Iowa

Peanut Butter Brownie Cups

Snuggled within each fudgy brownie is a tiny peanut butter cup candy. If you prefer cakelike brownies, bake the brownie cups a minute longer.

1 (21-ounce) package chewy fudge brownie mix (we tested with Duncan Hines)

15 miniature peanut butter cup candies

Prepare brownie mix according to package directions. Spoon batter into paper-lined muffin pans, filling two-thirds full. Unwrap candies, and place 1 in center of each muffin cup, pressing down until batter meets top edge of candy. Bake at 350° for 20 minutes. Carefully remove from pan, and let cool completely on wire racks. Yield: 15 brownie cups.

Teresa Meyer

Fire Gals' Hot Pans Cookbook
Garrison Emergency Services Auxiliary
Garrison, Iowa

Quick and Easy Pie

1 quart vanilla ice cream, softened
1 (6-ounce) chocolate-flavored crumb crust
1 (14.5-ounce) jar milk chocolate ice cream topping (we tested with Smucker's Dove Milk Chocolate Ice Cream Topping)

3 (1.4-ounce) English toffee-flavored candy bars, chopped (we tested with Heath bars)
Garnish: maraschino cherries with stems

Spread vanilla ice cream evenly in chocolate-flavored crumb crust. Freeze until firm. Spread ice cream topping evenly over ice cream, and sprinkle with chopped candy. Garnish, if desired. Serve immediately. Yield: one 9-inch pie.

Pat W. Jackson

Mounds of Cooking
Parkin Archeological Support Team
Parkin, Arkansas

Aw Nuts

Here's a timesaving trick we ran across while testing this soft-serve ice cream. Toast your pecans and coconut on opposite ends of the same pan at the same time at 350° for 7 minutes, stirring the coconut after 5 minutes.

½ gallon vanilla ice cream, softened

1 cup large pecan pieces, toasted

1 cup flaked coconut, toasted

¼ cup brandy or bourbon

Combine all ingredients in a large freezerproof bowl; cover and freeze at least 5 hours. To serve, spoon into individual dessert dishes. Yield: 8 cups.

Azaleas to Zucchini
Smith County Medical Society Alliance
Tyler, Texas

Frozen Raspberry Cream

1 (14-ounce) package frozen raspberries

1 (12-ounce) can frozen pink lemonade concentrate

1 quart vanilla ice cream, softened

Position knife blade in food processor bowl; add raspberries. Process until slushy, stopping once to scrape down sides. Add lemonade concentrate, and process until blended. Add ice cream, and process until smooth. Spoon mixture into a 13- x 9- x 2-inch pan. Cover and freeze at least 3 hours. Let stand 5 minutes before serving. To serve, use an ice cream scoop. Yield: 6 cups.   Joann Westin

150 Years of Good Eating
St. George Evangelical Lutheran Church
Brighton, Michigan

Meg's Crackly Sauce for Ice Cream

Make this sauce when you and a couple of friends are in the mood for something crunchy and chock-full of toasted nuts. The warm brown sugar and molasses sauce crackles when it hits cold ice cream. The contrast will delight your palate, and you'll want to eat it all, which is a good thing, because leftovers can't be successfully reheated to duplicate the effect.

1 cup firmly packed brown
   sugar
¼ cup butter
2 tablespoons molasses

1½ tablespoons water
⅛ teaspoon salt
1 tablespoon white vinegar
⅓ cup sliced almonds, toasted

Combine first 6 ingredients in a small saucepan; cook over medium heat, stirring constantly, 9 minutes or until mixture reaches soft crack stage or candy thermometer registers 280°. Remove from heat; stir in almonds. Spoon immediately over ice cream. Yield: 1½ cups.

Word of Mouth
Friends of the Humane Society of Knox County
Rockland, Maine

Ranch Home-Style Dressing Mix

1 cup buttermilk
1 cup mayonnaise
1 tablespoon dried parsley
   flakes

2 teaspoons dried minced
   onion
¼ teaspoon salt
⅛ teaspoon garlic powder

Combine all ingredients; stir well. Cover and chill. Serve with salad greens. Yield: 2 cups.
        Ruth Reynolds

A Recipe Runs Through It
Sula Country Life Club
Sula, Montana

Appetizers & Beverages

Fiesta Cheesecake, page 64

Mexi Spiced Nuts

You'll feast on the feisty chili-style flavors of this addictive nut mix.

2 cups pecan halves
2 cups salted roasted peanuts
1 egg white, lightly beaten
¼ cup butter or margarine,
   melted
1 tablespoon chili powder

1 teaspoon ground red pepper
½ teaspoon garlic powder
1 tablespoon Worcestershire
   sauce
1 teaspoon hot sauce

Combine pecans and peanuts in an ungreased 13- x 9- x 2-inch pan. Combine egg white and remaining 6 ingredients in a small bowl, stirring well; pour over nuts, stirring to coat. Bake, uncovered, at 350° for 30 minutes or until toasted; cool completely in pan on a wire rack. Store in an airtight container. Yield: 4 cups.   Lorene Culler

United Methodist Church Cookbook
Cairo United Methodist Church Women
Cairo, Nebraska

Nutty Brie with Tipsy Fruit

If you prefer Brie without the rind, just slice away the top rind; it's delectable either way. Decorate this melt-in-your-mouth appetizer with cranberries and nuts in alternating wagon-wheel wedges or simply mix the two ingredients together and sprinkle on top of the Brie.

½ cup dried cranberries (we
   tested with Craisins)
¼ cup dry white wine

⅓ cup chopped pecans
¼ cup butter, melted
1 (2-pound) round Brie

Combine cranberries and wine; cover and let stand at room temperature 8 hours.

Cook pecans in butter in a large skillet over medium-high heat, stirring constantly, until pecans are toasted; remove pecans from skillet with a slotted spoon. Drain and set aside.

Slice rind from top of Brie, if desired. Place Brie on an 8-inch circle of cardboard covered with aluminum foil. Place Brie and cardboard circle on an ungreased baking sheet. Bake, uncovered, at 325° for 12 minutes or until soft.

To serve, arrange cranberries and pecans, spoke fashion, creating a wheel design, if desired. Serve with assorted crackers. Yield: 16 appetizer servings.

Albertina's Exceptional Recipes
Albertina's
Portland, Oregon

Fruited Cheddar Ball

Sweet tidbits of dried fruit stud this Cheddar cheese ball. It's the perfect size (6 inches) for a large gathering, but the mixture can easily be divided into two 3-inch balls. Pop one in the freezer for later or give one as a gift.

¾ cup dried apricot halves
⅓ cup whole pitted dates
⅓ cup golden raisins
¼ cup cognac or brandy
1½ pounds mild Cheddar
   cheese, cut into ¾-inch cubes

12 ounces cream cheese,
   softened
¾ cup slivered almonds,
   toasted

Position knife blade in food processor bowl; add apricots and dates. Process until chopped. Combine chopped fruit, raisins, and cognac in a small bowl; cover and let stand 1 hour or until liquid is almost absorbed.

Place Cheddar cheese cubes in processor bowl; process until finely chopped. Add cream cheese, a third at a time; process until blended, stopping as needed to scrape down sides. Add fruit mixture and almonds; pulse several times or until fruit and almonds are finely chopped and mixture is combined.

Shape cheese mixture into a 6-inch ball. Wrap tightly with plastic wrap, and chill until firm. Let come to room temperature before serving. Serve with assorted crackers and fresh apple slices. Yield: one 6-inch cheese ball.

Shirley Calby

Curtain Calls
The Arts Society of the Norris Cultural Arts Center
St. Charles, Illinois

BLT Dip

If you're a BLT fan, you'll delight in this dip–it includes everything but the lettuce! For a spicier version, use salsa in place of the tomatoes. For a lighter version, use nonfat mayonnaise, fat-free sour cream, and turkey bacon. You'll even enjoy it over lettuce as a chunky salad dressing.

1 cup mayonnaise
1 (8-ounce) carton sour cream
1 pound bacon, cooked and
    crumbled

2 large tomatoes, chopped

Combine mayonnaise and sour cream in a medium bowl, stirring well with a wire whisk; stir in bacon and tomato. Serve immediately with melba toast rounds. Yield: 4 cups.

Savour St. Louis
Barnes-Jewish Hospital Auxiliary Plaza Chapter
St. Louis, Missouri

Orange Hummus

2 (15-ounce) cans chick-peas,
    drained
½ cup orange juice
¼ cup tahini (sesame seed
    paste)
4 green onions, minced
4 cloves garlic, crushed
1 tablespoon cider vinegar

1 teaspoon soy sauce
1½ teaspoons salt
¼ teaspoon ground cumin
¼ teaspoon ground coriander
¼ teaspoon ground ginger
¼ teaspoon dry mustard
¼ teaspoon ground turmeric
¼ teaspoon paprika

Position knife blade in food processor bowl; add all ingredients. Process until smooth, stopping once to scrape down sides. Serve with pita triangles. Yield: 3 cups.

Music, Menus & Magnolias
Charleston Symphony Orchestra League
Charleston, South Carolina

Fresh Crudités with Thai Peanut Dip

Sweet flaked coconut and brown sugar embrace the salty, spicy bravado of a blend of soy sauce and crushed red pepper. In this intensely seasoned dip, the nutty richness of peanut butter and dark sesame oil melds the flavors. Serve the dip with fresh crudités or chicken nuggets.

1 tablespoon minced shallots	¼ cup soy sauce
¾ teaspoon dark sesame oil	2 tablespoons flaked coconut
¾ cup creamy or chunky peanut butter	1 teaspoon dried crushed red pepper
½ cup water	2 cloves garlic, minced
¼ cup lemon juice	2½ tablespoons brown sugar

Cook shallot in sesame oil in a medium saucepan over medium-high heat, stirring constantly, until tender. Add peanut butter and next 6 ingredients, stirring well. Cook over medium-low heat 4 minutes, stirring constantly. Add brown sugar; cover, reduce heat, and simmer 10 minutes, stirring often. Serve warm with fresh crudités. Yield: 2 cups.

Capital Celebrations
The Junior League of Washington, DC

Hot Mexican-Style Spinach Dip

1 medium onion, chopped
2 tablespoons vegetable oil
2 medium tomatoes, peeled, seeded, and chopped
2 tablespoons chopped canned jalapeño pepper
1 (10-ounce) package frozen chopped spinach, thawed and well drained
2 cups (8 ounces) shredded Monterey Jack cheese
1 (8-ounce) package cream cheese, cut into ½-inch cubes
1 cup half-and-half
2 (2.2-ounce) cans sliced ripe olives, drained
1 tablespoon red wine vinegar
¼ teaspoon salt
¼ teaspoon black pepper

Cook onion in oil in a medium skillet over medium-high heat, stirring constantly, 4 minutes or until onion is tender. Add tomato and jalapeño pepper; cook 2 minutes. Transfer mixture to a large bowl; add spinach and remaining ingredients, stirring well. Spoon mixture into a greased 2-quart baking dish. Bake, uncovered, at 400° for 35 minutes or until golden and bubbly. Serve warm with tortilla chips. Yield: 6 cups.   Sandy Ricker

Our Sunrise Family Cookbook
Sunrise Drive Elementary School
Tucson, Arizona

Almond Ambrosia Spread

1 envelope unflavored gelatin
¼ cup cold water
12 ounces cream cheese, softened
½ cup sugar
½ cup butter, softened
½ cup sour cream
1 tablespoon grated lemon rind
1 tablespoon grated orange rind
½ cup golden raisins
½ cup currants
½ cup slivered almonds, toasted
½ cup chopped pecans
1 cup sliced almonds, toasted

Sprinkle gelatin over cold water in a small saucepan; let stand 1 minute. Cook over low heat, stirring until gelatin dissolves, about 2 minutes.

Beat cream cheese and next 5 ingredients at medium speed of an electric mixer until mixture is creamy; stir in gelatin mixture. Gently stir in raisins and next 3 ingredients.

Pour gelatin mixture into a 1-quart mold generously greased with mayonnaise. Cover and chill at least 6 hours.

Unmold gelatin mixture; gently press sliced almonds around sides and top. Serve with gingersnaps, assorted crackers, or apple wedges. Yield: 12 appetizer servings. Jackie Marble

Seasonings Change
Ohio State University Women's Club
Columbus, Ohio

Primarily Pine Shrimp Mousse

3 cups water
1 pound unpeeled medium-size
  fresh shrimp
2 envelopes unflavored gelatin
½ cup cold water
1 (8-ounce) package cream
  cheese, softened
3 tablespoons cocktail sauce
2 tablespoons chili sauce

1 cup mayonnaise
¾ cup minced celery
¼ cup minced green onions
1 tablespoon fresh lemon juice
1 tablespoon Worcestershire
  sauce
¼ teaspoon salt
¼ teaspoon pepper

Bring 3 cups water to a boil; add shrimp, and cook 3 to 5 minutes or until shrimp turn pink. Drain well; rinse with cold water.

Peel shrimp, and devein, if desired. Chop shrimp; cover and chill.

Sprinkle gelatin over cold water in a small saucepan; let stand 1 minute. Cook over low heat, stirring until gelatin dissolves, about 2 minutes. Let cool.

Beat cream cheese, cocktail sauce, and chili sauce at medium speed of an electric mixer until smooth; stir in gelatin mixture. Add shrimp, mayonnaise, and remaining ingredients, stirring well.

Rinse a 5-cup mold with cold water; drain but do not dry. Pour shrimp mixture into mold. Cover and chill at least 2 hours.

Unmold and serve with melba toast rounds or assorted crackers. Yield: 20 appetizer servings. Susie Smith

Blessed Isle
Episcopal Church Women of All Saints Parish
Pawleys Island, South Carolina

Tricolor Paté

The fruity essence of the almond-shaped kalamata olive is key in this recipe. Don't be tempted to substitute pitted ripe olives. You can easily pit the kalamata olives using a cherry pitter.

1 (8-ounce) package cream cheese, softened
1 (4-ounce) package feta cheese
1 cup loosely packed fresh basil leaves
1 cup loosely packed fresh parsley sprigs
¼ cup pine nuts, toasted
3 tablespoons olive oil
3 cloves garlic, divided
¾ cup oil-packed dried tomatoes, drained
Olivada

Line a 2½-cup mold or bowl with plastic wrap, leaving a 1-inch overhang around edges. Set aside.

Beat cream cheese and feta cheese at medium speed of an electric mixer until creamy; set aside. Combine basil and next 3 ingredients in container of an electric blender or food processor; add 2 cloves garlic. Process until smooth, stopping once to scape down sides; set aside.

Combine tomatoes and remaining clove garlic in container of an electric blender or food processor; process until smooth.

Spoon one-third of cream cheese mixture into prepared mold, spreading evenly; spread with basil mixture. Spoon one-third of cream cheese mixture over basil mixture, spreading evenly; spread with tomato mixture. Spread remaining cream cheese mixture over tomato mixture. Cover and chill at least 4 hours.

To serve, unmold onto a serving platter; peel off plastic wrap. Serve with Olivada and baguette slices or assorted crackers. Yield 2: cups.

Olivada

1 (16-ounce) jar kalamata olives, pitted
3 tablespoons olive oil
2 tablespoons pine nuts, toasted
2 large cloves garlic

Position knife blade in food processor bowl; add all ingredients. Process until smooth, stopping once to scrape down sides. Spoon mixture into a serving dish. Yield: 1 cup.

Beautiful, Bountiful Oregon
The Assistance League of Corvallis, Oregon

Artichoke Cheesecake

¼ cup fine, dry breadcrumbs
  (store-bought)
¼ cup grated Parmesan cheese
2 tablespoons dried Italian
  seasoning
2 (8-ounce) packages cream
  cheese, softened
1 cup crumbled feta cheese
3 large eggs
1 (8-ounce) carton sour cream
1 (14-ounce) can artichoke
  hearts, drained and chopped
¾ cup chopped sweet red
  pepper
¾ cup chopped green pepper
¾ cup chopped green onions
  (including ½-inch green tops)
1 large clove garlic, pressed
1 teaspoon dried tarragon
1 teaspoon dried basil

Generously butter a 9-inch springform pan. Combine first 3 ingredients; coat bottom of pan with breadcrumb mixture, and set aside remaining mixture.

Position knife blade in food processor bowl; add cream cheese. Process until smooth, stopping once to scrape down sides. Add feta cheese, eggs, and sour cream. Process until smooth, stopping once to scrape down sides. Add chopped artichoke and remaining 6 ingredients to processor bowl. Process until smooth, stopping once to scrape down sides. Pour mixture into prepared pan.

Bake, uncovered, at 375° for 45 to 50 minutes or until golden. Cool completely in pan on a wire rack. Cover and chill at least 2 hours.

Carefully remove sides of springform pan. Pat reserved breadcrumb mixture on sides of cheesecake. Serve with toast points or assorted crackers. Yield: one 9-inch cheesecake (16 appetizer servings).

Ambrosia
The Junior Auxiliary of Vicksburg, Mississippi

Fiesta Cheesecake

This Mexican cheesecake appetizer is destined to become your party favorite. It boasts an impressive wagon-wheel arrangement of toppings. If you're in a rush, sprinkle the toppings willy-nilly to create a fiesta of color and flavor.

1½ cups finely crushed tortilla chips
¼ cup butter, melted
2¾ cups (11 ounces) shredded Monterey Jack cheese, divided
2 (8-ounce) packages cream cheese, softened
2 large eggs
1 (4.5-ounce) can chopped green chiles, drained
¼ teaspoon ground red pepper
1 (8-ounce) carton sour cream
½ cup chopped green pepper
½ cup chopped sweet yellow pepper
½ cup chopped sweet red pepper
½ cup sliced green onions
½ cup seeded, chopped tomato
⅓ cup chopped ripe olives
⅓ cup chopped fresh cilantro

Combine tortilla chips, butter, and ¼ cup Monterey Jack cheese; firmly press mixture in bottom of a lightly greased 9-inch springform pan. Bake at 325° for 15 minutes. Set aside.

Beat cream cheese at medium speed of an electric mixer until creamy; add eggs, one at a time, beating after each addition. Stir in remaining 2½ cups Monterey Jack cheese, green chiles, and ground red pepper. Pour mixture into prepared pan.

Bake, uncovered, at 325° for 30 minutes. Let cool in pan on a wire rack 10 minutes. Carefully remove sides of springform pan; let cool completely on wire rack. Spread sour cream on top of cheesecake. Cover and chill thoroughly.

Arrange green pepper and remaining ingredients over sour cream, spoke fashion, creating a wheel design. Serve with tortilla chips. Yield: one 9-inch cheesecake (16 appetizer servings).

Sterling Service
The Dothan Service League
Dothan, Alabama

Greek Stuffed Mushrooms

Zesty feta cheese, spinach, and kalamata olives fill mushroom caps with distinctively Greek flavors. Different brands of feta can vary in salt content. If your cheese is on the mild side, you might want to add a bit of salt to the recipe to heighten the flavors.

1 (10-ounce) package frozen chopped spinach
1 cup crumbled feta cheese
½ cup finely chopped green onions

½ cup finely chopped fresh parsley
6 kalamata olives, pitted and finely chopped
12 large mushroom caps

Cook spinach according to package directions; drain well, pressing between layers of paper towels to remove excess moisture. Combine spinach, feta cheese, and next 3 ingredients; stir well.

Clean mushroom caps with damp paper towels. Place in an ungreased 11- x 7- x 1½-inch baking dish. Spoon spinach mixture evenly into mushroom caps. Bake, uncovered, at 350° for 10 to 15 minutes. Serve immediately. Yield: 12 servings.　　　Sherry Hils

A Cookbook
Life Education Department of the Cheshire Center of
Applied Science & Technology at Keene High School
Keene, New Hampshire

Beef Roulades with Watercress and Blue Cheese

This "two-bite" appetizer is worth the effort. Tender strips of grilled sirloin steak are wrapped around a blend of pungent blue cheese and fresh sprigs of watercress.

1 (4-ounce) package crumbled blue cheese
¼ cup sour cream
1 tablespoon fresh lemon juice
¾ teaspoon freshly ground pepper, divided
1 teaspoon salt
1½ pounds boneless sirloin steak (1½ inches thick)
48 small watercress sprigs

Combine first 3 ingredients in a small bowl; add ¼ teaspoon pepper, stirring well. Cover and chill.

Sprinkle salt and remaining ½ teaspoon pepper on both sides of steak. Grill steak, covered, over medium-hot coals (350° to 400°) 6 minutes on each side or to desired degree of doneness. Transfer to a cutting board, and let stand 7 minutes.

Cut steak diagonally across grain into 24 (¼-inch-thick) slices; spread 1 teaspoon blue cheese mixture on each slice. Place 2 sprigs watercress along 1 short edge of each slice; roll up each slice, beginning with short edge, and secure with a wooden pick. Serve immediately or cover and chill up to 1 hour. Yield: 2 dozen.

A Capital Affair
The Junior League of Harrisburg, Pennsylvania

Sherried Walnut-Chicken Appetizers

Serve a batch of these walnut-encrusted chicken nuggets with pretty wooden picks so that your guests can plunge them into the spiced plum sauce.

1¼ pounds skinned and boned chicken breast halves, cut into bite-size pieces
1 tablespoon dry sherry
2 to 2½ cups walnuts, finely chopped
1 teaspoon salt
⅛ teaspoon pepper
2 egg whites
¼ cup cornstarch
Vegetable oil
Plum-Good Sauce

Combine chicken and sherry in a small bowl; toss gently, and set aside. Combine walnuts, salt, and pepper in a shallow dish; set aside.

Beat egg whites at high speed of an electric mixer until foamy; add cornstarch, beating until stiff peaks form.

Press one-third of chicken pieces between paper towels to remove excess moisture. Dip chicken pieces in egg white mixture, and roll in walnut mixture.

Pour oil to depth of 2 inches in a large heavy skillet; heat to 350°. Fry chicken pieces until golden. Drain on paper towels. Repeat procedure with remaining chicken pieces, egg white mixture, and walnut mixture. Serve with Plum-Good Sauce. Yield: 3 dozen.

Plum-Good Sauce

1 cup plum jam or preserves
1 tablespoon ketchup
2 teaspoons grated lemon rind
1 tablespoon fresh lemon juice
2 teaspoons cider vinegar
½ teaspoon ground ginger
½ teaspoon anise seeds, crushed
¼ teaspoon dry mustard
¼ teaspoon ground cinnamon
⅛ teaspoon ground cloves
⅛ teaspoon hot sauce

Heat plum jam in a small saucepan over medium heat until melted, stirring often. Stir in ketchup and remaining ingredients; bring to a boil. Cook 1 minute, stirring constantly. Yield: 1 cup.

Here, There & Everywhere
Volunteers in Overseas Cooperative Assistance
Washington, DC

Mini Crab Cakes with Salsa Mayonnaise

We loved these little crab cakes, and the Salsa Mayonnaise is culinary creativity at its best. For a wonderful entrée, just make the patties larger.

3 tablespoons butter
¾ cup finely chopped onion
⅓ cup finely chopped celery
1 jalapeño pepper, seeded and minced
3 large eggs, beaten
¼ cup sour cream
1 pound fresh lump crabmeat, drained

1½ cups Italian-seasoned breadcrumbs
1 cup (4 ounces) shredded Monterey Jack cheese with jalapeño pepper
½ cup diced roasted red pepper
½ cup chopped fresh cilantro
2 tablespoons vegetable oil
Salsa Mayonnaise

Melt butter in a large skillet over medium heat. Add onion, celery, and jalapeño; cook, stirring constantly, 5 minutes or just until tender. Transfer to a large bowl; let cool.

Add eggs and sour cream to onion mixture. Gently stir in crabmeat and next 4 ingredients. Cover and chill 1 hour. Shape crab mixture into 36 (1½-inch-wide) patties.

Heat 1 teaspoon oil in a large skillet over medium heat; add 6 patties to skillet. Cook 4 minutes on each side or until golden. Set aside, and keep warm. Repeat procedure with remaining oil and patties. Serve crab cakes with Salsa Mayonnaise. Yield: 3 dozen.

Salsa Mayonnaise

1 cup mayonnaise
½ cup sour cream

½ cup picante sauce

Combine all ingredients in a small bowl; stir well. Cover and chill. Yield: 2 cups.

Taste of the Territory, The Flair and Flavor of Oklahoma
The Service League of Bartlesville, Oklahoma

Shrimp and Tortellini

1¼ cups olive oil
⅔ cup ketchup
½ cup white vinegar
1½ tablespoons prepared
   horseradish
5 cloves garlic, minced
1 tablespoon Dijon mustard
1 tablespoon lemon juice
1 teaspoon salt

1 teaspoon pepper
1 teaspoon hot sauce
2 (9-ounce) packages
   refrigerated cheese-filled
   tortellini
9 cups water
3 pounds unpeeled medium-
   size fresh shrimp
½ cup chopped celery

Combine first 10 ingredients in a large bowl, stirring with a wire whisk.
   Cook tortellini according to package directions; drain. Add to oil mixture in bowl.
   Bring 9 cups water to a boil; add shrimp, and cook 3 to 5 minutes or until shrimp turn pink. Drain well; rinse with cold water. Peel shrimp, and devein, if desired. Add shrimp and celery to tortellini mixture, tossing gently to coat. Cover and chill 8 hours. Yield: 16 appetizer servings.   Kay R. Fowler

Shared Treasures
First Baptist Church
Monroe, Louisiana

Orange Blush

Orange juice married with cranberry juice cocktail gives this beverage a rosy glow. It's the perfect partner for your favorite brunch fare.

1 (6-ounce) can frozen orange
   juice concentrate, thawed
   and undiluted

1 cup cranberry juice
¼ cup sugar
2 cups club soda, chilled

Combine first 3 ingredients in a pitcher, stirring until sugar dissolves. Cover and chill. Gently stir in club soda just before serving. Serve over ice. Yield: 4 cups.   Cindy Niedringhaus

Recipes & Remembrances
Frank P. Tillman Elementary P.T.O.
Kirkwood, Missouri

Mock Champagne Punch

Fresh strawberries
Fresh mint sprigs
Distilled water
2 cups cold water
½ (12-ounce) can frozen
   pineapple juice concentrate,
   thawed and undiluted
1 (6-ounce) can frozen
   lemonade concentrate,
   thawed and undiluted

1 (12-ounce) can or 1½ cups
   ginger ale, chilled
2 (6½-ounce) bottles sparkling
   water, chilled
1 (750-milliliter) bottle
   sparkling white grape juice
   cocktail, chilled

Arrange strawberries and mint in bottom of a ring mold; add just enough distilled water to cover fruit but not float it; freeze until firm. Fill remainder of mold with water; freeze until firm.

Combine 2 cups cold water and pineapple juice and lemonade concentrates in a punch bowl, stirring well. Dip ring mold into a sinkful of cold water. Turn ice ring out into juice mixture. Add ginger ale, sparkling water, and white grape juice; stir gently. Yield: 14 cups.

Azaleas to Zucchini
Smith County Medical Society Alliance
Tyler, Texas

Dreamsicle Punch

9 cups water
1 (12-ounce) can frozen
   lemonade concentrate,
   thawed and undiluted
1 (6-ounce) can frozen orange
   juice concentrate, thawed
   and undiluted

2½ quarts orange sherbet,
   softened
½ gallon vanilla ice cream,
   softened

Combine first 3 ingredients in a punch bowl. Add sherbet and ice cream, stirring until creamy. Yield: 22 cups.   Jan Applehaus

Culinary Classics
Hoffman Estates Medical Center Service League
Hoffman Estates, Illinois

Lamb's Wool

Bits of pureed apple add texture to this spiced apple cider beverage. Fluffy dollops of brown sugar-sweetened whipped cream float atop, hence the title "Lamb's Wool."

2 small Rome apples, peeled and quartered
1 gallon apple cider
½ cup sugar
½ teaspoon ground ginger
¼ teaspoon ground cinnamon
⅛ teaspoon ground nutmeg
2 cups whipping cream
2 tablespoons light brown sugar
¼ teaspoon salt

Position knife blade in food processor bowl; add apple. Process until pureed, stopping once to scrape down sides.

Combine pureed apple, apple cider, and next 4 ingredients in a large Dutch oven, stirring well. Cook over low heat until thoroughly heated.

Beat whipping cream until foamy; gradually add brown sugar and salt, beating until soft peaks form. Dollop whipped cream mixture on cider mixture. Serve immediately. Yield: 16 cups.   Dina Driggs

A Bite of the Best
The Relief Society Church of Jesus Christ of Latter Day Saints
Provo, Utah

Bloody Marys by the Gallon

This classic brunch favorite is strong and spicy.

½ cup fresh lime juice
¼ cup Worcestershire sauce
⅓ cup celery salt
3 tablespoons pepper
2 tablespoons prepared horseradish
2 (46-ounce) cans tomato juice
1 (750-milliliter) bottle vodka
Garnish: celery stalks

Combine first 5 ingredients in a large pitcher; stir well. Add tomato juice and vodka, stirring well. Serve over ice. Garnish, if desired. Yield: 16 cups.
Cissy Holloway

Texas Sampler
The Junior League of Richardson, Texas

Marshmallow Cream Eggnog

Here's a guilt-free take on a classic holiday indulgence.

4 cups fat-free milk
½ cup marshmallow cream
3 tablespoons sugar
½ vanilla bean, split lengthwise
1⅔ cups egg substitute
½ cup bourbon (optional)

½ teaspoon freshly grated
    nutmeg (optional)
2 cups low-fat vanilla ice
    cream, softened
Garnish: freshly grated nutmeg

Combine first 4 ingredients in a large saucepan, and cook over medium-low heat until marshmallow cream melts, stirring often.

Pour egg substitute into a bowl. Gradually stir about one-fourth of hot mixture into egg substitute; add to remaining hot mixture, stirring constantly. Cook over medium-low heat, stirring constantly, 3 to 4 minutes or until thickened; remove from heat. If desired, stir in bourbon and ½ teaspoon nutmeg. Let stand until cool. Cover and chill 3 hours; remove and discard vanilla bean.

Stir in ice cream just before serving. Garnish, if desired. Yield: 9 cups.

A Taste of the Good Life from the Heart of Tennessee
Saint Thomas Heart Institute
Nashville, Tennessee

Dynamite

1 gallon vanilla ice cream
1 (750-milliliter) bottle brandy
    or bourbon

Ground nutmeg

Soften ice cream in a large bowl. Add brandy, and stir with a wire whisk until smooth. Cover and freeze at least 24 hours (mixture will not freeze solid).

Stir with a wire whisk before serving. Serve immediately in punch cups; sprinkle with nutmeg. Yield: 17 cups.   Marwood H. Goetz

Nothing But the Best
College of Human Environmental Sciences/University of Alabama
Tuscaloosa, Alabama

Breads

Focaccia, page 89

Spiced Applesauce Bread

Warm and toasty spices give this applesauce quick bread its sweet, homespun character. A generous amount of chopped pecans tucked inside and a crunchy pecan and brown sugar topping ensure nutty flavor in every bite.

1¼ cups applesauce
1 cup sugar
½ cup vegetable oil
2 large eggs, lightly beaten
3 tablespoons milk
2 cups all-purpose flour
½ teaspoon baking powder
1 teaspoon baking soda
¼ teaspoon salt
½ teaspoon ground cinnamon
¼ teaspoon ground nutmeg
¼ teaspoon ground allspice
1 cup chopped pecans, divided
¼ cup firmly packed brown sugar
½ teaspoon ground cinnamon

Combine first 5 ingredients in a large bowl; stir well.

Combine flour and next 6 ingredients; add to applesauce mixture, stirring well. Fold in ½ cup pecans. Pour batter into a greased 9- x 5- x 3-inch loafpan. Combine remaining ½ cup pecans, brown sugar, and ½ teaspoon cinnamon; sprinkle over batter in pan.

Bake at 350° for 1 hour or until a wooden pick inserted in center comes out clean. Cool in pan on a wire rack 10 minutes; remove from pan. Cool completely on wire rack. Yield: 1 loaf.   Nancy H. Hamill

Fishing for Compliments
Shedd Aquarium Society
Chicago, Illinois

Hawaiian Pineapple Banana Bread

3 cups all-purpose flour
1 teaspoon baking soda
¾ teaspoon salt
2 cups sugar
1 cup chopped walnuts
1 teaspoon ground cinnamon
3 large eggs, beaten
2 cups mashed ripe banana
1 cup vegetable oil
1 (8-ounce) can crushed pineapple, drained
2 teaspoons vanilla extract

Combine first 6 ingredients in a bowl; make a well in center of mixture. Combine eggs and remaining 4 ingredients; add to dry ingredients, stirring just until moistened.

Spoon batter into two greased and floured 8½- x 4½- x 3-inch loaf-pans. Bake at 350° for 1 hour and 15 minutes or until a wooden pick inserted in center comes out clean. Cool in pans on wire racks 10 minutes; remove from pans, and let cool completely on wire racks. Yield: 2 loaves.   Dorothy Paterline

Let's Get Cooking
Monvale Health Resources Auxiliary
Monongahela, Pennsylvania

Cream Cheese Coffee Cake

½ cup butter, softened
1 (8-ounce) package cream
   cheese, softened
1½ cups sugar
2 large eggs
2 cups all-purpose flour

2 teaspoons baking powder
½ teaspoon baking soda
½ teaspoon salt
½ cup milk
1 teaspoon vanilla extract
Topping

Beat butter and cream cheese at medium speed of an electric mixer until creamy; gradually add sugar, beating well. Add eggs, one at a time, beating after each addition.

Combine flour, baking powder, soda, and salt; add to butter mixture alternately with milk, beginning and ending with flour mixture. Mix at low speed just until blended after each addition. Stir in vanilla.

Pour batter into a greased 13- x 9- x 2-inch pan. Sprinkle with Topping. Bake at 350° for 40 minutes or until a wooden pick inserted in center comes out clean. Cool in pan on a wire rack. Yield: 12 servings.

Topping

½ cup all-purpose flour
½ cup firmly packed brown
   sugar

½ cup chopped pecans
¼ cup butter, melted

Combine all ingredients. Yield: 1½ cups.   Michelle Jackson

Sharing Tasteful Memories
L.A.C.E. (Ladies Aspiring to Christian Excellence) of
First Church of the Nazarene
Longview, Texas

Grandma's Coffee Cake

Sugar and cinnamon are tossed with fresh blueberries and sprinkled atop this easy-to-make coffee cake. After baking, the sugar-cinnamon mix gets crisp and crunchy, in pleasing contrast to the plump berries.

1½ cups all-purpose flour	3 tablespoons butter, melted
2 teaspoons baking powder	1 teaspoon vanilla extract
1 cup sugar	½ cup sugar
1 large egg, beaten	1 teaspoon ground cinnamon
¾ cup milk	1 cup fresh blueberries

Combine first 3 ingredients in a medium bowl; stir well. Add egg and next 3 ingredients, stirring until smooth. Pour batter into a greased 9-inch round cakepan.

Combine ½ cup sugar and cinnamon, stirring well. Sprinkle over blueberries; toss gently. Spoon blueberry mixture evenly over batter.

Bake at 350° for 30 minutes or until a wooden pick inserted in center comes out clean. Let cool in pan on a wire rack. Yield: 8 servings.

Virginia Simson Nelson

Michigan Cooks
C.S. Mott Children's Hospital
Ann Arbor, Michigan

Peachy Sour Cream Coffee Cake

2 cups chopped pecans	2 cups all-purpose flour
⅓ cup firmly packed brown sugar	1½ teaspoons baking powder
3 tablespoons sugar	½ teaspoon baking soda
1 teaspoon ground cinnamon	½ teaspoon salt
½ cup butter, softened	1 (8-ounce) carton sour cream
1 cup sugar	1 teaspoon vanilla extract
2 large eggs	2 cups peeled, sliced fresh or frozen peaches, thawed

Combine first 4 ingredients in a small bowl, stirring well. Set pecan mixture aside.

Beat butter at medium speed of an electric mixer until creamy; gradually add 1 cup sugar, beating well. Add eggs, one at a time, beating after each addition.

Combine flour and next 3 ingredients; add to butter mixture alternately with sour cream, beginning and ending with flour mixture. Mix at low speed after each addition until blended. Stir in vanilla.

Pour half of batter into a greased 9-inch springform pan; sprinkle 1 cup pecan mixture over batter. Top with remaining half of batter, and sprinkle with ½ cup pecan mixture.

Bake at 350° for 30 minutes. Arrange peach slices in a ring on top of cake; sprinkle with remaining pecan mixture. Bake 40 additional minutes or until a wooden pick inserted in center comes out clean. Cool in pan on a wire rack 10 minutes; remove from pan, and let cool completely on wire rack. Yield: 12 servings.   Jeannie Baier

Cooking with the Lioness Club of Brown Deer
The Lioness Club of Brown Deer
Milwaukee, Wisconsin

Very Berry Muffins

Fresh blueberries and raspberries dot these fragrant muffins. A hint of orange and lemon complements the berry blend.

2 cups all-purpose flour	½ cup butter or margarine,
1 tablespoon baking powder	melted
½ teaspoon salt	½ cup fresh orange juice
½ cup sugar	¾ cup fresh blueberries
2 teaspoons grated lemon rind	¾ cup fresh raspberries
2 teaspoons grated orange rind	Vegetable cooking spray
1 large egg, beaten	

Combine first 6 ingredients in a large bowl; make a well in center of mixture.

Combine egg, butter, and orange juice; add to dry ingredients, stirring just until moistened. (Batter will be very thick.) Gently fold berries into batter. Spoon batter into muffin pans coated with cooking spray or paper-lined muffin pans, filling three-fourths full.

Bake at 400° for 18 to 20 minutes or until golden. Cool muffins in pan 1 minute; remove from pan, and let cool completely on a wire rack. Yield: 1 dozen.

Dawn to Dusk, A Taste of Holland
The Junior Welfare League of Holland, Michigan

Macadamia Nut Muffins

These tall, regal muffins are fit for a queen. They're bejeweled with buttery macadamia nuts and coconut. Brew a lovely pot of tea, and indulge.

¼ cup plus 2 tablespoons butter
¼ cup plus 2 tablespoons shortening
1 cup sugar
2 large eggs, beaten
1 cup milk
2 teaspoons vanilla extract

3 cups unbleached flour
4 teaspoons baking powder
¾ teaspoon salt
½ cup chopped macadamia nuts
½ cup flaked coconut
2 cups sifted powdered sugar
¼ cup fresh lemon juice

Beat butter and shortening at medium speed of an electric mixer until creamy. Gradually add 1 cup sugar, beating well.

Combine eggs, milk, and vanilla. Combine flour and next 4 ingredients. Add flour mixture to butter mixture alternately with egg mixture, beating after each addition.

Spoon batter into greased muffin pans, filling almost full. Bake at 350° for 25 minutes or until golden. Cool in pan 1 minute; remove from pan, and let cool 10 minutes on a wire rack.

Combine powdered sugar and juice. Drizzle over muffins. Cool completely on wire rack. Yield: 1 dozen.   The Berg Family, Asa Berg

Ka Mea 'Ai 'Ono Loa: Delicious Foods from
the Honolulu Waldorf School
Honolulu Waldorf School
Honolulu, Hawaii

Sunshine Muffins

Fresh orange juice, orange marmalade, and orange extract add a triple dose of citrus flavor to these hearty whole wheat and walnut muffins. We found that using paper-lined muffin pans produces prettier peaked muffins than greased muffin pans.

1⅔ cups sugar
1½ cups all-purpose flour
1 cup whole wheat flour
2 teaspoons baking powder
½ teaspoon salt
3 large eggs, beaten
¾ cup butter or margarine, melted

⅔ cup fresh orange juice
1 tablespoon orange marmalade
1 teaspoon orange extract
1 teaspoon vanilla extract
½ cup chopped walnuts

Combine first 5 ingredients in a medium bowl; make a well in center of mixture.

Combine eggs and next 5 ingredients; add to dry ingredients, stirring just until moistened. Gently stir in walnuts.

Spoon batter into paper-lined muffin pans, filling two-thirds full. Bake at 350° for 25 minutes or until golden. Remove from pans immediately. Cool on wire racks. Yield: 1½ dozen.   Carol Flickinger

Fire Gals' Hot Pans Cookbook
Garrison Emergency Services Auxiliary
Garrison, Iowa

Dried Cherry and Cream Scones

2 cups all-purpose flour
1 tablespoon baking powder
½ teaspoon salt
¼ cup sugar
¾ cup chopped dried cherries
1 tablespoon grated lemon rind

1¼ cups whipping cream
2 tablespoons unsalted butter, melted
2 tablespoons sugar
1 teaspoon grated lemon rind

Combine first 4 ingredients in a large bowl. Stir in cherries and 1 tablespoon lemon rind. Add whipping cream, stirring with a fork just until dry ingredients are moistened.

Turn dough out onto a lightly floured surface; knead lightly 4 or 5 times, just until dough holds together. Pat dough into an 8-inch circle on an ungreased baking sheet. Cut dough into 8 wedges; separate wedges slightly. Brush with melted butter. Combine 2 tablespoons sugar and 1 teaspoon lemon rind; sprinkle over dough.

Bake at 400° for 23 minutes or until golden. Remove from pan. Serve warm or let cool on a wire rack. Yield: 8 scones.

A Capital Affair
The Junior League of Harrisburg, Pennsylvania

Lavosh (Armenian Cracker Bread)

Irregularly shaped rounds of this flat, crispy bread are baked and then broken into serving-size pieces. Serve this unique cracker bread with soup, salad, or as an after-school snack.

1¾ cups whole wheat flour
1 cup all-purpose flour
½ teaspoon baking soda
½ teaspoon salt
¼ cup sugar
½ cup butter

1 cup buttermilk
Vegetable cooking spray
2 teaspoons poppy seeds, divided
2 teaspoons sesame seeds, divided

Combine first 5 ingredients in a large bowl; cut in butter with pastry blender until mixture is crumbly. Slowly add buttermilk, stirring with a fork until dry ingredients are moistened. Shape into 6 balls.

Place 1 portion of dough on a large baking sheet coated with cooking spray, and sprinkle with flour. Roll dough into a 12-inch circle, sprinkling with additional flour. (Dough will be very thin and irregularly shaped.) Sprinkle evenly with a rounded ¼ teaspoon each poppy seeds and sesame seeds; roll once to press in seeds.

Bake at 400° for 6 to 7 minutes or until golden. Carefully remove from baking sheet, and let cool completely on a wire rack. Repeat procedure with remaining portions of dough and seeds. Yield: 6 large crackers.

Jan Godfrey

A Bite of the Best
The Relief Society Church of Jesus Christ of Latter Day Saints
Provo, Utah

Salad Bread

Rounds of biscuit dough are dipped in melted butter and bits of onion, sweet red pepper, and celery, and then sprinkled with shredded Cheddar cheese before baking. The result is a wonderful cheese- and vegetable-laced pull-apart loaf.

½ cup chopped onion
½ cup chopped sweet red or
   green pepper
½ cup chopped celery
½ cup butter or margarine,
   melted

3 (12-ounce) cans flaky biscuits
   (we tested with Hungry Jack)
1 cup (4 ounces) shredded
   Cheddar cheese

Cook first 3 ingredients in melted butter in a large skillet until tender, stirring often.

Cut biscuits into fourths. Dip biscuit pieces in vegetable mixture, coating with butter and vegetables. Place pieces in a lightly greased 10-inch Bundt pan; sprinkle with cheese.

Bake at 350° for 40 minutes or until golden. Cool in pan 10 minutes; invert onto a serving platter, and serve immediately. Yield: one 10-inch ring.

Betty Gentry

Treasured Recipes
Chaparral Home Extension
Chaparral, New Mexico

Chocolate Babka

Traditional Polish babka is a rum-scented yeast bread studded with almonds, raisins, and orange peel. This cinnamon-scented version is filled with semisweet chocolate morsels. Walnuts and more morsels crown the pretty round loaf.

4 cups all-purpose flour, divided
2 (¼-ounce) envelopes active dry yeast
¾ cup sugar
⅔ cup water
½ cup butter
⅓ cup evaporated milk
4 egg yolks
1 cup (6 ounces) semisweet chocolate morsels
½ cup evaporated milk

2 tablespoons sugar
½ teaspoon ground cinnamon
½ cup all-purpose flour
⅓ cup firmly packed brown sugar
1 teaspoon ground cinnamon
¼ cup plus 2 tablespoons butter
½ cup (3 ounces) semisweet chocolate morsels
½ cup chopped walnuts or pecans

Combine 1½ cups flour and yeast in a large mixing bowl.

Combine ¾ cup sugar, water, butter, and ⅓ cup evaporated milk in a small saucepan; heat over medium heat, stirring constantly, just until hot (120° to 130°). Gradually add liquid mixture to flour mixture, beating at medium speed of a heavy-duty stand mixer. Beat 2 additional minutes. Add egg yolks, and beat at low speed 1 minute; beat at high speed 3 additional minutes. Gradually stir in remaining 2½ cups flour.

Place dough in a large well-greased bowl. Cover and let rise in a warm place (85°), free from drafts, 2 hours or until doubled in bulk.

Punch dough down; turn out onto a lightly floured surface, and let rest 10 minutes.

Combine 1 cup chocolate morsels, ½ cup evaporated milk, 2 tablespoons sugar, and ½ teaspoon cinnamon in a small saucepan; cook over low heat just until chocolate melts, stirring often. Let cool.

Roll dough into an 18- x 10-inch rectangle. Spread chocolate filling mixture to within ½-inch of edges of dough. Roll up dough carefully to contain filling, starting at long side; pinch ends together to seal. Place dough, seam side down, in a greased 10-inch tube pan.

Combine ½ cup flour, brown sugar, and 1 teaspoon cinnamon; cut in butter with pastry blender until mixture is crumbly. Stir in ½ cup chocolate morsels and nuts; sprinkle over dough. Cover and let rise in a warm place, free from drafts, 1 hour or until doubled in bulk.

Bake at 350° for 40 minutes or until loaf sounds hollow when tapped. Cool in pan 5 minutes; remove from pan, and let cool completely on a wire rack. Yield: one 10-inch loaf.

What's Cooking in Our Family?
Temple Beth-El
Providence, Rhode Island

Raisin Pumpernickel Bread

2 (¼-ounce) envelopes active dry yeast
1 teaspoon sugar or honey
2 cups warm water (110° to 115°)
3 cups all-purpose flour
6 tablespoons cocoa
⅓ cup dark molasses
¼ cup cider vinegar
1 tablespoon salt
2 tablespoons vegetable oil
1 tablespoon caraway seeds
1 teaspoon fennel seeds
½ cup raisins
3½ to 4 cups rye flour
2 tablespoons butter, melted
⅓ cup water
1 teaspoon cornstarch

Combine yeast, sugar, and warm water in a 2-cup liquid measuring cup; let stand 5 minutes.

Add 3 cups flour and next 7 ingredients. Beat at medium speed of an electric mixer 3 minutes or until blended. Stir in raisins. Gradually stir in enough rye flour to make a soft dough. Turn dough out onto a floured surface, and knead until smooth and elastic (about 8 to 10 minutes). Place in a well-greased bowl, turning to grease top.

Cover and let rise in a warm place (85°), free from drafts, 2 hours or until doubled in bulk. Punch dough down; divide in half. Shape each portion into an oval. Place in two greased 9- x 5- x 3-inch loafpans; make slashes on top of loaves, using a sharp knife. Brush with butter. Cover and let rise in a warm place, free from drafts, 1 hour or until almost doubled in bulk. Bake at 375° for 30 to 35 minutes.

Combine ⅓ cup water and cornstarch in a saucepan. Bring to a boil over medium-high heat; brush over loaves. Bake 15 additional minutes or until loaves sound hollow when tapped. Remove from pans immediately; cool on wire racks. Yield: 2 loaves.   Maureen Reed

Past Receipts, Present Recipes
Cumberland County Historical Society
Carlisle, Pennsylvania

Cinnamon English Muffin Bread

These simple little cinnamon-raisin loaves boast the same texture and flavor as English muffins. They're a little on the shallow side, making them perfectly suited to popping in the toaster.

Cornmeal
½ cup water
2 cups milk
5 cups all-purpose flour, divided
2 (¼-ounce) envelopes active dry yeast
¼ teaspoon baking soda
2 teaspoons salt
1 tablespoon sugar
1½ teaspoons ground cinnamon
1 cup raisins

Grease two 9- x 5- x 3-inch loafpans, and coat with cornmeal. Set aside.

Combine water and milk in a saucepan; heat over medium heat just until hot (120° to 130°).

Combine 3 cups flour, yeast, and next 4 ingredients in a large mixing bowl. Gradually add liquid mixture to flour mixture, beating at high speed of an electric mixer. Beat 2 additional minutes at medium speed. Stir in raisins. Gradually stir in remaining 2 cups flour to make a soft dough.

Spoon dough into prepared loafpans. Sprinkle tops with cornmeal. Cover and let rise in a warm place (85°), free from drafts, 45 minutes or until doubled in bulk.

Bake at 400° for 25 minutes. Remove bread from pans immediately; cool on wire racks. Yield: 2 loaves.   Pauline Moffatt

Party Pleasers
GFWC Philomathic Club
Duncan, Oklahoma

Honey-Yogurt Batter Bread

1 (16-ounce) carton plain
  nonfat yogurt
⅔ cup honey
½ cup water
½ cup butter or margarine
8 cups all-purpose flour,
  divided

2 (¼-ounce) envelopes active
  dry yeast
1 tablespoon salt
2 large eggs

Combine first 4 ingredients in a saucepan; heat until butter melts, stirring occasionally. Cool to 120° to 130°.

Combine 3 cups flour, yeast, and salt in a large mixing bowl. Gradually add yogurt mixture to flour mixture, beating at low speed of an electric mixer until blended. Beat 2 additional minutes at medium speed. Add eggs; beat well. Gradually stir in enough remaining flour to make a soft dough.

Turn dough out onto a floured surface, and knead until smooth and elastic (about 8 minutes). Place in a well-greased bowl, turning to grease top. Cover and let rise in a warm place (85°), free from drafts, 1 hour or until doubled in bulk.

Punch dough down; turn out onto a lightly floured surface, and knead lightly 4 or 5 times. Divide dough in half. Roll 1 portion of dough into a 14- x 7-inch rectangle. Roll up dough, starting at short side, pressing firmly to eliminate air pockets; pinch ends to seal. Place dough, seam side down, in a well-greased 9- x 5- x 3-inch loafpan. Repeat procedure with remaining dough.

Cover and let rise in a warm place, free from drafts, 45 minutes or until doubled in bulk.

Bake at 350° for 35 to 40 minutes or until loaves sound hollow when tapped. Remove bread from pans immediately; cool on wire racks. Yield: 2 loaves.

Dick Turnage

Blessed Isle
Episcopal Church Women of All Saints Parish
Pawleys Island, South Carolina

Olive and Cheese Baguettes

Food processor French bread is flattered by the addition of a pimiento-stuffed olive and Cheddar cheese filling. It can be served either warm or cooled, and makes the perfect addition to a tailgate party or picnic.

1 (¼-ounce) envelope active
  dry yeast
1 cup warm water (105° to 115°)
1 tablespoon sugar
3 cups all-purpose flour
½ teaspoon salt
2 tablespoons vegetable oil
1 (5¾-ounce) jar pimiento-stuffed
  olives, drained (about 1 cup)

1 (8-ounce) package block
  Cheddar cheese
Cornmeal
1 egg white, lightly beaten
1 tablespoon water
1 teaspoon poppy seeds

Combine first 3 ingredients in a 2-cup liquid measuring cup; let stand 10 minutes.

Position knife blade in food processor bowl; add flour, salt, and oil. Pulse 2 or 3 times or until mixture is combined. Pour yeast mixture through food chute with processor running. Process until dough is smooth and elastic (about 40 seconds).

Turn dough out onto a lightly floured surface, and shape into a ball. Place in a well-greased bowl, turning to grease top. Cover and let rise in a warm place (85°), free from drafts, 1 hour or until doubled in bulk.

Meanwhile, position knife blade in processor bowl; add olives. Pulse 2 or 3 times or until olives are coarsely chopped. Set aside.

Cut cheese into 6 pieces. Position shredding disc in processor bowl; push cheese through food chute with processor running, using medium pressure. Combine olives and cheese, tossing lightly; cover and set aside.

Grease two French bread pans or a baking sheet, and lightly sprinkle with cornmeal.

Punch dough down; turn out onto a lightly floured surface. Divide dough in half. Roll 1 portion of dough into a 14- x 8-inch rectangle. Spoon half of olive mixture along lower half of long side. Roll up dough, starting at long side, pressing gently to contain mixture; pinch ends, and turn under to seal. Place dough, seam side down, in prepared pan or on baking sheet. Repeat procedure with remaining dough and olive mixture. Cover and let rise in a warm place, free from drafts, 40 minutes or until doubled in bulk. Combine egg white and water, stirring until blended. Gently brush egg white mixture over loaves. Sprinkle evenly with poppy seeds.

Bake at 375° for 25 minutes or until golden. Remove bread from pans or baking sheet immediately, and cool on wire racks. Yield: 2 loaves.

Eleanor Magill

Our Favorite Recipes
The Claremont Society for the Prevention of Cruelty to Animals
Serving Sullivan County
Claremont, New Hampshire

Italian Rosemary Bread

2½ to 3 cups bread flour, divided
1 (¼-ounce) envelope active dry yeast
1 tablespoon dried rosemary, crushed
2 teaspoons salt
1 cup warm water (120° to 130°)
3 tablespoons olive oil
Additional olive oil
Freshly ground pepper

Combine 1½ cups flour, yeast, rosemary, and salt in a large mixing bowl. Gradually add warm water and 3 tablespoons olive oil, beating at medium speed of an electric mixer until well blended. Gradually stir in enough remaining flour to make a soft dough.

Turn dough out onto a lightly floured surface, and knead until smooth and elastic (about 5 minutes). Place in a well-greased bowl, turning to grease top. Cover and let rise in a warm place (85°), free from drafts, 1 hour or until doubled in bulk.

Punch dough down, and press into a 12-inch pizza pan coated with olive oil. Poke indentations in dough at 1-inch intervals with finger or handle of a wooden spoon. Brush dough with olive oil, and sprinkle with pepper. Let rise, uncovered, in a warm place, free from drafts, 30 minutes or until almost doubled in bulk.

Bake at 400° for 20 to 25 minutes or until golden. Brush bread with olive oil, if desired, and cut into wedges or squares to serve. Yield: 6 servings.

Sheila Hart

Waiting to Inhale
Pacific Coast Mothers Club
Huntington Beach, California

Red Pepper-Cheese Bread

1 large sweet red pepper
1 (¼-ounce) envelope active dry yeast
1¼ cups warm water (105° to 115°)
½ cup warm milk (105° to 115°)
1½ cups stone-ground whole wheat flour
2 teaspoons salt
1½ teaspoons dried dillweed
1 teaspoon brown sugar
1 teaspoon dried crushed red pepper
1 teaspoon sesame seeds
⅛ teaspoon ground red pepper
3½ cups all-purpose flour, divided
1 cup (4 ounces) shredded Monterey Jack cheese
1 tablespoon water

Cut sweet red pepper in half lengthwise; discard seeds and membrane. Place pepper, skin side up, on an ungreased baking sheet; flatten with palm of hand. Broil 5½ inches from heat (with electric oven door partially opened) 15 to 20 minutes or until charred. Place in ice water until cool; peel and discard skin. Finely chop pepper; set aside.

Combine yeast and warm water in a 2-cup liquid measuring cup; let stand 5 minutes. Combine yeast mixture and milk in a large bowl; stir in chopped pepper, whole wheat flour, and next 6 ingredients. Stir in 2 cups all-purpose flour and cheese. Turn dough out onto a floured surface; knead in remaining all-purpose flour, ¼ cup at a time, until smooth and elastic (about 10 minutes). Cover and let rest 5 minutes.

Divide dough in half. Press 1 portion into an 8- x 4-inch rectangle, pressing out air bubbles. Bring long edges together in center, pinching edges to close seam, and gently stretching loaf lengthwise. Pat dough flat; repeat pinching and stretching to make a 16-inch-long loaf about 2 inches in diameter. Place loaf, seam side down, on a large greased baking sheet. Repeat procedure with remaining dough.

Cover and let rise in a warm place (85°), free from drafts, 35 minutes or until almost doubled in bulk. Brush tops with 1 tablespoon water; make diagonal ¼-inch-deep slits down length of loaves, using a sharp knife.

Place a large shallow pan on bottom rack of oven; heat oven to 450°. Add 1 cup hot water to pan to create steam. Place baking sheet on oven rack above pan. Bake 20 minutes or until loaves sound hollow when tapped. Yield: two 16-inch loaves.   Melinda Littlejohn

Malibu's Cooking Again
Malibu's Cooking Again
Malibu, California

Focaccia

1¾ cups unbleached flour
1 (¼-ounce) envelope active
  dry yeast
1 teaspoon sugar

¾ teaspoon salt
¾ cup water
2½ tablespoons olive oil
Topping variations (choose 1)

Combine first 4 ingredients in a large bowl; stir well. Set aside. Combine water and oil in a saucepan; heat to 120° to 130°. Gradually add to flour mixture, stirring to form a sticky dough. Turn out onto a floured surface, and knead until smooth and elastic (about 10 minutes), adding additional flour as needed. Shape into a ball; place in a well-greased bowl, turning to grease top. Cover and let rise in a warm place (85°), free from drafts, 40 minutes or until doubled in bulk.

Punch dough down, and let rest 5 minutes; turn out onto a lightly floured surface, and knead 4 or 5 times. Roll into a 12-inch round; place on a greased baking sheet or in a greased 12-inch pizza pan. Cover and let rise in a warm place, free from drafts, 30 minutes. Poke indentations in dough at 1-inch intervals with finger or handle of a wooden spoon. For each topping, drizzle dough with olive oil, and sprinkle with remaining ingredients. Bake at 400° for 25 minutes or until lightly browned. Remove from oven, and let cool on baking sheet 5 minutes; cut into wedges, and serve warm. Yield: 6 servings.

Feta-Pesto-Tomato

1½ tablespoons olive oil
½ cup pesto

½ cup diced dried tomatoes
½ cup crumbled feta cheese

Garlic-Rosemary

3 tablespoons olive oil
2 tablespoons dried rosemary

1 teaspoon minced garlic

Gorgonzola-Pine Nut

2 tablespoons olive oil
½ cup crumbled Gorgonzola
  cheese

2 tablespoons pine nuts

Colorado Collage
The Junior League of Denver, Colorado

Mama Pick's Dinner Rolls

2 cups milk
½ cup sugar
½ cup shortening
1 (¼-ounce) envelope active
    dry yeast
¼ cup warm water (105° to 115°)

6½ cups all-purpose flour,
    divided
½ teaspoon baking powder
½ teaspoon baking soda
1 teaspoon salt

Combine first 3 ingredients in a saucepan; heat until shortening melts, stirring occasionally. Cool to 105° to 115°.

Combine yeast and warm water in a 1-cup liquid measuring cup; let stand 5 minutes.

Combine milk mixture, yeast mixture, and 2 cups flour in a large mixing bowl; beat at medium speed of an electric mixer until well blended. Gradually stir in 2 cups flour.

Cover and let rise in a warm place (85°), free from drafts, 45 minutes or until doubled in bulk.

Combine 2 cups flour, baking powder, soda, and salt in a large mixing bowl; add yeast mixture. Beat at medium speed until well blended.

Sprinkle remaining ½ cup flour evenly over work surface. Turn dough out onto floured surface, and knead until smooth and elastic (about 5 minutes). Roll dough to ¼-inch thickness; cut into rounds with a 2-inch biscuit cutter. Fold rounds in half, gently pressing edges to seal.

Arrange rolls in four greased 9-inch round cakepans. Cover and let rise in a warm place, free from drafts, 45 minutes or until doubled in bulk. Bake at 400° for 10 to 12 minutes or until golden. Yield: 5½ dozen.

Karon Pickering

The Best of West
The Junior Beta Club of West Jones Middle School
Laurel, Mississippi

Cakes

Chocolate Torte with Butter-Rum Sauce, page 114

Rave Reviews Coconut Cake

Coconut toasted in butter brings out the sweet richness of the flakes and the cream cheese frosting it flavors.

1 (18.25-ounce) package yellow cake mix (we tested with Duncan Hines)
1 (3.4-ounce) package vanilla instant pudding mix
1⅓ cups water
¼ cup vegetable oil
4 large eggs
5 cups flaked coconut, divided
1 cup chopped walnuts
3 tablespoons butter
1½ (8-ounce) packages cream cheese, softened
1 tablespoon milk
¾ teaspoon vanilla extract
5¼ cups sifted powdered sugar

Combine first 5 ingredients in a large mixing bowl; beat at low speed of an electric mixer until blended. Beat at medium speed 4 minutes. Stir in 2 cups coconut and walnuts. Pour batter into three greased and floured 9-inch round cakepans.

Bake at 350° for 25 to 30 minutes or until a wooden pick inserted in center comes out clean. Cool in pans on wire racks 10 minutes; remove from pans, and let cool completely on wire racks.

Cook remaining 3 cups coconut and butter in a large skillet over low heat, stirring constantly, until coconut is lightly browned. Spread browned coconut on paper towels; let cool.

Beat cream cheese at medium speed of an electric mixer until creamy. Add milk and vanilla; beat well. Gradually add powdered sugar, beating at low speed until well blended. Stir in 2½ cups browned coconut.

Spread frosting between layers and on top and sides of cake. Sprinkle remaining browned coconut on top of cake. Yield: one 3-layer cake.

Linda Windham

The Best of West
The Junior Beta Club of West Jones Middle School
Laurel, Mississippi

Fresh Grapefruit Cake

To impart a rosy glow to the cake and frosting try pink grapefruit. Use a hot knife to make a clean cut through the glossy frosting.

⅔ cup butter, softened
1¾ cups sugar
2 large eggs
3 cups sifted cake flour
2½ teaspoons baking powder
½ teaspoon salt

½ cup fresh grapefruit juice
¾ cup milk
1 teaspoon grated grapefruit
  rind
1½ teaspoons vanilla extract
Grapefruit Frosting

Beat butter at medium speed of an electric mixer until creamy; gradually add sugar, beating well. Add eggs, one at a time, beating after each addition.

Combine flour, baking powder, and salt; add to butter mixture alternately with grapefruit juice, beginning and ending with flour mixture. Mix at low speed after each addition until blended. Gradually add milk, beating well. Stir in grapefruit rind and vanilla. Pour batter into two greased and floured 9-inch round cakepans.

Bake at 350° for 25 minutes or until a wooden pick inserted in center comes out clean. Cool in pans on wire racks 10 minutes; remove from pans, and cool completely on wire racks. Spread frosting between layers and on top and sides of cake. Yield: one 2-layer cake.

Grapefruit Frosting

1½ cups sugar
⅛ teaspoon salt
⅓ cup fresh grapefruit juice
2 egg whites

1 tablespoon light corn syrup
1 tablespoon grated grapefruit
  rind
2 teaspoons vanilla extract

Combine first 5 ingredients in top of a double boiler. Beat at low speed of an electric mixer 30 seconds or just until blended. Place over boiling water; beat constantly at high speed 7 to 9 minutes or until stiff peaks form and temperature reaches 160°. Remove from heat. Add rind and vanilla; beat 1 to 2 minutes or until thick enough to spread. Spread immediately. Yield: 3¾ cups.   John E. Troha

Dinner Bells for Handbells
Umatilla Presbyterian Church
Umatilla, Florida

Chocolate Praline Cake

1 cup firmly packed brown sugar
½ cup butter
¼ cup whipping cream
½ cup finely chopped pecans
1 (18.25-ounce) package devil's food cake mix with pudding (we tested with Pillsbury Plus)
1¼ cups water
⅓ cup vegetable oil
3 large eggs
Filling and Topping
Pecan halves
Chocolate curls

Combine first 3 ingredients in a medium saucepan; cook over medium heat until sugar and butter melt, stirring occasionally. Pour mixture evenly into two 9-inch round cakepans. Sprinkle evenly with chopped pecans.

Combine cake mix, water, oil, and eggs in a large mixing bowl. Beat at high speed of an electric mixer 2 minutes or until blended. Pour into prepared pans.

Bake at 325° for 35 to 40 minutes or until a wooden pick inserted in center comes out clean. Cool in pans on wire racks 5 minutes. Turn out carefully onto racks, spooning any praline mixture remaining in pans over cake layers. Let cool completely.

Spread Filling and Topping mixture between layers and on top of cake. Top with pecan halves and chocolate curls. Store in refrigerator. Yield: one 2-layer cake.

Filling and Topping

¾ cup whipping cream
¼ cup sifted powdered sugar
¼ teaspoon vanilla extract

Beat whipping cream until foamy; gradually add sugar and vanilla, beating until soft peaks form. Yield: 1¼ cups.   Anne Ciurila

Healthy Cooking for Kids–and You!
The Children's Wish Foundation
West Melbourne, Florida

Kahlúa White Russian Cake

3 tablespoons Kahlúa
2 tablespoons vodka
2 (1-ounce) white chocolate
   baking squares, chopped
½ cup butter, softened
2 tablespoons shortening
1¼ cups sugar

3 large eggs
1¾ cups all-purpose flour
¾ teaspoon baking soda
½ teaspoon baking powder
¾ cup buttermilk
⅓ cup apricot preserves or jam
White Russian Cream

Combine first 3 ingredients in a small heavy saucepan. Cook over low heat until white chocolate melts, stirring occasionally; let cool.

Beat butter and shortening at medium speed of an electric mixer until creamy; gradually add sugar, beating well. Add eggs, one at a time, beating after each addition.

Combine flour, baking soda, and baking powder; add to butter mixture alternately with buttermilk, beginning and ending with flour mixture. Mix at low speed after each addition until blended. Stir in white chocolate mixture. Pour batter into three greased and floured 8-inch round cakepans.

Bake at 350° for 16 to 18 minutes or until a wooden pick inserted in center comes out clean. Cool in pans on wire racks 10 minutes; remove from pans, and let cool completely on wire racks.

Place 1 cake layer on a serving plate, and spread with half of apricot preserves and 1 cup White Russian Cream. Top with second cake layer. Spread with remaining preserves and 1 cup White Russian Cream. Top with remaining cake layer. Spread remaining White Russian Cream on top and sides of cake. Chill before serving. Store in refrigerator. Yield: one 3-layer cake.

White Russian Cream

2 cups whipping cream
½ cup sifted powdered sugar

¼ cup Kahlúa
2 teaspoons vodka

Chill mixing bowl and beaters. Beat cream until foamy; gradually add powdered sugar, beating until thickened. Add Kahlúa and vodka; beat until soft peaks form. Yield: 5½ cups.   Robyn Leyden

Just Peachey, Cooking Up a Cure
Catherine Peachey Fund
Warsaw, Indiana

Grandma's Hint-of-Mint Chocolate Cake

If you're a chocolate-mint combo fan, you'll adore this rich double-frosted sheet cake. Underneath the fudgy frosting lies a layer of melted peppermint patties. If you're in a rush, you can skip the frosting and let the swirled peppermint patty layer stand sublimely solo.

2 cups all-purpose flour
2 cups sugar
¼ cup cocoa
1 teaspoon ground cinnamon
1 cup butter
1 cup water
1 teaspoon baking soda
1 large egg, lightly beaten
½ cup buttermilk
1 teaspoon vanilla extract
1 (13-ounce) package miniature chocolate-covered peppermint patties, unwrapped (we tested with York)
Chocolate Frosting

Combine first 4 ingredients; set aside.

Combine butter and water in a saucepan; bring to a boil. Remove from heat; stir in baking soda. Add to flour mixture, stirring well.

Combine egg, buttermilk, and vanilla; stir into flour mixture. Pour batter into a greased and floured 13- x 9- x 2-inch pan. Bake at 350° for 30 minutes.

Top with peppermint patties, and bake 2 to 3 additional minutes or until patties melt. Gently spread melted patties over top of cake. Let cool completely. Spread Chocolate Frosting over top of cake. Yield: 15 servings.

Chocolate Frosting

½ cup butter
⅓ cup milk
1 (16-ounce) package powdered sugar, sifted
¼ cup cocoa
1 teaspoon vanilla extract

Combine butter and milk in a saucepan; bring to a boil.

Combine powdered sugar and cocoa; add to butter mixture, stirring until smooth. Stir in vanilla. Yield: 2 cups.   Carol Gockel

Texas Sampler
The Junior League of Richardson, Texas

Ponderosa Cake

1 cup butter, softened
2 cups sugar
2 large eggs
2 cups mashed very ripe
   banana (about 4 large)
1 teaspoon vanilla extract
3 cups all-purpose flour
2 teaspoons baking powder

2 teaspoons baking soda
1 (8-ounce) carton sour cream
½ cup firmly packed brown
   sugar
1 teaspoon ground cinnamon
1½ cups (9 ounces) semisweet
   chocolate morsels, divided

Beat butter at medium speed of an electric mixer until creamy; gradually add 2 cups sugar, beating well. Add eggs, one at a time, beating after each addition. Add mashed banana and vanilla, beating until smooth.

Combine flour, baking powder, and baking soda. Add to banana mixture alternately with sour cream, beginning and ending with flour mixture. Mix at low speed after each addition until blended. Spread half of batter into a greased 13- x 9- x 2-inch pan. Combine brown sugar and cinnamon; sprinkle half of brown sugar mixture over batter. Sprinkle ¾ cup chocolate morsels over brown sugar mixture. Repeat procedure with remaining batter, brown sugar mixture, and chocolate morsels. Bake at 350° for 55 to 60 minutes or until a wooden pick inserted in center comes out clean. Let cool in pan on a wire rack. Yield: 15 servings.

Nelson Yoshina

Renaissance of Recipes
Iao Intermediate School Renaissance Ke 'ala hou
Wailuku, Hawaii

Turtle Cake

Caramel, chocolate, and pecans–what's not to love? This decadent, rich cake is worth every calorie.

1 (18.25-ounce) package German chocolate cake mix with pudding (we tested with Betty Crocker)
3 cups chopped pecans, divided
¾ cup butter, melted
⅓ cup evaporated milk
1 (14-ounce) package caramels (about 50 caramels)
½ cup evaporated milk
2 cups (12 ounces) semisweet chocolate morsels

Combine cake mix, 2 cups pecans, butter, and ⅓ cup evaporated milk in a large bowl; stir well. Reserve half of cake mix mixture for topping. Press remaining half of mixture into a greased and floured 13- x 9- x 2-inch pan. Bake at 350° for 8 minutes. Remove pan from oven, and set aside.

Meanwhile, combine caramels and ½ cup evaporated milk in a small heavy saucepan. Cook over low heat until caramels melt, stirring often.

Sprinkle remaining 1 cup pecans and chocolate morsels evenly over cake. Drizzle caramel mixture over pecans and chocolate morsels. Crumble reserved cake mix mixture evenly over caramel mixture. Bake at 350° for 20 additional minutes. Let cool in pan on a wire rack. Yield: 12 servings.   Cyndi Bradt

Moments, Memories & Manna
Restoration Village
Rogers, Arkansas

Lemon Buttermilk Cake with Lemon Curd Sauce

1 cup butter, softened
2⅓ cups sugar, divided
3 large eggs
3 cups all-purpose flour
½ teaspoon baking soda
½ teaspoon salt
1 cup buttermilk

1½ tablespoons grated lemon rind
½ cup plus 3 tablespoons fresh lemon juice, divided
3 tablespoons fine, dry breadcrumbs (store-bought)
Lemon Curd Sauce

Beat butter at medium speed of an electric mixer until creamy; gradually add 2 cups sugar, beating well. Add eggs, one at a time, beating after each addition.

Combine flour, baking soda, and salt; add to butter mixture alternately with buttermilk, beginning and ending with flour mixture. Mix at low speed after each addition until blended. Stir in rind and 3 tablespoons juice. Pour into a buttered 12-cup Bundt pan coated with breadcrumbs. Bake at 350° for 1 hour to 1 hour and 15 minutes or until a wooden pick inserted in center comes out clean. Cool in pan on a wire rack 10 minutes; remove from pan, and place on wire rack.

Combine remaining ⅓ cup sugar and ½ cup lemon juice in a saucepan; cook over medium-low heat until sugar dissolves, stirring often. Prick cake at 1-inch intervals with a long wooden skewer or cake tester. Spoon juice mixture over top of warm cake; cool completely on wire rack. Serve with Lemon Curd Sauce. Yield: one 10-inch cake.

Lemon Curd Sauce

2 cups sugar
6 large eggs, lightly beaten
¼ cup grated lemon rind

¾ cup fresh lemon juice
¾ cup butter, softened

Combine first 4 ingredients in top of a double boiler; bring water to a boil. Reduce heat to medium; cook, stirring constantly, until mixture coats a spoon. Cool slightly. Add butter, a tablespoon at a time, whisking until blended. Serve immediately or chill. Yield: 4 cups.

Savour St. Louis
Barnes-Jewish Hospital Auxiliary Plaza Chapter
St. Louis, Missouri

Orange Liqueur Cake

Dress up a plain-Jane yellow cake mix with sour cream and orange-flavored liqueur plus a shiny golden marmalade glaze–instant glamour.

1 (18.25-ounce) package yellow cake mix with pudding (we tested with Betty Crocker)
3 large eggs
1 tablespoon grated orange rind
1 cup fresh orange juice
⅓ cup vegetable oil
⅓ cup sour cream
1 tablespoon lemon juice
1 tablespoon Cointreau or other orange-flavored liqueur
⅓ cup firmly packed brown sugar
⅓ cup fresh orange juice
2 tablespoons butter
⅓ cup Cointreau or other orange-flavored liqueur
½ cup apricot preserves
2 tablespoons orange marmalade
Garnish: orange rind slivers

Combine first 8 ingredients in a large mixing bowl; beat at low speed of an electric mixer 2 minutes. Pour batter into a greased 12-cup Bundt pan.

Bake at 350° for 35 to 40 minutes or until a wooden pick inserted in center comes out clean. Transfer cake in pan to a wire rack.

While cake bakes, combine brown sugar, ⅓ cup orange juice, and butter in a small saucepan. Cook over medium heat until sugar dissolves and butter melts, stirring occasionally. Remove from heat, and stir in ⅓ cup Cointreau.

Prick warm cake to bottom of pan at 1-inch intervals with a long wooden skewer or cake tester. Spoon warm orange juice mixture over warm cake. Let cool at least 3 hours in pan on wire rack.

Combine apricot preserves and orange marmalade in a small saucepan. Cook over medium heat, stirring constantly, just until preserves and marmalade melt. Pour mixture through a wire-mesh strainer into a bowl, discarding solids.

Invert cake onto a serving plate. Brush preserve mixture evenly over cake. Garnish, if desired. Yield: one 10-inch cake.

Noteworthy Two
Ravinia Festival Association
Highland Park, Illinois

Orange Carrot Cake

The personality of this out-of-the-ordinary carrot cake comes from an orange, rind and all. Use a navel orange (no seeds), and grind it in the food processor. You can even use your processor to grate the carrots and chop the nuts. A slathering of honey-sweetened cream cheese frosting heightens the flavors.

1 large navel orange, unpeeled and quartered
2 cups all-purpose flour
2 cups sugar
2 teaspoons baking powder
2 teaspoons baking soda
1 teaspoon salt
2 teaspoons ground cinnamon
2 teaspoons ground nutmeg
1¼ cups vegetable oil
4 large eggs
2 cups grated carrot
½ cup chopped walnuts
½ cup raisins
Cream Cheese Icing

Position knife blade in food processor bowl; add quartered orange, and process until pureed, stopping once to scrape down sides. Set orange puree aside.

Combine flour and next 6 ingredients in a large bowl. Add orange puree, oil, and eggs; mix well. Stir in carrot, walnuts, and raisins. Pour batter into a greased and floured 10-inch tube pan.

Bake at 350° for 1 hour. Let cool completely in pan on a wire rack. Remove cake from pan. Frost top of cake with Cream Cheese Icing. Cover and store in refrigerator. Yield: one 10-inch cake.

Cream Cheese Icing

1 (8-ounce) package cream cheese, softened
2 tablespoons honey
½ teaspoon vanilla extract

Beat cream cheese in a medium mixing bowl at medium speed of an electric mixer until creamy. Add honey and vanilla, and beat until blended. Yield: 1 cup.

Centennial Cookbook 1895-1995
Rogers Memorial Library
Southampton, New York

Pumpkin Spice Cake

Superbly spiced plus moist and pumpkiny—the perfect autumn/winter cake selection. Moisture-added baking raisins, new to the marketplace, go into the cake batter, plumped and perfect. Regular raisins work fine, too.

1½ cups butter, softened
2 cups sugar
4 large eggs
3 cups plus 2 tablespoons all-purpose flour, divided
2 teaspoons baking powder
1 teaspoon baking soda
1 teaspoon salt
2 teaspoons ground cinnamon
2 teaspoons ground allspice
1 teaspoon ground nutmeg

1 teaspoon ground cloves
2 cups canned mashed pumpkin
2 teaspoons vanilla extract
2 teaspoons rum extract
1 cup chopped pecans
1 cup moisture-added baking raisins (we tested with Sun-Maid)
Raisin Frosting

Beat butter at medium speed of an electric mixer until creamy; gradually add sugar, beating well. Add eggs, one at a time, beating after each addition.

Combine 3 cups flour, baking powder, and next 6 ingredients; add to butter mixture alternately with pumpkin, beginning and ending with flour mixture. Mix at low speed after each addition just until blended. Stir in flavorings. Combine remaining 2 tablespoons flour, pecans, and raisins; stir into batter. Pour batter into a greased and floured 12-cup Bundt or 10-inch tube pan.

Bake at 350° for 1 hour or until a wooden pick inserted in center comes out clean. Cool in pan on a wire rack 10 minutes; remove from pan, and let cool completely on wire rack. Spread Raisin Frosting on top and sides of cake. Yield: one 10-inch cake.

Raisin Frosting

1 cup firmly packed brown sugar
1 cup evaporated milk
½ cup butter
3 egg yolks, lightly beaten
1 teaspoon vanilla extract
1 teaspoon rum extract

1 cup moisture-added baking raisins (we tested with Sun-Maid)
¾ cup flaked coconut
¾ cup finely chopped pecans

Combine first 6 ingredients in a medium saucepan. Cook over medium heat 12 minutes, stirring constantly. Stir in raisins, coconut, and pecans. Let cool. Yield: 3 cups.

Ambrosia
The Junior Auxiliary of Vicksburg, Mississippi

Bourbon Pound Cake

Have two large mixing bowls at the ready to create this big and beautiful melt-in-your-mouth pound cake. One bowl is for beating the egg whites to fluffy perfection and the other is for blending the batter.

½ cup chopped pecans
8 large eggs, separated
3 cups sugar, divided
2 cups butter, softened
3 cups all-purpose flour

⅓ cup bourbon
2 teaspoons vanilla extract
2 teaspoons almond extract
Sifted powdered sugar

Generously grease a 10-inch tube pan; sprinkle pecans in pan.

Beat egg whites at high speed of an electric mixer until foamy. Gradually add 1 cup sugar, 1 tablespoon at a time, beating until stiff peaks form and sugar dissolves (2 to 4 minutes). Set aside.

Beat butter in a large mixing bowl at medium speed about 2 minutes or until creamy; gradually add remaining 2 cups sugar, beating at medium speed 5 to 7 minutes. Add egg yolks, one at a time, beating just until yellow disappears.

Add flour to butter mixture alternately with bourbon, beginning and ending with flour. Mix at low speed just until blended after each addition. Stir in flavorings. Fold in one-third of beaten egg white mixture. Gently fold in remaining two-thirds egg white mixture, and spoon into prepared pan.

Bake on bottom rack of oven at 350° for 1 hour and 20 minutes or until a wooden pick inserted in center comes out clean. (Cover with aluminum foil to prevent excessive browning, if necessary.) Cool in pan on a wire rack 10 to 15 minutes; remove from pan, and let cool completely on wire rack. Sprinkle top of cake with powdered sugar. Yield: one 10-inch cake.

Elli Fleming

With Love from the Shepherd's Center of North Little Rock
Shepherd's Center of North Little Rock, Arkansas

Chocolate-Nut Pound Cake

2 cups butter, softened
3 cups sugar
5 large eggs
4 cups all-purpose flour
½ cup cocoa

½ teaspoon baking powder
1 cup milk
½ cup chopped pecans
1 teaspoon vanilla extract
1 teaspoon almond extract

Beat butter at medium speed of a heavy-duty mixer about 2 minutes or until creamy. Gradually add sugar, beating at medium speed 5 to 7 minutes. Add eggs, one at a time, beating just until yellow disappears.

Combine flour, cocoa, and baking powder; add to butter mixture alternately with milk, beginning and ending with flour mixture. Mix at low speed just until blended after each addition. Stir in pecans, vanilla, and almond extract. Pour batter into a greased and floured 10-inch tube pan.

Bake at 300° for 1 hour and 45 minutes or until a wooden pick inserted in center comes out clean. Cool in pan on a wire rack 10 to 15 minutes; remove from pan, and let cool completely on wire rack. Yield: one 10-inch cake.   Meg Wright

Blessed Isle
Episcopal Church Women of All Saints Parish
Pawleys Island, South Carolina

Orange Chiffon Cake

2¾ cups sifted cake flour
1 tablespoon baking powder
1 teaspoon salt
1⅓ cups sugar
½ cup vegetable oil
5 egg yolks
1 teaspoon grated orange
  rind

¾ cup fresh orange juice
1 teaspoon orange extract
1 teaspoon vanilla extract
8 egg whites
½ teaspoon cream of tartar
Orange Filling
Whipped Cream Frosting

Combine first 4 ingredients in a large mixing bowl. Make a well in center; add oil and next 5 ingredients. Beat at high speed of an electric mixer about 1 minute or until smooth.

Beat egg whites and cream of tartar in a large mixing bowl until stiff peaks form.

Pour egg yolk mixture in a thin, steady stream over entire surface of egg whites; then gently fold whites into yolk mixture. Pour batter into an ungreased 10-inch tube pan, spreading evenly with a spatula.

Bake at 325° for 55 minutes or until cake springs back when lightly touched. Invert pan; cool 40 minutes. Loosen cake from sides of pan, using a narrow metal spatula; remove from pan.

Cut cake horizontally into 3 layers. Spread Orange Filling between layers. Frost top and sides of cake with Whipped Cream Frosting. Top cake with reserved oranges. Yield: one 10-inch cake.

Orange Filling

¼ cup sugar
¼ cup cornstarch
1 cup fresh orange juice
¼ cup water

1 (11-ounce) can mandarin oranges, drained and finely chopped (reserve 12 segments for top of cake)

Combine sugar and cornstarch in a small heavy saucepan; stir in orange juice and water. Bring to a boil, stirring constantly; cook 1 minute. Remove from heat. Stir in chopped oranges; cover and chill. Yield: 1½ cups.

Whipped Cream Frosting

1¼ teaspoons unflavored gelatin
¼ cup cold water
2 cups whipping cream

2 tablespoons sugar
½ teaspoon orange extract
½ teaspoon vanilla extract

Sprinkle gelatin over cold water in a small saucepan; let stand 1 minute. Cook over low heat, stirring constantly, until gelatin dissolves, about 2 minutes. Remove from heat; gradually stir in whipping cream. Cover and chill.

Beat chilled whipping cream mixture, sugar, and flavorings in a large mixing bowl at high speed of an electric mixer until stiff peaks form. Yield: 4½ cups.   Wilda L. Holloway

Just Desserts
Amsterdam Free Library
Amsterdam, New York

Light-As-Air Sponge Cake

This airy cake has a wonderful texture and flavor. Be sure to cool the cake upside down to prevent shrinking and falling. If the cake pan is footed, invert it and let the cake cool on the feet. If not, set the pan over a long-necked bottle so that air can flow underneath it.

6 large eggs, separated
½ cup cold water
1½ cups sugar
1 teaspoon vanilla extract

1¾ cups sifted cake flour
¼ teaspoon salt
¾ teaspoon cream of tartar

Beat egg yolks in a large mixing bowl at high speed of an electric mixer until thick and pale. Add water, and beat 5 minutes or until thick. Add sugar and vanilla, and beat well. Combine flour and salt; gently fold one-fourth of the flour mixture at a time into the egg yolk mixture. Set aside.

Beat egg whites and cream of tartar at high speed until stiff peaks form. Gently fold beaten egg white into yolk mixture. Pour batter into an ungreased 10-inch tube pan, spreading evenly with a spatula.

Bake at 350° for 50 minutes or until cake springs back when lightly touched. Invert pan; cool 40 minutes. Loosen cake from sides of pan, using a narrow metal spatula; remove cake from pan. Yield: 12 servings.   Olga Newkirk

Seasoning the Fox Valley
Public Action to Deliver Shelter Ministry at Hesed House
Aurora, Illinois

Hot Milk Sponge Cake

A tantalizing mix of coconut, brown sugar, and pecans is broiled atop this easy sponge cake to create a crunchy Praline Topping. This cake forgoes beating and folding in the egg whites as in traditional sponge cakes in favor of a quick rise ensured by the warm milk mixture and baking powder.

4 large eggs
2 cups sugar
2 teaspoons vanilla extract
2 cups sifted cake flour
2 teaspoons baking powder

½ teaspoon salt
1 cup milk
2 tablespoons butter
Praline Topping

Grease bottom and sides of a 13- x 9- x 2-inch pan; flour bottom of pan. Set aside.

Beat eggs, sugar, and vanilla at medium speed of an electric mixer about 2 minutes or until pale. Combine flour, baking powder, and salt; add to egg mixture. Mix at low speed until blended.

Bring milk and butter to a boil in a medium saucepan. Quickly add to batter, mixing at low speed until blended. (Batter will be thin.) Pour batter into prepared pan.

Bake at 350° for 25 minutes or until a wooden pick inserted in center comes out clean. Cool in pan on a wire rack.

Spread cake with Praline Topping. Broil 5½ inches from heat (with electric oven door partially opened) 3 minutes or until coconut is lightly toasted. Yield: 15 servings.

Praline Topping

¾ cup firmly packed brown
  sugar
¼ cup butter, softened
2 tablespoons milk

¼ teaspoon vanilla extract
1 cup flaked coconut
½ cup chopped pecans

Combine first 4 ingredients in a medium mixing bowl; beat at medium speed of an electric mixer about 2 minutes or until blended. Stir in coconut and pecans. Yield: 1½ cups.　　　　Alta Jenkins

A Taste of Gem Valley Country Living
North Gem Valley Development Corporation

Apricot Upside-Down Cake

¼ cup butter
1 cup firmly packed brown
  sugar
1 (15¼-ounce) can apricot
  halves, drained
3 large eggs, separated

1 cup sugar
1 cup all-purpose flour
1 teaspoon baking powder
⅛ teaspoon salt
½ cup apricot nectar

Melt butter in a 10-inch cast-iron skillet over medium heat, and sprinkle with brown sugar. Place apricot halves, rounded side down, over brown sugar mixture. Beat egg yolks until thick and pale; gradually add 1 cup sugar, beating well. Combine flour, baking powder, and salt. Add to yolk mixture, beating just until blended. Stir in nectar.

Beat egg whites until stiff peaks form; gently fold into batter. Spoon batter evenly over apricot halves in skillet.

Bake at 350° for 40 minutes or until a wooden pick inserted in center comes out clean. Run a knife around edge of cake to loosen; cool in pan on a wire rack 30 minutes. Invert cake onto a serving plate. Yield: one 10-inch cake.   Ila Thierolf

Kitchen Keepsakes
United Methodist Church Women
Beloit, Kansas

Macaroon Angel Cakes

1 cup sugar
¾ cup all-purpose flour
½ teaspoon baking powder
½ teaspoon salt
6 egg whites

½ teaspoon cream of tartar
⅓ cup sugar
½ teaspoon vanilla extract
½ teaspoon almond extract
1 cup flaked coconut

Combine first 4 ingredients; set aside.

Beat egg whites and cream of tartar at high speed of an electric mixer until foamy. Add ⅓ cup sugar, 1 tablespoon at a time, beating until stiff peaks form and sugar dissolves (2 to 4 minutes). Add flavorings, beating well.

Sift flour mixture over egg white mixture, ¼ cup at a time, and gently fold in after each addition; fold in coconut. Spoon batter evenly into paper-lined muffin pans, filling half-full.

Bake at 300° for 45 minutes or until golden. Remove from pans immediately. Serve warm or let cool completely on wire racks. Yield: 2 dozen.

Janet Johnson

A Gardener Cooks
Danbury Garden Club
New Milford, Connecticut

Charlie Cakes

These darling little cakes begin with a mix. But an eye-catching glaze and a showy walnut crown belie their humble beginnings.

1 (22-ounce) package brownie mix with walnuts (we tested with Duncan Hines)
1 large egg
⅓ cup water
⅓ cup vegetable oil
1 (16-ounce) package powdered sugar, sifted

⅓ to ½ cup milk
24 walnut halves
⅓ cup (2 ounces) semisweet chocolate morsels
1 tablespoon shortening

Combine first 4 ingredients in a large bowl; mix well. Stir in walnuts from mix, if packaged separately. Spoon about 2 level tablespoons batter into each of 24 foil cupcake liners arranged on a large baking sheet.

Bake at 350° for 25 minutes. Cool in liners on wire racks 5 minutes; remove from liners, and invert cakes onto wire racks. Let cool completely. Place a sheet of wax paper under racks.

Combine powdered sugar and enough milk to make a spoonable glaze, stirring until smooth. Spoon evenly over cakes, letting excess drip down sides. Top each cake with a walnut half. Let stand until glaze is set.

Place chocolate morsels and shortening in a small heavy-duty, zip-top plastic bag. Place bag in a bowl of hot water until chocolate and shortening melt. Gently knead bag until mixture is blended. Snip a tiny hole in one corner of bag. Drizzle chocolate mixture over cakes. Let stand until chocolate is set. Store in an airtight container. Yield: 2 dozen.

Cathy Schembechler

Michigan Cooks
C.S. Mott Children's Hospital
Ann Arbor, Michigan

Bananas Foster Cheesecake

All the flavors of bananas Foster, the quintessential New Orleans dessert, are incorporated in this creamy delight of a cheesecake.

¾ cup all-purpose flour
¾ cup finely chopped pecans
3 tablespoons brown sugar
2 tablespoons sugar
¼ cup unsalted butter, melted
1½ tablespoons vanilla extract, divided
2 (8-ounce) packages cream cheese, softened
1½ cups sugar, divided
2 tablespoons cornstarch
3 large eggs
2 cups mashed very ripe banana (about 4 large)

1 (16-ounce) carton sour cream, divided
2 tablespoons fresh lemon juice
1½ teaspoons ground cinnamon, divided
⅛ teaspoon salt
½ teaspoon sugar
2 very ripe bananas
1 (12-ounce) jar caramel sauce (we tested with Smucker's)
¼ cup dark rum

Combine first 5 ingredients in a bowl; stir well. Stir in 2 teaspoons vanilla. Press in bottom of a 10-inch springform pan; set aside.

Beat cream cheese at medium speed of an electric mixer until creamy. Gradually add 1¼ cups sugar and cornstarch, beating well. Add eggs, one at a time, beating after each addition. Stir in mashed banana, half the sour cream, lemon juice, 2 teaspoons vanilla, 1 teaspoon cinnamon, and salt. Pour batter into prepared pan.

Bake at 350° for 1 hour or until center is set. Remove from oven, and set aside.

Combine remaining sour cream, ¼ cup sugar, and ½ teaspoon vanilla a small bowl, stirring well. Spread over warm cheesecake; return to oven, and bake 10 additional minutes. Turn oven off; let cheesecake cool in oven 2 hours or until room temperature. Cover and chill 8 hours.

Carefully remove sides of springform pan. Combine ½ teaspoon sugar and remaining ½ teaspoon cinnamon in a small bowl; sprinkle over cheesecake. Peel and slice 2 bananas; arrange slices on top of cheesecake. Combine caramel sauce and rum in a small saucepan; cook over medium heat until warm. Drizzle some warm sauce over cheesecake, and serve with remaining sauce. Yield: 12 servings.

Capital Celebrations
The Junior League of Washington, DC

Chamboreo Cheesecake

Oreo cookies and Chambord (raspberry-flavored liqueur) star in this memorable chocolate-raspberry cheesecake. A hint of cinnamon in the crust brings out the best in both ingredients.

1½ cups graham cracker crumbs
¼ cup firmly packed brown sugar
2 teaspoons ground cinnamon
¼ cup plus 1 tablespoon butter, softened
4 (8-ounce) packages cream cheese, softened
1¼ cups sugar
2 tablespoons all-purpose flour
6 large eggs
2 egg yolks
⅓ cup whipping cream
¼ cup Chambord or other raspberry-flavored liqueur
1 teaspoon vanilla extract
1½ cups chopped cream-filled chocolate sandwich cookies (we tested with 15 Oreos)
1 (16-ounce) carton sour cream
¼ cup sugar
1 tablespoon vanilla extract
Chocolate curls

Combine first 4 ingredients in a small bowl; press mixture in bottom and 1-inch up sides of a 10-inch springform pan. Cover and chill 45 minutes.

Beat cream cheese at low speed of an electric mixer until creamy; gradually add 1¼ cups sugar and flour, beating well. Add eggs and egg yolks, one at a time, beating after each addition. Stir in whipping cream, liqueur, and vanilla, mixing well.

Pour half of batter into prepared pan. Sprinkle evenly with chopped cookies. Carefully pour remaining batter evenly over cookie layer. Bake at 425° for 15 minutes. Reduce oven temperature to 350°; bake 45 additional minutes or until center is almost set. Remove from oven, and place pan on a wire rack.

Combine sour cream, ¼ cup sugar, and vanilla; spread over warm cheesecake. Let cool completely in pan on wire rack; cover and chill at least 8 hours.

Carefully remove sides of springform pan; top with chocolate curls. Yield: 12 servings.

Carol Reimann

Favorite Recipes II
St. Isaac Jogues Senior Guild, St. Mary's of the Hills Catholic Church
Rochester Hills, Michigan

Famous Cheesecake

Start spreading the news–this thick and creamy New York-style cheese-cake is a towering temptation that must be experienced to be believed.

1 cup all-purpose flour
2 cups sugar, divided
2½ teaspoons grated lemon
  rind, divided
2½ teaspoons grated orange
  rind, divided
½ cup butter
1 egg yolk
¼ teaspoon vanilla extract
5 (8-ounce) packages cream
  cheese, softened

3 tablespoons all-purpose flour
5 large eggs
2 egg yolks
¼ cup whipping cream
½ teaspoon vanilla extract
3 cups strawberries or other
  fruit (optional)
½ cup red currant jelly, melted
  (optional)

Combine 1 cup flour, ¼ cup sugar, and 1 teaspoon each of lemon and orange rind in a medium bowl, stirring well. Cut in ½ cup butter with pastry blender until mixture is crumbly; add 1 egg yolk and ¼ teaspoon vanilla, stirring with a fork until dry ingredients are moistened. Shape into a ball; cover and chill 1 hour.

Press one-third of dough in bottom of a lightly buttered 9-inch springform pan. Bake at 350° for 10 minutes; cool in pan on a wire rack. Press remaining two-thirds of dough 2 inches up sides of pan.

Combine cream cheese, remaining 1¾ cups sugar, and 3 table-spoons flour in a large mixing bowl; beat at medium speed of an electric mixer until smooth. Add eggs and 2 egg yolks, one at a time, beating after each addition. Add remaining 1½ teaspoons each lemon and orange rind, whipping cream, and ½ teaspoon vanilla; beat at low speed until smooth.

Pour batter into prepared pan. Bake at 475° for 10 minutes; reduce oven temperature to 200°, and bake 1 hour and 10 minutes. Turn oven off; leave cheesecake in oven 1 hour. Partially open oven door, and leave cheesecake in oven 30 minutes. Let cool to room temperature on wire rack; cover and chill at least 8 hours.

Carefully remove sides of springform pan. If desired, arrange fruit on top of cheesecake, and brush with melted jelly. Yield: 12 servings.

Delta Informal Gardeners Cook
Delta Informal Gardeners
Brentwood, California

Crème de Cacao Torte

Pair this lush bittersweet chocolate torte with a robust java.

⅔ cup butter, softened
1⅔ cups sugar
3 large eggs
2 cups all-purpose flour
⅔ cup cocoa
1¼ teaspoons baking soda
¼ teaspoon baking powder

1⅓ cups milk
½ teaspoon vanilla extract
1 cup whipping cream
¼ cup crème de cacao, divided
1 tablespoon cocoa
Chocolate Ganache Glaze

Beat butter at medium speed of an electric mixer until creamy; gradually add sugar, beating well. Add eggs, one at a time, beating after each addition.

Combine flour and next 3 ingredients; add to butter mixture alternately with milk, beginning and ending with flour mixture. Mix at low speed after each addition until blended. Stir in vanilla. Pour batter into two greased and floured 9-inch round cakepans.

Bake at 350° for 30 to 35 minutes or until a wooden pick inserted in center comes out clean. Cool in pans on wire racks 10 minutes; remove from pans, and let cool completely on wire racks.

Meanwhile, beat whipping cream, 2 tablespoons crème de cacao, and 1 tablespoon cocoa until soft peaks form. Cover and chill.

Split each cake layer in half horizontally. Sprinkle remaining 2 tablespoons liqueur evenly over each layer. Place 1 layer on a cake plate; spread with one-third of whipped cream mixture. Repeat procedure twice. Top with remaining cake layer. Cover and chill at least 8 hours.

Spoon Chocolate Ganache Glaze over top of torte, allowing glaze to drizzle down sides. Serve immediately or cover and chill. Yield: one 9-inch torte.

Chocolate Ganache Glaze

1 (7-ounce) bar special dark
    mildly sweet chocolate,
    broken into pieces (we tested
    with Hershey's)

¼ cup whipping cream
1 tablespoon butter
1½ teaspoons crème de cacao

Combine first 3 ingredients in a saucepan. Cook over low heat, stirring constantly, until smooth. Stir in crème de cacao. Yield: 1 cup.

Landmark Entertaining
The Junior League of Abilene, Texas

Chocolate Torte with Butter-Rum Sauce

This easy-to-prepare single-layer torte has presence and panache. Made with just a little bit of flour, it resembles a brownie. Nestle a chocolaty wedge in a puddle of the to-die-for Butter-Rum Sauce, and await the raves.

½ cup butter
2 (1-ounce) squares
  unsweetened chocolate
2 large eggs
1 cup sugar

¼ teaspoon salt
1 teaspoon vanilla extract
½ cup all-purpose flour
Butter-Rum Sauce

Combine butter and chocolate in top of a double boiler; bring water to a boil. Reduce heat to low; cook until chocolate and butter melt, stirring occasionally. Set aside, and let cool to room temperature.

Beat eggs in a medium bowl at medium speed of an electric mixer 3 minutes. Gradually add sugar, and beat until thick and pale (about 4 minutes). Add salt and vanilla, beating well. Gradually add flour, beating at low speed just until blended. Add melted chocolate mixture; beat at low speed until blended. Spread batter into a greased 9-inch springform pan. Bake at 325° for 30 minutes. Carefully remove sides of pan; let cool on pan bottom on a wire rack. Spoon Butter-Rum Sauce onto dessert plates; top with wedges of torte. Yield: 8 servings.

Butter-Rum Sauce

1 cup whipping cream
¾ cup firmly packed brown
  sugar

½ cup butter
3 tablespoons dark rum
½ teaspoon vanilla extract

Combine first 3 ingredients in a small saucepan; cook over medium-low heat until mixture comes to a boil, stirring often (about 10 minutes). Boil 5 minutes (do not increase heat). Remove from heat; stir in rum and vanilla. Yield: 2 cups.

Classic Favorites
P.E.O., Chapter SB
Moraga, California

Cookies & Candies

Tempt-Me Truffles, page 128

Forgotten Raspberry Kiss Cookies

These pretty-in-pink meringue cookies owe their blush to raspberry-flavored gelatin. Use lime-flavored gelatin to make a batch in celebration of St. Patrick's Day.

3 egg whites
¾ cup sugar
3½ tablespoons raspberry-
    flavored gelatin

1 tablespoon white vinegar
1 cup (6 ounces) semisweet
    chocolate mini-morsels
Vegetable cooking spray

Beat egg whites at high speed of an electric mixer until foamy. Combine sugar and gelatin, stirring well. Gradually add sugar mixture to egg whites, 1 tablespoon at a time, beating until stiff peaks form and sugar dissolves (2 to 4 minutes). Gently stir in vinegar; fold in chocolate morsels.

Drop dough by heaping teaspoonfuls onto cookie sheets coated with cooking spray or lined with parchment paper. Bake at 250° for 25 minutes. Turn oven off, and let cookies cool in oven 20 minutes (do not open oven door). Remove cookies to a wire rack, and let cool completely. Store in an airtight container up to 5 days. Yield: 44 cookies.

Flavor of Nashville
Home Economists in Home and Community
Nashville, Tennessee

Grand Slams

1 cup shortening
1 cup sugar
1 cup firmly packed brown
    sugar
2 large eggs
2½ cups all-purpose flour

1 teaspoon baking soda
½ teaspoon baking powder
1 teaspoon salt
1 cup crispy rice cereal
1 cup flaked coconut
½ cup chopped pecans

Beat shortening at medium speed of an electric mixer until fluffy. Gradually add sugars, beating mixture well. Add eggs, one at a time, beating well.

Combine flour and next 3 ingredients; gradually add to sugar mixture, beating until smooth. Stir in cereal, coconut, and pecans. Cover and chill 10 minutes.

Drop dough by rounded teaspoonfuls onto ungreased cookie sheets. Bake at 325° for 10 minutes. Cool slightly on cookie sheets; remove to wire racks, and let cool completely. Yield: 6 dozen.

Bully's Best Bites
The Junior Auxiliary of Starkville, Mississippi

The Very Best Oatmeal Cookies

Wholesome wheat flour, oats, and pecans give these cookies their hearty texture. The raisins studding these mighty morsels are soaked in egg and vanilla to plump them up before adding them to the dough.

4 egg whites, lightly beaten	1½ cups all-purpose flour
1 large egg, lightly beaten	1 cup whole wheat flour
1 teaspoon vanilla extract	2 teaspoons baking soda
1 cup raisins	1 teaspoon salt
1 cup butter or margarine, softened	1 teaspoon ground cinnamon
1 cup sugar	2 cups regular oats, uncooked
1 cup firmly packed brown sugar	¾ cup chopped pecans

Combine first 3 ingredients, stirring well. Add raisins; cover and chill 1 hour to rehydrate raisins.

Beat butter at medium speed of an electric mixer until creamy; gradually add sugars, beating well.

Combine flours and next 3 ingredients; add to butter mixture, beating well. Add raisin mixture, beating well; stir in oats and pecans.

Drop dough by rounded teaspoonfuls onto greased cookie sheets. Bake at 350° for 10 to 12 minutes or until lightly browned. Cool slightly on cookie sheets; remove to wire racks, and let cool completely. Yield: 7 dozen.

Mary Lou Eitzman

Recipes from Our Home to Yours
Hospice of North Central Florida
Gainesville, Florida

Oatmeal-Cranberry-White Chocolate Chunk Cookies

1 cup butter, softened
1 cup firmly packed brown
  sugar
2 large eggs
2 cups all-purpose flour
2 cups regular oats, uncooked
1 teaspoon baking soda
½ teaspoon salt
1½ cups dried cranberries (we
  tested with Craisins)
1 cup coarsely chopped white
  chocolate (we tested with
  Baker's premium white
  chocolate baking squares)

Beat butter at medium speed of an electric stand mixer until creamy; gradually add sugar, beating well. Add eggs; beat well.

Combine flour and next 3 ingredients; gradually add to butter mixture, beating well. Stir in cranberries and chocolate.

Drop dough by heaping teaspoonfuls 2 inches apart onto ungreased cookie sheets. Bake at 375° for 8 minutes or until lightly browned. Cool slightly on cookie sheets; remove to wire racks, and let cool completely. Yield: 2½ dozen. Dianne Cook

Simply Cape Cod
The Sandwich Junior Women's Club
Sandwich, Massachusetts

Date Nugget Cookies

Chewy cookie lovers stop here! These brown sugar and walnut wonders trace their winning texture to chopped dates.

1 cup shortening
1¼ cups firmly packed brown
  sugar
3 large eggs
2½ cups all-purpose flour
1 teaspoon baking soda
½ teaspoon salt
3 teaspoons ground cinnamon
2 cups chopped walnuts
1½ cups chopped dates
1 teaspoon vanilla extract

Beat shortening at medium speed of an electric mixer until fluffy; gradually add sugar, beating well. Add eggs; beat well.

Combine flour and next 3 ingredients; gradually add to shortening mixture, beating well. Stir in walnuts, dates and vanilla. Shape dough into 1-inch balls; place 2 inches apart on greased cookie sheets. Bake at 350° for 12 minutes or until lightly browned. Cool slightly on cookie sheets; remove to wire racks, and let cool completely. Yield: 3 dozen.   Ruth Bosi

Seasoned with Love
United Methodist Women of United Methodist
Church of Sepulveda
North Hills, California*

Lemon Cheese Logs (Zitronen Stangerl)

1 cup butter, softened
1 (3-ounce) package cream
  cheese, softened
1 cup sugar
1 egg yolk
2½ cups all-purpose flour

1 cup finely chopped walnuts
½ teaspoon salt
½ teaspoon grated lemon rind
6 (1-ounce) squares semisweet
  chocolate or 1 cup (6 ounces)
  semisweet chocolate morsels

Beat butter and cream cheese at medium speed of an electric mixer until creamy; gradually add sugar, beating well. Add egg yolk, and beat well.

Combine flour and next 3 ingredients; gradually add to butter mixture, beating well. Cover and chill at least 2 hours.

Shape dough into 1-inch logs, using 1 teaspoon dough per cookie. Place 2 inches apart on ungreased cookie sheets. Bake at 325° for 12 minutes or until lightly browned. Cool slightly on cookie sheets; remove to wire racks, and let cool completely.

Cook chocolate in a small saucepan over low heat, stirring constantly, until chocolate melts. Dip 1 end of each cookie into chocolate; return to wire racks, and let stand until chocolate is firm. Store in an airtight container in refrigerator. Yield: 8 dozen.   Brigitte Hoppe

A Taste of Leavenworth
Washington State Autumn Leaf Festival Association
Leavenworth, Washington

Glazed Orange-Spice Cookies

½ cup shortening
½ cup margarine, softened
1 cup sugar
½ cup finely chopped almonds
3 tablespoons grated orange
  rind
1¾ cups all-purpose flour
1 teaspoon baking powder

¼ teaspoon salt
½ teaspoon ground nutmeg
¼ teaspoon ground cloves
¼ teaspoon ground cinnamon
1 cup sifted powdered sugar
⅓ cup orange marmalade
Garnish: sliced almonds

Beat shortening and margarine at medium speed of an electric mixer until creamy; gradually add sugar, beating well. Add almonds and orange rind; beat well.

Combine flour and next 5 ingredients; gradually add to shortening mixture, beating well.

Place dough on a lightly floured surface; roll into a 14- x 12-inch rectangle. Cut into 2- x 1-inch rectangles; place on ungreased cookie sheets. Bake at 350° for 12 to 13 minutes or until lightly browned. Cool slightly on cookie sheets; remove to wire racks, and let cool completely.

Combine powdered sugar and marmalade; stir well. Spread glaze on cookies. Garnish, if desired. Yield: 4 dozen.   Marilyn Drnevich

Sampler Cookbook
Clarence Log Cabin Quilters
Clarence, New York

Hattie's Tea Cakes

1½ cups butter or margarine,
  softened
1½ cups sugar
3 large eggs

2 tablespoons lemon extract
4 cups all-purpose flour
1 tablespoon baking powder

Beat butter at medium speed of an electric mixer until creamy; gradually add sugar, beating mixture well. Add eggs and lemon extract; beat well.

Combine flour and baking powder; gradually add to butter mixture, beating well. Cover and chill at least 1 hour.

Divide dough into fourths. Work with 1 portion of dough at a time, storing remainder in refrigerator. Roll each portion of dough to

¼-inch thickness on a lightly floured surface. Cut with a 2¾-inch cookie cutter; place on ungreased cookie sheets.

Bake at 350° for 15 to 16 minutes or until edges are lightly browned. Cool slightly on cookie sheets; remove to wire racks, and let cool completely. Yield: 4 dozen.   Kathy Robinson

The Best of West
The Junior Beta Club of West Jones Middle School
Laurel, Mississippi

Fruit-Filled Spritz

1 cup butter, softened
1½ cups sugar, divided
½ cup firmly packed brown
  sugar
3 large eggs
½ teaspoon vanilla extract
½ teaspoon almond extract
4 cups all-purpose flour
½ teaspoon baking soda

½ teaspoon salt
1¼ cups whole pitted dates,
  chopped
1 cup water or orange juice
2 teaspoons grated orange rind
1 cup chopped walnuts
½ cup flaked coconut
½ cup chopped red candied
  cherries

Beat butter at medium speed of an electric mixer until creamy; gradually add 1 cup sugar and ½ cup brown sugar, beating well. Add eggs and flavorings, beating well. Combine flour, soda, and salt; add to butter mixture, beating well. Cover and chill 1 hour.

Combine dates, remaining ½ cup sugar, water, and orange rind in a saucepan; bring to a boil over medium-high heat. Reduce heat, and cook, stirring constantly, until thick. Cool 5 minutes; stir in walnuts, coconut, and cherries.

Use a cookie gun with the sawtooth edge, following manufacturer's directions, to shape dough in long strips on ungreased cookie sheets. Spoon a thin layer of date mixture on each strip, and shape a second dough strip over filling.

Bake at 375° for 10 to 12 minutes. Cool slightly on cookie sheets, and cut into 2-inch bars. Remove to wire racks, and let cool completely. Yield: 6 dozen.   Karen Dougherty

Bearing Our Cupboard
Brain Tumor Support Group
Richmond, Virginia

Butterflies

These old favorites require a butterfly iron (check kitchen specialty shops). The hot iron is placed in thin batter, and then plunged into hot oil. The batter releases from the iron in the butterfly shape, creating a light and crispy cookie.

1 cup all-purpose flour
1 tablespoon sugar
½ teaspoon salt
1 cup milk

1 large egg
1½ pounds shortening
  (3⅔ cups)
¼ cup sifted powdered sugar

Combine first 5 ingredients in a large bowl; stir with a wire whisk until smooth.

Heat shortening in a large heavy skillet to 360°. Heat butterfly iron in oil about 1 minute; drain excess oil. Working quickly, dip iron into batter, being careful not to coat top of iron with batter.

Dip iron into hot oil, shaking gently to release butterfly from iron. Fry butterflies, 4 at a time, until golden, turning once. Drain upside-down on paper towels. Reheat iron in oil for a few seconds, and repeat procedure with remaining batter, keeping oil at 360°. Dust pastries with powdered sugar. Store in an airtight container. Yield: 5 dozen.

The Many Tastes of Haverstraw Middle School
Home and Career Skills Department, Haverstraw Middle School
Haverstraw, New York

Zucchini Brownies

Grate your garden overrun of zucchini to add moistness and texture to these fudgy brownies. A generous spoonful of ground cinnamon adds a warm flavor note.

3 cups all-purpose flour
¼ cup cocoa
1 teaspoon baking soda
½ teaspoon salt
2 teaspoons ground cinnamon
2 cups grated zucchini (about
  ¾ pound)
½ cup butter, melted

1¾ cups sugar
1 cup vegetable oil
2 large eggs, lightly beaten
1 teaspoon vanilla extract
2 cups (12 ounces) semisweet
  chocolate morsels
½ cup chopped walnuts

Combine first 5 ingredients in a bowl, stirring well. Combine zucchini and butter; add to flour mixture, stirring well. Combine sugar and next 3 ingredients; add to zucchini mixture, stirring 2 minutes.

Pour batter into a greased 15- x 10- x 1-inch jellyroll pan; top with chocolate morsels and walnuts. Bake at 350° for 30 minutes. Cut into bars. Yield: 32 brownies.   Florence Deeley

Howey Cook
Howey-in-the-Hills Garden and Civic Club
Howey-in-the-Hills, Florida

Cranberry-Orange-Ginger-Oat Bars

1 (12-ounce) package fresh or
   frozen cranberries, thawed
¾ cup sugar
¾ cup water
1 tablespoon grated fresh
   ginger
1 tablespoon grated orange
   rind
1 cup butter or margarine,
   softened

1 cup firmly packed brown
   sugar
2 large eggs
1¾ cups all-purpose flour
1½ cups regular oats,
   uncooked
1 teaspoon baking powder
½ teaspoon salt
2 teaspoons ground ginger

Combine first 5 ingredients in a medium saucepan; bring to a boil. Reduce heat to medium-low; simmer, uncovered, 10 minutes or until thickened, stirring occasionally. Let cool.

Beat butter at medium speed of an electric mixer until creamy; gradually add sugar, beating mixture well. Add eggs, one at a time, beating well.

Combine flour and remaining 4 ingredients; add to butter mixture, beating well.

Press half of dough in bottom of a buttered 13- x 9- x 2-inch pan. Spoon cranberry mixture over dough, spreading evenly. Spoon remaining dough by tablespoonfuls over filling. Bake at 350° for 35 minutes or until golden. Let cool completely in pan on a wire rack. Cut into bars. Yield: 3 dozen.   Hazel Warren

Food for Thought
Friends of Centerville Public Library
Centerville, Massachusetts

Toffee-Coconut Bars

A brown sugar cookie base and a chewy top note of coconut and almonds make these buttery bar cookies something special.

½ cup butter, softened
1½ cups firmly packed brown
 sugar, divided
1 cup all-purpose flour
2 large eggs, beaten
1 cup flaked coconut

1 cup sliced almonds
2 tablespoons all-purpose flour
1 teaspoon baking powder
½ teaspoon salt
1 teaspoon vanilla extract

Beat butter at medium speed of an electric mixer until creamy; gradually add ½ cup brown sugar, beating well. Add 1 cup flour, beating until blended. Press mixture into a lightly greased 13- x 9- x 2-inch baking dish. Bake at 350° for 10 minutes.

Combine remaining 1 cup brown sugar, eggs, and remaining 6 ingredients in a medium bowl; stir well. Pour mixture over crust in pan; bake 20 minutes or until lightly browned. Let cool completely in pan on a wire rack. Cut into bars. Yield: 16 bars.   Emilie Fritz

A Cookbook
Life Education Department of the Cheshire Center of
Applied Science & Technology at Keene High School
Keene, New Hampshire

Symphony Tea Bars

Take these triple-layered marvels with you to a symphony-in-the-park picnic or tailgate party. They start with a butter-pecan cookie base, segue into a splendid chocolate center, and end with a luscious vanilla frosting.

1 cup butter, softened
2 cups sugar
4 large eggs
½ teaspoon vanilla extract
2 cups all-purpose flour
2 cups chopped pecans

½ teaspoon salt
2 (1-ounce) squares
   unsweetened chocolate,
   melted
Frosting

Beat butter at medium speed of an electric mixer until creamy; gradually add 2 cups sugar, beating mixture well. Add eggs and vanilla; beat well.

Combine flour, pecans, and salt; add to butter mixture, beating well. Pour half of batter into a greased 13- x 9- x 2-inch pan. Add melted chocolate to remaining half of batter, mixing well. Spread chocolate mixture over batter in pan. Bake at 350° for 30 minutes. Let cool completely in pan on a wire rack. Spread frosting over cooled batter. Cut into bars. Yield: 20 bars.

Frosting

1 cup milk
¼ cup plus 1 tablespoon
   all-purpose flour

1 cup butter, softened
1 cup sugar
2 teaspoons vanilla extract

Combine milk and flour in top of a double boiler; bring water to a boil. Reduce heat to low; cook, stirring constantly, until mixture forms a paste. Cool 10 minutes. Beat butter, 1 cup sugar, and vanilla at medium speed of an electric mixer until blended. Add milk mixture, and beat 5 minutes. Yield: 3 cups.

Carol Juntunen

Seasoning the Fox Valley
Public Action to Deliver Shelter Ministry at Hesed House
Aurora, Illinois

White Christmas Bark

White chocolate is swirled with semisweet chocolate and then embellished with jewels of dried cranberries, slices of almonds, and flakes of coconut.

1 pound white chocolate, coarsely chopped (we tested with Baker's premium white chocolate baking squares)

1 cup dried cranberries, divided (we tested with Craisins)

½ cup flaked coconut, toasted and divided

⅓ cup sliced almonds, toasted and divided

2 (1-ounce) squares semisweet chocolate, coarsely chopped

¼ teaspoon butter or margarine

Place white chocolate in a medium-size microwave-safe bowl. Microwave at HIGH for 3 minutes or until chocolate melts, stirring at 1-minute intervals. Stir in half each of cranberries, coconut, and almonds; set aside.

Place semisweet chocolate and butter in a small microwave-safe bowl. Microwave at HIGH for 30 seconds or until chocolate melts; stir to blend.

Line a large baking sheet with a 12- x 8-inch piece of aluminum foil. Spread white chocolate mixture evenly over foil. Spoon semisweet chocolate by spoonfuls over white chocolate mixture; swirl chocolate gently with a knife. Sprinkle with remaining half of cranberries, coconut, and almonds, pressing gently. Chill 30 minutes or until firm. Break into pieces. Yield: about 1½ pounds.   Grace Loesch

Tasty Temptations
Our Lady of the Mountains Church
Sierra Vista, Arizona

Golden Nugget Fudge

3 cups sugar

1½ cups milk

3 tablespoons light corn syrup

¾ teaspoon salt

3 tablespoons butter

2 teaspoons vanilla extract

½ cup chopped dried apricot halves

½ cup marshmallow cream

⅓ cup chopped walnuts or pecans

Butter sides of a 3-quart saucepan. Combine first 4 ingredients in saucepan. Cook over medium heat, stirring constantly, until sugar dissolves (about 10 minutes). Bring mixture to a boil; cover and cook 2 to 3 minutes to wash down sugar crystals from sides of pan. Uncover and cook, without stirring, until candy thermometer registers 236°. (Be sure to keep mixture at a rolling boil.) Remove from heat, and add butter and vanilla. Let mixture cool, without stirring, until lukewarm (about 110°).

Stir in chopped apricot, and beat with a wooden spoon 3 minutes.

Quickly stir in marshmallow cream and walnuts. Beat until mixture begins to thicken and lose its gloss (about 3 minutes). Quickly pour mixture into a buttered 9-inch square pan, spreading evenly. Cool; cut into squares. Yield: 2 pounds.   Mrs. Walter W. (Saress) Gregg

Carolina Cuisine: Nothin' Could Be Finer
The Junior Charity League of Marlboro County
Bennettsville, South Carolina

Chocolate-Peanut Butter Cups

2 cups (12 ounces) milk
   chocolate morsels
2 tablespoons shortening
24 (1½-inch) paper candy cups

¾ cup sifted powdered sugar
¾ cup creamy peanut butter
1 tablespoon butter, melted

Place chocolate morsels and shortening in top of a double boiler. Bring water to a boil. Reduce heat to low; cook until chocolate melts and mixture is smooth, stirring often. Remove from heat.

Spoon 1 teaspoon chocolate mixture into each candy cup, and coat bottom and sides, using a small rubber spatula. Chill 30 minutes or until firm. Cover melted chocolate mixture, and keep over warm water in double boiler.

Combine sugar, peanut butter, and butter in a bowl; stir well. Spoon a heaping teaspoonful of peanut butter mixture into each cup. Spoon a level teaspoonful of chocolate mixture on top; smooth over to seal. Cover and chill 45 minutes or until firm; serve chilled. Store in an airtight container in refrigerator. Yield: 2 dozen.   Cyndi Bradt

Moments, Memories & Manna
Restoration Village
Rogers, Arkansas

Tempt-Me Truffles

These elegant chocolate candies are deceptively easy to make. Finely chopped toasted almonds, powdered sugar, and cocoa offer different looks and cloak the truffles in style.

1 (8-ounce) package cream cheese, softened
4 cups sifted powdered sugar
5 (1-ounce) squares unsweetened chocolate, melted

1 teaspoon vanilla extract
Finely chopped toasted almonds
Cocoa
Powdered sugar

Beat cream cheese at medium speed of an electric mixer until creamy; gradually add 4 cups powdered sugar, beating well after each addition. Stir in melted chocolate and vanilla. Cover and chill 2 hours or until firm.

Shape mixture into 1-inch balls; roll in almonds, cocoa, or powdered sugar. Cover and chill at least 1 hour; serve chilled. Store in an airtight container in refrigerator. Yield: 4 dozen.   Josh Day

a la Park
Park School Parent-Teachers Association
Mill Valley, California

Desserts

Lake Country Poached Pears with Delicious Sauces, page 132

Cream Cheese Crêpes with Apricot Sauce

1 (8-ounce) package cream
  cheese, softened
¼ cup plus 2 tablespoons
  butter, softened and divided
¼ cup sugar
3 teaspoons grated orange
  rind, divided
1 teaspoon vanilla extract
1 teaspoon almond extract

8 prepared 8-inch crêpes
⅔ cup apricot jam or preserves
⅓ cup fresh orange juice
1 tablespoon fresh lemon juice
1 teaspoon orange-flavored
  liqueur or orange juice
¼ cup plus 2 tablespoons
  sliced almonds, toasted

Position knife blade in food processor bowl; add cream cheese, ¼ cup butter, sugar, 2 teaspoons orange rind, and flavorings, and process until fluffy. Spread 1 heaping tablespoon cream cheese mixture over 1 side of each crêpe. Fold sides of each crêpe into center, and then roll up. Place crêpes, seam side down, in a buttered 13- x 9- x 2-inch pan. Bake, uncovered, at 350° for 10 minutes.

Meanwhile, combine jam, remaining 2 tablespoons butter, remaining 1 teaspoon orange rind, ⅓ cup orange juice, lemon juice, and liqueur in a small saucepan; cook over medium heat 5 minutes or until mixture is smooth and slightly thickened, stirring often. Spoon over warm crêpes, and sprinkle with almonds. Serve immediately. Yield: 8 servings.

Colorado Collage
The Junior League of Denver, Colorado

Cherry Berries on a Cloud

6 egg whites
½ teaspoon cream of tartar
¼ teaspoon salt
1¾ cups sugar
2 (3-ounce) packages cream
  cheese, softened
1 cup sugar
1 teaspoon vanilla extract

2 cups whipping cream,
  whipped
2 cups miniature marshmallows
1 (21-ounce) can cherry pie
  filling
2 cups fresh strawberries,
  hulled and sliced
1 teaspoon lemon juice

Beat first 3 ingredients at high speed of an electric mixer until foamy. Gradually add 1¾ cups sugar, 1 tablespoon at a time, beating until stiff peaks form and sugar dissolves (2 to 4 minutes). Spread meringue evenly in a greased 13- x 9- x 2-inch pan. Bake at 275° for 1 hour; turn oven off (do not open oven door). Let meringue cool in oven at least 12 hours.

Beat cream cheese, 1 cup sugar, and vanilla at medium speed until smooth. Gently fold in whipped cream and marshmallows. Spread mixture over meringue. Cover and chill 4 hours. Cut into squares.

Combine cherry pie filling, strawberries, and lemon juice in a bowl, stirring gently to combine; spoon evenly over each serving. Yield: 15 servings.   Anne Goodman

Quad City Cookin'
Queen of Heaven Circle of OLV Ladies Council
Davenport, Iowa

Swedish Cream

A sublime blend of whipping cream and sour cream creates the perfect cushion for a sprinkling of fresh berries.

1 cup sugar	2 (8-ounce) cartons sour cream
1 envelope unflavored gelatin	1 teaspoon vanilla extract
2 cups whipping cream	Fresh berries

Combine sugar and gelatin in a medium saucepan; stir in whipping cream, and let stand 1 minute. Cook over medium heat, stirring constantly with a wire whisk, 5 minutes or until gelatin dissolves. Remove from heat, and let cool.

Stir sour cream and vanilla into gelatin mixture. Pour into a serving bowl; cover and chill 3 hours or until set. To serve, spoon mixture into dessert dishes, and top with berries. Yield: 4 servings.   Ruth Bliss

700 lbs. of Marmalade
The Woman's Club of Winter Park, Florida

Lake Country Poached Pears with Delicious Sauces

A drizzle of the sauce of your choosing over these lemony poached pears is perfection. For a different look, pool the raspberry sauce on a plate and top with a pear and additional sauce, or flatten a scoop of vanilla ice cream in a dish and top with a pear and the warm chocolate sauce.

3 cups water
2 cups sugar
1 tablespoon grated lemon rind
2 tablespoons fresh lemon juice
1 teaspoon vanilla extract
4 ripe Bartlett or Anjou pears
Raspberry Cardinal Sauce
Belle-Helene Chocolate Sauce

Combine first 5 ingredients in a large saucepan. Peel pears, leaving stems intact; place in saucepan. Bring to a boil; cover, reduce heat, and simmer 10 minutes or until pears are slightly tender, turning occasionally. (Do not overcook.) Uncover and let pears cool. Cover and chill in cooking liquid 3 hours.

To serve, remove pears from liquid, and stand upright on dessert plates. Drizzle with chilled Raspberry Cardinal Sauce or warm Belle-Helene Chocolate Sauce. Yield: 4 servings.

Raspberry Cardinal Sauce

2 cups fresh or frozen raspberries, thawed
2 tablespoons sugar
1 tablespoon light rum, orange-flavored liqueur, or orange juice

Press raspberries through a wire-mesh strainer into a bowl, discarding seeds. Add sugar and rum, and stir well. Cover and chill. Yield: ¾ cup.

Belle-Helene Chocolate Sauce

2 (1-ounce) squares bittersweet chocolate
¼ cup whipping cream
1 tablespoon butter
1 teaspoon vanilla extract, light rum, or cognac

Combine chocolate and whipping cream in top of a double boiler; bring water to a boil. Reduce heat to low; cook until chocolate melts, stirring often. Add butter and vanilla, stirring until sauce is smooth. Serve warm. Yield: ½ cup.   Betty Evans

Foods and Flowers
Hermosa Garden Club
Hermosa Beach, California

Strawberries Romanoff: The Easy Way

Ease of preparation belies the elegance of this classic dessert. It's worthy of being served in your best silver or crystal bowl.

1 **quart fresh strawberries**
¼ **cup sugar**
1 **cup whipping cream, whipped**
1 **cup vanilla ice cream, softened**

¼ **cup Cointreau or other orange-flavored liqueur or orange juice**

Set aside the 6 prettiest strawberries for garnish. Wash and hull remaining strawberries, and place in a bowl; sprinkle with sugar. Cover and chill at least 3 hours.

Fold whipped cream into softened ice cream; add Cointreau and sugared strawberries, and fold gently. Garnish with reserved strawberries. Serve immediately. Yield: 6 servings.   Anne Lyles

The Parkway Palate
San Joaquin River Parkway & Conservation Trust
Fresno, California

Hot Apple Sundaes

Sweetly spiced apple slices are cooked until tender and warm, and then spooned over scoops of vanilla ice cream to cause a coveted ice cream meltdown. Dish the mixture over waffles to formulate another delicious duo.

1 cup sugar	10 cups peeled, sliced cooking
1 cup orange juice	apple (we tested with Granny
½ cup lemon juice	Smith)
½ teaspoon ground cinnamon	1½ quarts vanilla ice cream

Combine first 4 ingredients in a small saucepan. Bring to a boil; reduce heat to low; simmer, uncovered, 5 minutes. Add apple; return to a boil. Reduce heat to low; cover and simmer 10 minutes or until apple is tender. Serve warm over ice cream. Chill leftover sauce up to 3 days; reheat as needed. Yield: 12 servings.   Bertha Johnson

First Baptist Church Centennial Cookbook
First Baptist Church
Cushing, Oklahoma

Peach Melba Ice Cream Cake

If fresh peaches are not in season when you get a yen to make this fruity frozen cake, simply substitute thawed frozen peach slices.

1 cup melba toast crumbs
⅓ cup sugar
⅓ cup flaked coconut
¼ cup plus 2 tablespoons butter, melted
1 quart raspberry sherbet, softened
1 quart vanilla ice cream, softened

1 (10-ounce) package frozen raspberries, thawed
½ cup sugar
2 tablespoons cornstarch
1 tablespoon lemon juice
1 cup sliced fresh peaches, chilled

Combine first 4 ingredients, stirring well. Press mixture in bottom and up sides of a 9-inch springform pan. Bake at 350° for 10 minutes or until golden. Cool completely in pan on a wire rack. Cover and freeze at least 1 hour.

Spread raspberry sherbet in frozen crust. Freeze 30 minutes or until firm. Spread vanilla ice cream over sherbet. Cover and freeze 8 hours.

Drain raspberries, reserving liquid. Set raspberries aside. Combine ½ cup sugar and cornstarch in a saucepan. Add water to raspberry liquid to equal 1 cup. Stir liquid into sugar and cornstarch mixture. Cook over medium heat, stirring constantly, until mixture thickens and comes to a boil. Boil 1 minute, stirring constantly. Remove from heat; stir in raspberries and lemon juice. Let cool; cover and chill.

To serve, carefully remove sides of springform pan. Arrange peach slices on top of vanilla ice cream. Drizzle a small amount of raspberry sauce over peaches. Cut ice cream cake into wedges. Serve immediately with additional raspberry sauce spooned over each serving. Yield: 12 servings.

Here, There & Everywhere
Volunteers in Overseas Cooperative Assistance
Washington, DC

Margarita Ice Cream Torte

2½ dozen chocolate sandwich cookies (we tested with Oreos)
¼ cup butter or margarine, melted
½ cup frozen lemonade concentrate, thawed
¼ cup plus 2 tablespoons tequila
1 teaspoon grated lime rind
2 tablespoons plus 2 teaspoons fresh lime juice
2 tablespoons Triple Sec or other orange-flavored liqueur
5 drops of green food coloring
2 quarts vanilla ice cream, softened

Position knife blade in food processor bowl; add cookies, and process until crumbly. Pour butter through food chute with processor running. Process until crumbs resemble coarse meal; set aside 2 tablespoons crumb mixture. Press remaining crumb mixture in bottom of a 9-inch springform pan. Bake at 350° for 10 minutes. Let cool in pan on a wire rack.

Combine lemonade concentrate and next 5 ingredients in a large bowl; stir well. Add ice cream, stirring until blended. Pour immediately into prepared crust. Sprinkle reserved crumb mixture around top edge of torte. Cover and freeze at least 8 hours or up to 1 week.

To serve, carefully remove sides of springform pan. Cut into wedges; serve immediately. Yield: 12 servings.

Celebrate Chicago! A Taste of Our Town
The Junior League of Chicago, Illinois

Kiwi Icebergs

A refreshing dessert lies ahead when you create our kiwifruit ice. Orange-flavored liqueur complements the elusive flavor of the kiwifruit, while a fresh strawberry garnish brings out the kiwifruit's brilliant green color.

1½ cups peeled, mashed kiwifruit (about 6 medium)
¾ cup sugar
1 cup sparkling water
½ cup orange-flavored liqueur or rum
¼ cup fresh lemon juice
12 slices peeled kiwifruit (about 2 medium)
6 fresh strawberries

Combine mashed kiwifruit and sugar in a medium bowl; cover and let stand 20 minutes. Stir in sparkling water, liqueur, and lemon juice. Pour mixture into a 9-inch square pan. Cover and freeze until firm around the edges (about 2 hours).

Spoon mixture into a mixing bowl. Beat at medium speed of an electric mixer until smooth. Return mixture to pan. Cover and freeze until firm (about 4 hours).

To serve, scoop mixture evenly into six stemmed dessert dishes; top each serving with 2 kiwifruit slices and a strawberry. Serve immediately. Yield: 6 servings.   Joyce Jensen

Kenwood Lutheran Church Cookbook
Kenwood Women of the Evangelical Lutheran Church in America
Duluth, Minnesota

Lemon Ice in Lemon Cups

6 large lemons
1 envelope unflavored gelatin
2¼ cups cold water, divided

1 cup sugar
Garnish: fresh mint sprigs

Grate rind from top half of each lemon (the half around stem end); reserve rind. Cut lemons in half crosswise. Squeeze juice from grated top halves of lemons, reserving juice and discarding tops. Scoop pulp from bottom halves of lemons, reserving pulp for another use. Cut a thin slice of rind from bottom of each lemon cup so cups will stand upright. Cover and chill lemon cups.

Sprinkle gelatin over ¼ cup cold water in a medium saucepan; let stand 1 minute. Stir in remaining 2 cups cold water and sugar. Cook over low heat, stirring until gelatin dissolves, about 2 minutes. Remove from heat, and add reserved lemon rind and lemon juice. Pour mixture into a mixing bowl; cover and freeze 3 hours or until partially frozen.

Beat at medium speed of an electric mixer until smooth. Cover and freeze 2 hours; beat at medium speed until smooth. Cover and freeze until firm.

To serve, let stand at room temperature 10 minutes; scoop into lemon cups. Garnish, if desired. Serve immediately. Yield: 6 servings.

Take the Tour
St. Paul's Episcopal Church Women
Edenton, North Carolina

Sherbet and Ice Cream Fantasy

Bitsy balls of orange, lime, and raspberry sherbet are suspended like polka dots in a sea of vanilla ice cream. This unique dessert will have your guests asking, "How did you do that?"

2 cups orange sherbet	1 gallon vanilla ice cream
2 cups lime sherbet	2 cups whipping cream,
2 cups raspberry sherbet	whipped

Scoop sherbets into 1-inch balls with a scoop or melon baller. Place balls on a cookie sheet, and freeze until firm.

Place vanilla ice cream in a large bowl, and let stand until melted. Place sherbet balls into a 2-quart glass bowl or mold. Pour vanilla ice cream over balls, filling all spaces and gaps. Cover and freeze at least 8 hours. Unmold onto a freezer-proof serving plate; frost with whipped cream. Cover and freeze at least 3 hours. Let stand at room temperature 10 minutes before serving. Cut into wedges, and serve immediately. Yield: 12 servings.　　　　　Debbie Bernheim

Bone Appetit: A Second Helping
Operation Kindness
Carrollton, Texas

Watermelon Dessert

Layers of sherbet make up the rind and strawberry frozen yogurt the flesh of this watermelon look-alike. Since no watermelon experience is complete without the seeds, chocolate mini-morsels play the part.

1 quart lime sherbet, softened	2 quarts strawberry frozen yogurt, softened
1 quart lemon or orange sherbet, softened	1 cup (6 ounces) semisweet chocolate mini-morsels

Line a 5-quart freezer-proof bowl with wax paper, leaving a 1-inch overhang around edges. Spread lime sherbet in bottom and up sides of prepared bowl, forming an even layer; cover and freeze until firm. Spread lemon sherbet over lime sherbet, forming an even layer; cover and freeze until firm. Combine frozen yogurt and mini-morsels; spoon over lemon sherbet in center of bowl. Cover and freeze at least 8 hours.

Remove bowl from freezer; immerse up to rim in warm water 10 seconds. Invert onto a serving plate; peel off wax paper. Cut into wedges; serve immediately. Yield: 10 servings.   Jeannine Panunzio

Culinary Classics
The Hoffman Estates Medical Center Service League
Hoffman Estates, Illinois

Chocolate Snowball

2 (8-ounce) packages semisweet chocolate
2 cups sugar
1 cup water
2 cups butter, softened
8 large eggs

1 cup pecans or walnuts, chopped
2 tablespoons vanilla extract
2 cups whipping cream
¼ cup sugar
1 teaspoon vanilla extract

Line a 2½-quart ovenproof bowl with a double layer of aluminum foil; set aside.

Combine chocolate, 2 cups sugar, and water in top of a double boiler; bring water in bottom to a boil. Reduce heat to low; cook until chocolate and sugar melt, stirring often. Set aside.

Beat butter at medium speed of an electric mixer until creamy; add chocolate mixture, and beat until blended. Add eggs, one at a time, beating after each addition. Add pecans and 2 tablespoons vanilla, beating well. Pour chocolate mixture into prepared bowl.

Bake at 350° for 1 hour and 10 minutes or until set. (Top will be cracked.) Remove from oven, and let cool completely in bowl on a wire rack. (Top will collapse.) Cover and chill until firm.

Beat whipping cream until foamy; gradually add ¼ cup sugar and 1 teaspoon vanilla, beating until soft peaks form. Spoon whipped cream mixture into a decorating bag fitted with a large star tip. Remove chocolate mixture from refrigerator; invert onto a serving platter, and peel off aluminum foil. Pipe whipped cream mixture in rosettes over entire surface of dessert. Cut dessert into wedges; serve immediately. Store in refrigerator up to 1 week or freeze up to 2 weeks. Yield: 10 servings.   Joan Carson

The Club's Choice . . . A Second Helping
The Fuquay-Varina Woman's Club
Fuquay-Varina, North Carolina

Chocolate Truffle Loaf with Raspberry Sauce

A simple slice of this luxuriously decadent chocolate loaf drizzled with a brilliant red raspberry sauce will please the eye as well as the palate of the most ardent dessert lover.

2 cups whipping cream, divided
3 egg yolks, lightly beaten
2 (8-ounce) packages semisweet chocolate
1 cup light corn syrup, divided
½ cup butter or margarine
¼ cup sifted powdered sugar
1 teaspoon vanilla extract
2 (6-ounce) packages fresh raspberries

Line a 9- x 5- x 3-inch loafpan with heavy-duty plastic wrap; set aside.

Combine ½ cup whipping cream and egg yolks in a large bowl, stirring well.

Combine chocolate, ½ cup corn syrup, and butter in a 3-quart saucepan; cook over medium heat until chocolate and butter melt, stirring often. Stir in egg yolk mixture, and cook 3 minutes, stirring constantly. Remove from heat, and let cool completely.

Beat remaining 1½ cups whipping cream, powdered sugar, and vanilla at medium speed of an electric mixer until soft peaks form. Gently fold into chocolate mixture. Pour into prepared pan. Cover and freeze 3 hours or chill at least 8 hours.

Place raspberries in container of an electric blender, and process until smooth. Pour pureed raspberries through a wire-mesh strainer into a bowl, discarding seeds. Stir in remaining ½ cup corn syrup.

To serve, unmold loaf onto a serving platter; peel off plastic wrap. Cut loaf into slices, and serve with sauce. Yield: 18 servings.

Treasures of the Great Midwest
The Junior League of Wyandotte and Johnson Counties
Kansas City, Kansas

Chocolate Pâté

Here's an unusual approach to dessert. This spreadable chocolate "pâté" is spiked with bourbon and crowned with chopped pecans. Served with an assortment of cookies or fresh fruit, it makes a delightful end to a meal or addition to a dessert buffet. As a bonus, it can be repeatedly refrozen up to one month.

2 (8-ounce) packages semisweet chocolate

2 cups whipping cream

¼ cup plus 2 tablespoons bourbon

1 tablespoon plus 1 teaspoon vanilla extract

2½ cups sifted powdered sugar

¼ cup finely chopped pecans

Line an 8½- x 4½- x 3-inch loafpan with heavy-duty plastic wrap; set aside.

Combine chocolate and whipping cream in a heavy saucepan. Cook over medium heat, stirring constantly, until chocolate melts and mixture is smooth. Stir in bourbon and vanilla. Add powdered sugar, stirring with a wire whisk until smooth.

Pour mixture into prepared pan. Cover and freeze at least 4 hours or until firm (mixture will not freeze solid).

Unmold onto a serving platter; peel off plastic wrap. Sprinkle pecans over pâté. Serve with gingersnaps, shortbread cookies, sugar wafers, or apple wedges. Yield: 24 servings.   Steven Stolman

Centennial Cookbook 1895–1995
Rogers Memorial Library
Southampton, New York

Pear and Apple Pandowdy

Slices of apple and pear are sweetened with brown sugar, spiced with cinnamon and nutmeg, and then topped with a sweet biscuit batter that becomes browned and crisped after baking. A dollop of whipped cream atop each serving melds the medley.

3 large Granny Smith apples, peeled and sliced (about 4 cups)
3 large firm ripe pears, peeled and sliced (about 4 cups)
½ cup firmly packed brown sugar
¼ cup plus 2 tablespoons butter or margarine
2 tablespoons lemon juice
½ teaspoon ground cinnamon
½ teaspoon ground nutmeg
2 cups all-purpose flour
½ cup sugar
2 teaspoons baking powder
½ teaspoon salt
1 cup butter or margarine
½ cup water
2 teaspoons sugar
Whipped cream

Combine first 7 ingredients in a large saucepan; cook over medium heat until thoroughly heated, stirring occasionally. Pour hot filling into a greased 13- x 9- x 2-inch baking dish.

Combine 2 cups flour and next 3 ingredients in a small bowl, mixing well. Cut in butter with a pastry blender until mixture is crumbly. Add water, stirring just until dry ingredients are moistened. Drop by rounded tablespoonfuls onto hot filling; sprinkle with 2 teaspoons sugar. Bake, uncovered, at 375° for 30 minutes or until golden. Serve warm with whipped cream. Yield: 18 servings.   Terry L. Williams

Vermont Children's Aid Society Cookbook
The Vermont Children's Aid Society
Winooski, Vermont

Apple-Nut Pudding with Hot Rum Sauce

This homey apple dessert is a cross between a cake and a pudding. Slice it into squares or scoop spoonfuls into dessert dishes before blanketing it with a generous amount of rum sauce.

½ cup butter, softened
2 cups sugar
2 large eggs
2 tablespoons water
2 teaspoons vanilla extract
½ teaspoon butter flavor
2 cups all-purpose flour
2 teaspoons baking soda
½ teaspoon salt
2 teaspoons ground cinnamon
5 cooking apples, peeled and finely chopped (we tested with Granny Smith)
1 cup chopped pecans
Hot Rum Sauce

Beat butter at medium speed of an electric mixer until creamy; gradually add sugar, beating well. Add eggs, one at a time, beating after each addition. Add water and flavorings, beating well.

Combine flour and next 3 ingredients; add to butter mixture, beating well. Stir in apple and pecans. Spoon mixture into a greased and floured 13- x 9- x 2-inch pan. Bake at 350° for 1 hour. Cut into squares or spoon into dessert dishes. Serve warm with warm Hot Rum Sauce. Yield: 18 servings.

Hot Rum Sauce

1 cup sugar
1 cup water
½ cup butter
2 tablespoons all-purpose flour
⅛ teaspoon salt
2 teaspoons rum extract
1 teaspoon vanilla extract
¼ teaspoon butter flavor

Combine first 5 ingredients in a medium saucepan, and bring mixture to a boil over medium-high heat, stirring constantly. Stir in flavorings, and return to a boil, stirring constantly. Serve warm. Yield: 2⅓ cups.

Jennean McCutchen

Mounds of Cooking
Parkin Archeological Support Team
Parkin, Arkansas

Upside-Down Date Pudding

1 cup whole pitted dates, chopped
1 cup boiling water
½ cup sugar
2 cups firmly packed brown sugar, divided
1 large egg, lightly beaten
3 tablespoons butter, divided
1½ cups all-purpose flour
1 teaspoon baking soda
½ teaspoon baking powder
½ teaspoon salt
1 cup chopped walnuts or pecans
1½ cups boiling water
Whipped cream

Combine dates and 1 cup boiling water in a small bowl; set aside.

Combine ½ cup sugar, ½ cup brown sugar, egg, and 2 tablespoons butter in a mixing bowl; beat at medium speed of an electric mixer until blended.

Combine flour and next 3 ingredients; stir well. Add to sugar mixture, beating well. (Mixture will be crumbly.) Stir in cooled date mixture and walnuts.

Spoon batter into a lightly greased 13- x 9- x 2-inch pan. Combine remaining 1½ cups brown sugar, 1½ cups boiling water, and remaining 1 tablespoon butter, stirring well. Pour mixture over batter in pan. (Do not stir.) Bake, uncovered, at 375° for 35 to 40 minutes. Serve warm with whipped cream. Yield: 12 servings.   Ruby Perau

The St. Ansgar Heritage Cookbook
St. Ansgar Heritage Association
St. Ansgar, Iowa

Orange Caramel Flan

½ cup sugar
¼ cup water
2 cups milk
1 (1-inch) stick cinnamon
Peel of 1 medium orange
3 large eggs, lightly beaten

2 egg yolks, lightly beaten
½ cup sugar
1 teaspoon Grand Marnier or
    other orange-flavored liqueur
Garnish: fresh orange slices

Combine ½ cup sugar and water in a small saucepan, stirring well. Bring to a boil over medium heat; cook, without stirring, until sugar melts and mixture turns amber. Immediately pour caramelized sugar into six 6-ounce custard cups; set aside to cool.

Combine milk, cinnamon stick, and orange peel in a small saucepan; bring just to a boil over medium heat. Remove from heat, and let cool 10 minutes. Pour mixture through a wire-mesh strainer into a 2-cup liquid measuring cup, discarding cinnamon stick and orange peel; set milk mixture aside.

Combine eggs, egg yolks, ½ cup sugar, and liqueur in a small bowl, stirring well. Gradually add about 1 cup reserved warm milk into egg mixture; add remaining milk mixture, stirring constantly. Pour mixture through a wire-mesh strainer into a bowl; spoon into prepared cups. Cover each cup with aluminum foil, and place in a large pan; add hot water to pan to depth of 1 inch. Bake at 350° for 30 minutes or until a knife inserted in center comes out clean. Remove cups from water; remove foil, and let cool in cups on a wire rack.

To serve, unmold onto individual dessert plates. Garnish, if desired. Yield: 6 servings.

Texas Ties
The Junior League of North Harris County
Spring, Texas

Easy Tiramisù

1 (3-ounce) package vanilla
  pudding mix
2 cups milk
Homemade Mascarpone
2¾ cups frozen whipped
  topping, thawed
1½ teaspoons instant coffee
  granules
½ cup hot water

¼ cup brandy
¼ cup Kahlúa or other coffee-
  flavored liqueur
28 ladyfingers (about three
  3.5-ounce packages)
1 cup frozen whipped topping,
  thawed
1 teaspoon cocoa

Combine pudding and milk in a saucepan; cook over medium heat just until pudding comes to a boil and thickens, stirring often. Transfer mixture to a mixing bowl, and let cool. Add Homemade Mascarpone to pudding; beat at low speed until smooth. Fold in 2¾ cups whipped topping; set aside.

Dissolve coffee granules in water; stir in brandy and Kahlúa. Line bottom of an 11- x 7- x 1½-inch dish with ladyfingers. Brush one-third of coffee mixture over ladyfingers. Spread one-third of pudding mixture evenly over ladyfingers. Repeat layering procedure twice. Cover and chill 8 hours.

Remove from refrigerator; spread 1 cup whipped topping evenly over pudding mixture, and dust with cocoa. Yield: 8 servings.

Homemade Mascarpone

1 (8-ounce) package cream
  cheese, softened

3 tablespoons sour cream
2 tablespoons milk

Beat cream cheese at low speed of an electric mixer until creamy. Add sour cream and milk, beating until smooth. Yield: 1¼ cups.

Gracious Goodness Christmas in Charleston
Bishop England High School Endowment Fund
Charleston, South Carolina

Eggs & Cheese

Corn, Ham, and Cheese Soufflé, page 159

Smoked Ham and Potato Frittata

2 medium-size red potatoes,
  unpeeled
3 tablespoons olive oil
1 small onion, thinly sliced
4 ounces thinly sliced smoked
  ham, cut into 1-inch squares

10 large eggs, beaten
¼ cup chopped fresh parsley
¼ cup chopped fresh chives
½ cup grated Parmesan cheese
¼ teaspoon freshly ground
  pepper

Cook potatoes in boiling salted water to cover 30 minutes or until tender; drain and let cool. Cut into ¼-inch slices.

Spoon olive oil into an 11- x 7- x 1½-inch baking dish; brush oil on bottom and up sides of dish. Arrange onion slices in dish. Bake, uncovered, at 400° for 12 minutes or until onion is tender and beginning to brown. Remove baking dish from oven; reduce oven temperature to 350°.

Place ham on top of onion slices; top with potato slices. Combine eggs, parsley, and chives; pour over layered mixture. Sprinkle evenly with cheese and pepper. Bake, uncovered, 25 additional minutes or until set and golden. Yield: 6 servings.

Treasures of the Great Midwest
The Junior League of Wyandotte and Johnson Counties
Kansas City, Kansas

Quick Crab Quiche

Fast and fabulous describe this scrumptious quiche. It's sure to become a standby because it's a breeze to prepare with a few refrigerator and pantry staples.

Pastry for 9-inch pie
3 large eggs, beaten
1 (8-ounce) carton sour cream
1 (6-ounce) can crabmeat,
  drained and flaked

1 cup (4 ounces) shredded
  Cheddar cheese
1 (2.8-ounce) can French fried
  onions

Line a 9-inch pieplate with pastry. Trim off excess pastry along edges. Fold edges under, and crimp. Prick bottom and sides of pastry with a fork. Bake at 400° for 8 minutes. Remove from oven; reduce oven temperature to 350°.

Combine eggs and remaining 4 ingredients, stirring well. Spoon crabmeat mixture into prepared pastry shell. Bake, uncovered, 35 minutes or until set. Let stand 10 minutes before serving. Yield: one 9-inch quiche. Margaret Balentine

Nothing But the Best
College of Human Environmental Sciences/University of Alabama
Tuscaloosa, Alabama

Crispy Potato Quiche

1 (26-ounce) package frozen country-style shredded potatoes, thawed (we tested with Ore-Ida)
⅓ cup butter, melted
1 cup (4 ounces) shredded Monterey Jack cheese with jalapeño pepper

1 cup (4 ounces) shredded Swiss cheese
1 cup diced cooked ham
2 large eggs, beaten
½ cup half-and-half
¼ teaspoon seasoned salt

Press potato between paper towels to remove excess moisture. Press potato in bottom and up sides of a greased 10-inch pieplate. Brush with melted butter. Bake, uncovered, at 425° for 25 minutes; remove from oven. Reduce oven temperature to 350°.

Sprinkle cheeses and ham over crust. Combine eggs, half-and-half, and seasoned salt; pour over cheese mixture. Bake, uncovered, 35 minutes or until set. Yield: one 10-inch quiche. Barbara Bundy

Tasty Temptations
Our Lady of the Mountains Church
Sierra Vista, Arizona

Spinach Quiche with Cheddar Crust

Shreds of sharp Cheddar cheese meld with a bit of flour and butter to create a crisp and flavor-packed crust. It's just the right partner to embrace an earthy mix of spinach and mushrooms.

1 cup (4 ounces) shredded
  sharp Cheddar cheese
2 tablespoons butter
2 tablespoons all-purpose flour
¼ teaspoon salt
Vegetable cooking spray
1 (10-ounce) package frozen
  chopped spinach, cooked
  and drained

2 large eggs, beaten
½ cup chopped green onions
½ cup sliced fresh mushrooms
½ cup evaporated skimmed
  milk
¼ cup water
¼ teaspoon salt
½ teaspoon pepper
¼ teaspoon ground nutmeg

Position knife blade in food processor bowl; add first 4 ingredients, and process until blended.

Coat a 7¾-inch tart pan with removable bottom with cooking spray. Firmly press cheese mixture in bottom and up sides of pan; set aside.

Press spinach between paper towels to remove excess moisture. Combine spinach, eggs, and remaining 7 ingredients in a medium bowl; stir well. Pour spinach mixture into prepared tart pan. Bake, uncovered, at 400° for 15 minutes; reduce oven temperature to 350°, and bake 30 additional minutes or until set and golden. Serve immediately. Yield: one 7¾-inch quiche.

Herbal Harvest Collection
The Herb Society of America, South Texas Unit
Houston, Texas

Greek Spinach Pie

No, your eyes aren't playing tricks on you. There really is 1½ pounds of creamy, tangy feta cheese in this Mediterranean classic. We relished every ounce of it.

1 pound fresh spinach
3 tablespoons olive oil
1¼ cups finely chopped onion
¾ cup chopped green onions
½ cup butter or margarine,
   melted
1½ pounds feta cheese,
   crumbled

4 large eggs, beaten
½ cup chopped fresh parsley
1 tablespoon dried dillweed
¼ teaspoon pepper
1 (17¼-ounce) package frozen
   phyllo pastry, thawed
1 cup unsalted butter, melted

Remove stems from spinach; wash leaves thoroughly, and pat dry. Coarsely chop spinach leaves. Cook spinach in hot oil in a large skillet over medium heat until wilted, stirring often; drain and set aside.

Cook onion and green onions in ½ cup melted butter in a large skillet over medium-high heat, stirring constantly, until tender. Combine onion mixture, spinach, cheese, and next 4 ingredients; set aside.

Stack 36 sheets of phyllo on a damp towel; reserve remaining phyllo for another use. Place an 8-inch square pan on top of phyllo; cut around pan with a small sharp knife or pizza cutter to make 36 (8-inch) squares phyllo. Cover squares with a damp towel.

Butter the inside of pan; place 2 sheets of phyllo in bottom of pan, and brush lightly with melted unsalted butter. Layer 10 additional sheets of phyllo over first sheets, lightly brushing each sheet with butter. Spread half of spinach mixture over phyllo.

Layer 12 additional sheets of phyllo over spinach mixture, lightly brushing each sheet with butter. Spread remaining spinach mixture over phyllo. Layer remaining 12 sheets of phyllo over spinach mixture, lightly brushing each sheet with butter. Score (cut) top of phyllo into 12 squares.

Bake, uncovered, at 400° for 1 hour or until golden. Let stand 10 minutes before serving. Cut into squares. Yield: 12 servings.

Dawn to Dusk, A Taste of Holland
The Junior Welfare League of Holland, Michigan

Crustless Grits and Ham Pie

No need for a traditional piecrust when you can whip together this grits, ham, and cheese combo that makes its own crust. It's a winner– simple to prepare and easy to slice.

1 cup water
⅓ cup quick-cooking grits, uncooked
1 cup evaporated skimmed milk
1 cup chopped cooked lean ham
1 cup (4 ounces) shredded Cheddar cheese
3 large eggs, beaten
1 tablespoon chopped fresh parsley
½ teaspoon dry mustard
Vegetable cooking spray

Bring water to a boil in a small saucepan; stir in grits. Cover, reduce heat, and simmer 5 minutes or until liquid is absorbed.

Combine grits, milk, and next 5 ingredients; stir well. Spoon into a 9-inch pieplate coated with cooking spray. Bake, uncovered, at 350° for 35 minutes or until set. Let stand 10 minutes before serving. Yield: 6 servings.

Sue Briggs

Second Helpings
Deerfoot Community Bible Church
Pinson, Alabama

Eggs Presnov

This puffy egg and cheese dish is right at home alongside some fresh fruit and a tender muffin.

6 large eggs, beaten
1 cup milk
8 ounces Monterey Jack cheese, cubed
1 cup large-curd cottage cheese
3 tablespoons butter or margarine, cubed
2 teaspoons sugar
½ to 1 teaspoon salt
½ cup all-purpose flour
1 teaspoon baking powder
½ cup chopped fresh chives or parsley

Combine first 7 ingredients in a large bowl. Stir in flour, baking powder, and chives.

Pour into a greased 11- x 7- x 1½-inch baking dish. Bake, uncovered, at 325° for 45 to 47 minutes or until set in center and edges are golden. Serve immediately. Yield: 6 servings.

Classic Favorites
P.E.O., Chapter SB
Moraga, California

Broccoli Egg Puff

Bacon and broccoli meet up with eggs and cheese in this satisfying dish. If you aren't a Cheddar lover, use Swiss instead.

1 pound fresh broccoli
2 tablespoons all-purpose flour
½ teaspoon baking powder
5 large eggs, beaten
1 cup small-curd cottage
   cheese

4 slices bacon, cooked and
   crumbled
½ cup (2 ounces) shredded
   sharp Cheddar cheese

Remove leaves, and cut off tough ends of broccoli stalks; discard. Cut off broccoli flowerets, cutting large flowerets into small pieces; set aside. Coarsely chop remaining stalks; cook stalks in boiling salted water 5 minutes. Add flowerets, and cook 5 additional minutes; drain. Arrange broccoli evenly in a lightly greased 11- x 7- x 1½-inch baking dish; set aside.

Combine flour and baking powder in a small bowl; stir flour mixture into beaten eggs with a wire whisk. Stir in cottage cheese and bacon. Pour egg mixture evenly over broccoli.

Bake, uncovered, at 350° for 25 minutes or until set. Sprinkle with cheese, and bake 3 additional minutes. Yield: 6 servings.

Delta Informal Gardeners Cook
Delta Informal Gardeners
Brentwood, California

Breakfast Pizza

Make your next breakfast to order with this morning version of America's favorite pie. Crescent rolls create the crust, while pork sausage stands in for Italian.

1 pound ground pork sausage
½ cup chopped green pepper
1 (8-ounce) package refrigerated crescent rolls
1 cup frozen shredded potatoes, thawed
½ cup chopped onion
1 cup (4 ounces) shredded sharp Cheddar cheese
5 large eggs, beaten
¼ cup milk
½ teaspoon salt
½ teaspoon black pepper
2 tablespoons grated Parmesan cheese

Brown sausage in a large skillet, stirring until it crumbles, adding green pepper during the last 2 minutes of cooking; drain and set aside.

Press crescent roll dough in bottom of an ungreased 13- x 9- x 2-inch pan; sprinkle with sausage and pepper mixture. Top with potato and onion; sprinkle with Cheddar cheese.

Combine eggs and next 3 ingredients; pour over potato mixture. Sprinkle with Parmesan cheese. Bake, uncovered, at 375° for 25 minutes or until set. Yield: 8 servings.   Linda Bough

Owensburg Spring Festival Cookbook 1996
Owensburg Fire Department
Owensburg, Indiana

Superpan! Skillet Breakfast!

Top this hash brown-based egg, bacon, and cheese creation with salsa, and serve it with lots of enthusiasm! It deserves it!

6 slices bacon
1 (12-ounce) package frozen shredded potatoes
6 large eggs, beaten
¼ cup milk
½ teaspoon salt
Dash of pepper
1 cup (4 ounces) shredded Cheddar cheese
Salsa

Cook bacon in a large skillet until crisp; remove bacon, reserving drippings in skillet. Crumble bacon, and set aside.

Cook potato in drippings until bottom is crisp and browned. Combine eggs and next 3 ingredients; pour over potato. Sprinkle with cheese; top with bacon. Cover and cook over low heat 18 minutes or until set. Cut into wedges; serve with salsa. Yield: 6 servings.

Waiting to Inhale
Pacific Coast Mothers Club
Huntington Beach, California

Brie Strata with Fresh Fruit Salsa

8 to 10 slices French or Italian
  bread
3 tablespoons butter or
  margarine, softened
1 (15-ounce) Brie

4 large eggs, beaten
1½ cups milk
1 teaspoon salt
Dash of paprika
Fresh Fruit Salsa

Remove and discard crusts from bread. Butter 1 side of each slice of bread. Place half of bread slices, buttered side up, in a lightly greased 11- x 7- x 1½-inch baking dish. Remove and discard rind from Brie. Cut cheese into 1-inch cubes. Arrange half of cheese cubes on top of bread. Repeat layers with remaining bread slices and cheese cubes.

Combine eggs, milk, and salt in a small bowl; stir well. Pour egg mixture evenly over bread mixture; cover and chill 30 minutes.

Remove from refrigerator; let stand at room temperature 30 minutes. Uncover and sprinkle with paprika. Bake, uncovered, at 350° for 35 minutes or until set and lightly browned. Serve immediately; top with Fresh Fruit Salsa. Yield: 12 servings.

Fresh Fruit Salsa

2 cups fresh strawberries,
  hulled and diced
1 ripe pear, unpeeled, cored,
  and diced

1 tablespoon honey
1 tablespoon Key lime juice

Combine all ingredients; toss well. Cover and chill. Yield: 3 cups.

Special Selections of Ocala
Ocala Royal Dames for Cancer Research, Inc.
Ocala, Florida

Gruyère Cheese Pudding

18 slices whole wheat bread,
  toasted
1 pound Gruyère cheese, sliced
¼ cup finely chopped shallots
¼ cup chopped fresh parsley

4 large eggs, beaten
2 cups whipping cream
½ teaspoon salt
½ teaspoon ground nutmeg
¼ teaspoon ground red pepper

Place 6 toast slices in bottom of a buttered 13- x 9- x 2-inch baking dish. Layer cheese and remaining toast slices evenly in dish, ending with cheese. Sprinkle shallot and parsley over cheese.

Combine eggs and remaining 4 ingredients, stirring with a wire whisk; pour over cheese mixture. Cover and bake at 325° for 30 minutes; uncover and bake 15 additional minutes or until browned. Serve immediately. Yield: 6 servings.

Compliments of the Chef
Friends of the Library of Collier County, Inc.
Naples, Florida

Spring Brunch Bake

½ pound fresh asparagus
1 medium-size sweet red
  pepper, chopped
1 medium onion, cut into thin
  strips
¼ cup butter or margarine,
  melted
8 ounces French bread, cut
  into 1-inch cubes (about 8
  cups)

2 cups (8 ounces) shredded
  sharp Cheddar cheese,
  divided
1 cup cubed cooked ham
8 large eggs, beaten
2½ cups milk
½ teaspoon salt
½ teaspoon dried marjoram
⅛ teaspoon pepper

Snap off tough ends of asparagus. Remove scales from stalks with a vegetable peeler, if desired. Cut asparagus into 1-inch pieces. Cook asparagus, red pepper, and onion in butter in a large skillet, stirring constantly, until asparagus is crisp-tender.

Combine asparagus mixture, bread cubes, 1 cup cheese, and ham; toss well. Spoon mixture into a buttered 13- x 9- x 2-inch baking dish.

Combine eggs and remaining 4 ingredients in a medium bowl, stirring well. Pour egg mixture over bread mixture. Cover and chill 8 hours.

Bake, uncovered, at 350° for 45 minutes or until puffed and golden. Sprinkle with remaining 1 cup cheese; bake 5 additional minutes or until cheese melts. Let stand 5 minutes before serving. Yield: 10 servings.   Patricia Adlhoch

Dancers for Doernbecher Present Recipes from the Heart
Dancers for Doernbecher
Milwaukie, Oregon

Poached Eggs with Roquefort Cheese

A poached egg is nestled inside each hollowed crusty French roll lined with buttery Swiss. An assertive Roquefort topping crowns each serving in style. Serve these lovelies with salty slices of Canadian bacon and generous slabs of grilled garden tomato.

4 (1-ounce) round French
   bread rolls
3 tablespoons butter, softened
   and divided
2 tablespoons shredded Swiss
   cheese

4 large eggs
3 tablespoons crumbled
   Roquefort cheese

Cut ¼ inch from top of each roll; hollow out centers of bottoms, leaving ¼-inch shells. Reserve roll centers for another use. Spread 2 tablespoons butter evenly in bottom of rolls. Sprinkle Swiss cheese evenly in bottom of rolls. Place rolls on an ungreased baking sheet; bake, uncovered, at 375° for 5 minutes or until golden.

Lightly grease a large saucepan; add water to depth of 2 inches. Bring to a boil; reduce heat, and maintain a light simmer. Break eggs, one at a time, into a saucer; slip into water, holding saucer close to water. Simmer 5 minutes or until cooked. Remove eggs with a slotted spoon; trim edges of eggs, if desired.

Place a poached egg in each prepared roll. Combine remaining 1 tablespoon butter and Roquefort cheese; sprinkle evenly over eggs. Bake, uncovered, 3 minutes or until thoroughly heated. Yield: 4 servings.   Rayetta Graham Bovay

Newport Cooks & Collects
The Preservation Society of Newport County
Newport, Rhode Island

Smoked Salmon and Onion Cheesecake

A smoky wedge of this rich salmon cheesecake and a fresh green salad make memorable luncheon fare. If you prefer, serve the cheesecake in small wedges as a plated appetizer.

¼ cup grated Parmesan cheese, divided
2 tablespoons fine, dry breadcrumbs (store-bought)
1 small Vidalia or other sweet onion, chopped
1 cup chopped green pepper
3 tablespoons butter or margarine, melted
3 (8-ounce) packages cream cheese, softened

⅓ cup evaporated milk
4 large eggs
¼ teaspoon salt
¼ teaspoon freshly ground black pepper
½ pound smoked salmon, finely chopped
½ cup (2 ounces) shredded Swiss cheese

Combine 2 tablespoons Parmesan cheese and breadcrumbs. Sprinkle crumb mixture evenly in bottom and up sides of a buttered 8-inch springform pan; set aside.

Cook onion and green pepper in butter in a skillet over medium heat 3 minutes or just until tender, stirring occasionally; set aside.

Combine cream cheese, milk, and eggs in a large mixing bowl; beat at medium speed of an electric mixer until smooth. Stir in onion mixture, salt, and ground pepper; fold in salmon and Swiss cheese. Pour mixture into prepared pan.

Bake, uncovered, at 300° for 1 hour and 40 minutes or until center is almost set. Turn oven off. Leave cheesecake in oven 1 hour. Remove from oven, and let cool to room temperature on a wire rack; sprinkle top with remaining 2 tablespoons Parmesan cheese. Carefully remove sides of springform pan. Serve at room temperature, or cover and chill. Yield: 16 servings.

Carolina Sunshine, Then & Now
The Charity League of Charlotte, North Carolina

Corn, Ham, and Cheese Soufflé

Vegetable cooking spray
2 teaspoons fine, dry
  breadcrumbs (store-bought)
1½ cups fresh corn, cut
  from cob (2 large ears)
⅓ cup thinly sliced green
  onions
⅔ cup diced cooked maple-
  glazed ham (about 3 ounces)

¼ cup all-purpose flour
¾ cup fat-free milk
½ cup (2 ounces) shredded
  sharp Cheddar cheese
¼ teaspoon ground red pepper
2 egg yolks, beaten
4 egg whites
½ teaspoon cream of tartar

Cut a piece of aluminum foil long enough to fit around a 1½-quart soufflé dish, allowing a 1-inch overlap; fold foil lengthwise into thirds. Coat one side of foil and bottom of dish with cooking spray. Wrap foil around outside of dish, coated side against dish, allowing it to extend 3 inches above rim to form a collar; secure with string. Sprinkle breadcrumbs in bottom of dish; set aside.

Coat a large nonstick skillet with cooking spray. Place over medium-high heat until hot. Add corn and green onions; cook, stirring constantly, 5 minutes or until tender. Stir in ham. Remove from heat, and set aside.

Place flour in a small saucepan; gradually add milk, stirring with a wire whisk until blended. Cook over medium heat, stirring constantly, 3 minutes or until mixture thickens. Remove from heat; stir in cheese and pepper. Gradually stir cheese mixture into egg yolks; stir in corn mixture.

Beat egg whites and cream of tartar at high speed of an electric mixer until stiff peaks form. Fold one-fourth of beaten whites into cheese mixture. Fold in remaining egg whites. Pour mixture into prepared dish.

Bake, uncovered, at 325° for 55 minutes or until puffed and golden. Remove foil collar from dish, and serve immediately. Yield: 6 servings.

Deborah Walsh

Exclusively Corn Cookbook
Coventry Historical Society
Coventry, Connecticut

Florentine Egg Torte

Prepare this recipe when nothing but a showstopper will do. Colorful layers of spinach, ham, sweet red pepper, and cheesy scrambled eggs comprise the torte. For extra-pretty slices, cut with an electric knife.

¼ cup plus 3 tablespoons butter, divided
3 large shallots, chopped
2 (10-ounce) packages frozen chopped spinach, thawed and drained
2 egg whites, beaten
½ teaspoon salt
¼ teaspoon freshly grated nutmeg
¼ teaspoon freshly ground black pepper
3 slices firm white bread, crusts removed

3 large green onions, cut into 1-inch pieces
½ cup chopped fresh parsley
1 cup milk
12 large eggs
½ pound Swiss cheese, divided
¾ teaspoon salt
¾ pound sliced lean cooked ham
3 sweet red peppers, roasted and quartered*

Melt 3 tablespoons butter in a skillet over medium-high heat. Add shallot, and cook 5 minutes or until tender, stirring occasionally. Combine shallot, spinach, and next 4 ingredients in a large bowl; stirring well.

Tear bread into pieces. Position knife blade in food processor bowl. Add bread, green onions, and parsley to processor bowl. Process 5 seconds. Place bread mixture in a small bowl; add milk, and let stand 5 minutes. Drain milk from bread mixture, and place milk in processor bowl. Set bread mixture aside.

Add eggs to processor bowl; process 10 seconds.

Coarsely chop ¼ pound Swiss cheese; set aside. Melt remaining ¼ cup butter in a large skillet over medium-high heat. Add egg mixture and ¾ teaspoon salt; cook until eggs are softly scrambled but not runny. Remove eggs from heat; stir in chopped Swiss cheese and reserved bread mixture.

Place half of egg mixture in a greased 9-inch springform pan. Top with half of spinach mixture. Arrange ham slices over spinach mixture. Arrange roasted peppers evenly over ham slices. Top with remaining egg mixture. Slice remaining ¼ pound Swiss cheese. Layer cheese slices on top of egg mixture.

Cover base of springform pan with aluminum foil to catch any drippings. Bake at 400° for 30 minutes. Remove from oven, and let stand

10 minutes. Carefully remove sides of springform pan. Serve immediately. Yield: 8 servings.

*You can purchase commercially roasted red peppers at most grocery stores. Find them on the aisle with other condiments like olives.

Capital Celebrations
The Junior League of Washington, DC

Caramel-Pecan French Toast

12 (1-inch-thick) slices French bread
8 large eggs, beaten
1 cup milk
1 cup half-and-half
2 teaspoons vanilla extract
½ teaspoon ground nutmeg
½ teaspoon ground mace
½ teaspoon ground cinnamon
¾ cup butter or margarine, softened
1⅓ cups firmly packed brown sugar
3 tablespoons light corn syrup
1⅓ cups chopped pecans

Arrange bread slices in a buttered 13- x 9- x 2-inch baking dish.

Combine eggs and next 6 ingredients in a large bowl; stir well with a wire whisk. Pour egg mixture over bread slices. Cover and chill 8 hours.

Beat butter, brown sugar, and corn syrup at medium speed of an electric mixer until blended. Stir in pecans. Top bread slices with nut mixture, spreading evenly.

Bake, uncovered, at 350° for 45 minutes or until golden. Yield: 10 servings.

Cheryl Tveit

Ashland County Fair Centennial Cookbook 1895–1995
Ashland County Fair Association
Ashland, Wisconsin

Stuffed French Toast

A dozen eggs, a loaf of bread, and a block of cream cheese go into this French toast fantasy. Maple syrup and cinnamon add just the right touch of sweetness.

12 large eggs, beaten
4 cups milk
1 cup maple syrup
¼ cup butter or margarine, melted
1 (1-pound) loaf unsliced white bread or French bread, cut into 1-inch cubes

1 (8-ounce) package cream cheese, softened
¼ cup sugar
¼ teaspoon ground cinnamon

Combine first 4 ingredients in a large bowl; stir well, and set aside.

Place half of bread cubes in a greased 13- x 9- x 2-inch pan. Spread cream cheese over bread cubes; top with remaining half of bread cubes. Pour egg mixture over bread mixture.

Combine sugar and cinnamon in a small bowl; sprinkle over bread mixture. Bake, uncovered, at 350° for 50 to 55 minutes or until almost set in center. Let stand 5 minutes before serving. Yield: 10 servings.

Vicky Furness, Sharon Furness Ulrici, Kathleen (Norris) Sullivan

Morrisonville's 125th Anniversary Cookbook
Morrisonville Historical Society & Museum
Morrisonville, Illinois

Fish & Shellfish

Mussels with Spaghettini, page 178

Cornmeal-Crusted Catfish on Mixed Greens

Mixed salad greens, lightly wilted by a warm dressing, cradle crusty nuggets of catfish in this summer supper. We suggest serving thick slices of juicy vine-ripe tomatoes on the side.

3 cups loosely packed mixed salad greens
½ cup thinly sliced purple onion
¼ cup yellow cornmeal
¼ teaspoon salt
⅛ teaspoon pepper
12 ounces catfish fillets, cut into 1-inch pieces

2 tablespoons vegetable oil
½ teaspoon grated lemon rind
2 tablespoons fresh lemon juice
1½ teaspoons honey
1½ teaspoons Dijon mustard

Combine salad greens and onion in a large bowl; set aside.

Combine cornmeal, salt, and pepper. Rinse fish in cold water; drain. Dredge fish in cornmeal mixture. Cook fish in hot oil in a large skillet over medium-high heat 6 minutes or until golden, turning occasionally; remove from skillet.

Add lemon rind and next 3 ingredients to skillet; cook over medium-high heat 30 seconds, stirring constantly. Pour lemon juice mixture over greens mixture; toss gently.

Spoon greens mixture onto two serving plates; top with fish. Serve immediately. Yield: 2 servings.   Dr. and Mrs. Robert Roberts

Memorial Hospital Associates Favorites
Memorial Hospital Activities Committee
York, Pennsylvania

Rafe's Fried Grouper

A dusting of cornmeal is key to the crispy crust on these panfried grouper fillets. Serve them with a squirt of fresh lemon juice or a dollop of tangy tartar sauce.

1 cup milk
1 small onion, minced (about ¾ cup)
1 clove garlic, minced
1 pound grouper or other firm white fish fillets
⅔ cup all-purpose flour
⅓ cup white cornmeal
½ teaspoon dried basil
½ teaspoon dried oregano
¼ teaspoon salt
⅛ teaspoon black pepper
⅛ teaspoon ground red pepper
Vegetable oil
Lemon wedges

Combine first 3 ingredients in a large bowl; add fish fillets. Cover and marinate in refrigerator 30 minutes.

Combine flour and next 6 ingredients; stir well. Dredge fillets in flour mixture. Fry in ½ inch hot oil in a skillet over medium-high heat 5 to 6 minutes on each side or until golden. Drain on paper towels. Serve with lemon wedges. Yield: 4 servings.　　　Rafael Rosengarten

McClellanville Coast Seafood Cookbook
McClellanville Arts Council
McClellanville, South Carolina

Halibut with Papaya-Ginger Salsa

1 teaspoon mayonnaise
1 pound halibut fillets (1 inch thick)
½ teaspoon dried dillweed
1 ripe papaya, peeled and diced
¼ cup chopped fresh cilantro
2 tablespoons brown sugar
2 tablespoons chopped green onions
2 tablespoons grated fresh ginger
3 tablespoons lime juice
2 tablespoons oyster sauce
1 teaspoon hot sauce
Vegetable cooking spray

Spread mayonnaise over both sides of fish; sprinkle with dillweed. Cover and chill 30 minutes.

Combine papaya and next 7 ingredients in a small bowl, stirring well; cover and let stand at room temperature 30 minutes.

Coat grill rack with cooking spray; place on grill over medium-hot coals (350° to 400°). Place fish on rack. Grill, covered, 7 minutes on each side or until fish flakes easily when tested with a fork. Serve with salsa. Yield: 4 servings.   Suzanne Glickman

Tuvia's Tasty Treats
Tuvia School of Temple Menorah
Redondo Beach, California

Fish à la Lulu

Halibut fillets are seared in olive oil and then finished off in the oven while you make the topping. This recipe boasts the bright flavors of fresh tomato, basil, garlic, and shallot.

4 (4-ounce) halibut fillets
3 tablespoons minced garlic, divided
7 plum tomatoes
2 tablespoons olive oil, divided
½ cup loosely packed fresh basil leaves, chopped
2 tablespoons minced shallots
1 tablespoon drained capers
1 teaspoon fresh lemon juice
¼ teaspoon salt
¼ teaspoon pepper

Rub fillets on both sides with 1 tablespoon garlic. Cover and marinate in refrigerator 1 hour.

Dice tomatoes, and drain well. Place tomato, remaining 2 tablespoons garlic, 1 tablespoon olive oil, basil, and next 5 ingredients in a small bowl; set aside.

Cook fillets in remaining 1 tablespoon olive oil in a large ovenproof skillet over medium-high heat about 2 minutes on each side or until browned. Place skillet in oven. Bake, uncovered, at 350° for 6 minutes or until fish flakes easily when tested with a fork.

To serve, place fillets on individual serving plates, and top evenly with tomato mixture. Yield: 4 servings.   Lou Siemons

Malibu's Cooking Again
Malibu's Cooking Again
Malibu, California

Quick and Easy Mahimahi

Mayonnaise keeps the mahimahi fillets moist while baking. A grating of sharp Italian cheeses plus a touch of oregano adds subtle flavor interest to this uncomplicated entrée.

2 **pounds mahimahi fillets (1½ inches thick)**
¼ **teaspoon salt**
¼ **teaspoon pepper**
⅓ **cup mayonnaise**
2 **tablespoons grated Parmesan cheese**

2 **tablespoons grated Romano cheese**
1½ **teaspoons dried oregano or basil**

Sprinkle fillets with salt and pepper. Place on a lightly greased baking sheet.

Combine mayonnaise and remaining 3 ingredients in a small bowl. Spread mixture evenly over 1 side of fillets.

Bake, uncovered, at 350° for 15 minutes or until fish flakes easily when tested with a fork. Yield: 4 servings.   Shirley Rizzuto

Ka Mea 'Ai 'Ono Loa: Delicious Foods from the
Honolulu Waldorf School
Honolulu Waldorf School
Honolulu, Hawaii

Grilled Redfish with Mango Salsa

Mango salsa gets an intriguing boost from toasted cumin seeds. The salsa is a standout with grilled chicken, too.

½ teaspoon cumin seeds
1¼ cups diced mango (about 1 small)
½ cup diced sweet red pepper
¼ cup minced purple onion
1 tablespoon fresh lime juice

¼ teaspoon hot sauce
2 pounds redfish fillets (½ inch thick)
½ teaspoon salt
½ teaspoon pepper
Vegetable cooking spray

Toast cumin seeds in a small skillet over medium-low heat until fragrant, stirring often. Transfer to a small bowl; add mango and next 4 ingredients, stirring well. Cover and chill.

Sprinkle fillets with salt and pepper. Coat grill rack with cooking spray; place on grill over medium-hot coals (350° to 400°). Arrange fillets on rack; grill, covered, 5 minutes on each side or until fish flakes easily when tested with a fork. Transfer to a serving platter; spoon salsa over fillets. Yield: 4 servings.

Beneath the Palms
The Brownsville Junior Service League
Brownsville, Texas

Baked Salmon in Phyllo

1 (14.75-ounce) can red salmon, drained and flaked
1 cup soft breadcrumbs (homemade)
¾ cup sour cream
⅓ cup chopped pecans
¼ cup sliced green onions
¼ cup chopped celery
2 tablespoons chopped pimiento

½ teaspoon salt
¼ teaspoon ground red pepper
2 large eggs, lightly beaten
8 sheets frozen phyllo pastry, thawed
⅓ cup butter or margarine, melted
Garnishes: lemon slices, green onion fans

Combine first 10 ingredients; stir well, and set aside.

Place 1 sheet of phyllo on a damp towel, keeping remaining phyllo covered with a damp towel. Brush phyllo sheet lightly with butter.

Layer 3 additional sheets of phyllo over bottom sheet, brushing each sheet lightly with butter. Cut stack of phyllo in half lengthwise. Place phyllo strips lengthwise in a greased 9- x 5- x 3-inch loafpan. Repeat procedure, using remaining phyllo sheets and butter, but placing phyllo strips crosswise in pan.

Spoon salmon mixture into pan. Fold ends of phyllo over top of salmon mixture. Brush top with remaining butter. Bake, uncovered, at 375° for 20 minutes. Invert loafpan into a lightly greased 15- x 10- x 1-inch jellyroll pan. Bake 20 additional minutes or until golden. Garnish, if desired. Yield: 4 servings.   Marianne Gienger

Favorite Recipes
Tillamook County Dairy Women
Tillamook, Oregon

Salmon with Basil, Tomato, and Capers

1 **pound plum tomatoes, seeded and chopped**	1 **tablespoon drained capers**
¾ **cup lightly packed fresh basil leaves, chopped**	⅛ **teaspoon salt**
	⅛ **teaspoon pepper**
½ **cup olive oil**	4 **(6-ounce) salmon fillets**
1 **shallot, chopped**	1 **tablespoon olive oil**
(2 tablespoons)	**Vegetable cooking spray**
1½ **tablespoons lemon juice**	**Garnish: lemon wedges**
	(1 small lemon)

Combine first 8 ingredients in a small bowl, stirring well; set aside.

Brush both sides of salmon with 1 tablespoon olive oil. Place salmon on a rack of broiler pan coated with cooking spray. Broil 3 inches from heat (with electric oven door partially opened) 10 minutes or until fish flakes easily when tested with a fork.

To serve, transfer salmon to a serving plate; top with tomato mixture, and garnish, if desired. Yield: 4 servings.

Special Selections of Ocala
Ocala Royal Dames for Cancer Research, Inc.
Ocala, Florida

Grilled Salmon with Yogurt-Dill Sauce

1 (16-ounce) carton plain
   nonfat yogurt
2 cloves garlic, minced
1 tablespoon chopped fresh dill
   or 1 teaspoon dried dillweed
1 tablespoon lemon juice
⅛ teaspoon salt
⅛ teaspoon pepper
⅛ teaspoon hot sauce
⅔ cup peeled, thinly sliced
   cucumber (about ½ medium)
Vegetable cooking spray
6 (8-ounce) salmon fillets or
   steaks

Combine first 7 ingredients in a small bowl; stir well. Gently stir in cucumber; set aside.

Coat grill rack with cooking spray; place on grill over medium-hot coals (350° to 400°). Place salmon on rack; grill, covered, 8 minutes on each side or until fish flakes easily when tested with a fork. Serve with sauce. Yield: 6 servings.
                                         Julie Rehfeld

Bartlett Memorial Hospital's 25th Anniversary Cookbook
Bartlett Memorial Hospital
Juneau, Alaska

Honey-Glazed Salmon Burgers

Rose-hued flakes of canned salmon transform into gourmet burgers with a basting of a sassy honey-horseradish glaze as they grill.

⅔ cup honey
⅔ cup ketchup
1 tablespoon cider vinegar
2 teaspoons prepared
   horseradish
½ teaspoon minced garlic
¼ teaspoon dried crushed red
   pepper
1 (14¾-ounce) can salmon,
   drained and flaked
1 cup fine, dry breadcrumbs
   (store-bought)
½ cup finely chopped onion
½ cup finely chopped green
   pepper
3 egg whites
Vegetable cooking spray
4 hamburger buns

Combine first 6 ingredients in a small bowl; stir well. Reserve half of sauce to serve with burgers; set remaining sauce aside.

Combine salmon and next 4 ingredients; add 2 tablespoons sauce, and stir until combined. Divide mixture into 4 patties.

Coat grill rack with cooking spray; place on grill over medium-hot coals (350° to 400°). Place burgers on rack; grill, covered, 4 minutes on each side or until browned, basting with additional sauce.

To serve, top bottom halves of each bun with a patty. Spoon reserved sauce over patties, and cover patties with bun tops. Yield: 4 servings.   Mary Ann Myers

Star-Spangled Recipes
American Legion Auxiliary, Department of West Virginia
Belmont, Ohio

Sole with Herbs

This simple sauté of sole fillets takes on a distinctive air with a clever sprinkling of four dried herbs–chives, parsley, tarragon, and chervil. A short simmer in white wine and lemon juice completes this classy entrée.

4 (4-ounce) sole fillets
½ teaspoon salt
⅛ teaspoon pepper
2 tablespoons all-purpose flour
¼ teaspoon dried chives
¼ teaspoon dried parsley
   flakes
¼ teaspoon dried tarragon
¼ teaspoon dried chervil
¼ teaspoon paprika
2 tablespoons butter or
   margarine
½ cup dry white wine
1 tablespoon lemon juice

Sprinkle fillets with salt and pepper; dredge in flour.

Combine chives and next 4 ingredients; set aside.

Melt butter in a large skillet over medium-high heat. Add fillets; cook until lightly browned on bottom. Turn fillets; sprinkle with herb mixture. Add wine and lemon juice to skillet. Bring just to a simmer; cover and simmer 5 minutes or until fish flakes easily when tested with a fork. Serve immediately. Yield: 4 servings.   Marianne Muellerleile

From ANNA's Kitchen
Adams-Normandie Neighborhood Association (ANNA)
Los Angeles, California

Garlicky Swordfish en Papillote

4 cloves garlic, thinly sliced
½ teaspoon fennel seeds,
    crushed
1 tablespoon olive oil,
    divided
¼ cup fresh lemon juice
1 (10-ounce) bag shredded
    carrot (about 4 cups)
4 (6-ounce) swordfish steaks
    (1 inch thick)
¼ teaspoon salt

Cook garlic and fennel seeds in 2 teaspoons olive oil in a small skillet over medium-high heat 3 minutes, stirring constantly. Remove from heat, and let cool slightly; stir in lemon juice, and set aside.

Cut four 15-inch squares of parchment paper; fold each square in half, and trim each into a large heart shape. Place parchment hearts on an ungreased baking sheet, and open out flat. Place 1 cup carrot on each parchment heart near the crease; set aside.

Brown fish in remaining 1 teaspoon olive oil in a large skillet over medium-high heat 1 minute on each side. Place a fish steak on top of carrot on each parchment heart. Spoon about 1 tablespoon garlic mixture over each fish steak. Sprinkle fish and vegetables evenly with salt.

Fold paper edges over to seal securely. Starting with rounded edges of hearts, pleat and crimp edges of parchment paper to make an airtight seal.

Bake at 375° for 20 minutes or until packets are puffed and lightly browned.

Place packets on individual serving plates; cut an opening in the top of each packet, and fold paper back. Serve immediately. Yield: 4 servings.

A Capital Affair
The Junior League of Harrisburg, Pennsylvania

Grilled Swordfish with Herbs

2 (8-ounce) swordfish steaks
½ cup Chardonnay or other
    dry white wine
¼ cup chopped fresh cilantro
1 tablespoon dry mustard
1 tablespoon chili powder
2 tablespoons lime juice
1 tablespoon olive oil
1 teaspoon mustard seeds
1 teaspoon pepper
Vegetable cooking spray

Place fish in a heavy-duty, zip-top plastic bag. Combine wine and next 7 ingredients, stirring well; pour over fish in bag. Seal bag securely, and shake bag gently to coat. Marinate in refrigerator 15 minutes. Drain fish, reserving marinade. Bring marinade to a boil in a small saucepan; set aside.

Coat grill rack with cooking spray; place on grill over medium-hot coals (350° to 400°). Place fish on rack; grill, covered, 5 minutes on each side or until fish flakes easily when tested with a fork, basting twice with marinade. Yield: 2 servings.　　　　　Wendy Nelson

Waiting to Inhale
Pacific Coast Mothers Club
Huntington Beach, California

Tilapia with Lemon-Caper Butter

The fine-textured flesh of tilapia is white and sweet. In this unpretentious yet elegant dish, the fillets are topped with slices of lemon-caper butter to complement.

½ cup unsalted butter,
  softened
¼ cup drained capers
1 teaspoon grated lemon rind
¼ teaspoon fresh lemon juice

⅛ teaspoon ground white
  pepper
¼ cup all-purpose flour
4 (6-ounce) tilapia fillets
2 tablespoons olive oil

Combine first 5 ingredients in a small bowl, stirring until blended. Shape butter mixture into a 3-inch log. Wrap in wax paper; freeze until firm.

Place flour in a large heavy-duty, zip-top plastic bag; add fish. Seal bag securely; shake until fish is coated. Fry fish in hot olive oil in a large skillet 3 minutes on each side or until fish flakes easily when tested with a fork.

Remove wax paper from butter log, and cut log into 4 slices. Place a slice of butter mixture on top of each fillet. Serve immediately. Yield: 4 servings.

Celebrate Chicago! A Taste of Our Town
The Junior League of Chicago, Illinois

Baked Fish with Lemon-Parsley Stuffing

1 (1½-pound) pan-dressed bass
Lemon-Parsley Stuffing
Vegetable cooking spray

1 tablespoon fresh lemon juice
Garnishes: fresh parsley sprigs,
lemon wedges

Rinse fish, and pat dry. Fill cavity of fish with Lemon-Parsley Stuffing, and secure with skewers. Place fish in a 13- x 9- x 2-inch baking dish coated with cooking spray. Sprinkle with lemon juice.

Bake, uncovered, at 350° for 40 minutes or until fish flakes easily when tested with a fork. Garnish, if desired. Yield: 4 servings.

Lemon-Parsley Stuffing

¼ cup chopped onion
¼ cup chopped celery
1 clove garlic, minced
1 tablespoon butter or
margarine, melted
2 tablespoons chopped fresh
parsley
1 tablespoon fresh lemon juice

1 tablespoon dry white wine
½ teaspoon grated lemon rind
¼ teaspoon dried thyme,
crushed
¼ teaspoon salt
⅛ teaspoon pepper
1½ cups soft whole wheat
breadcrumbs (homemade)

Cook first 3 ingredients in butter in a medium skillet over medium-high heat, stirring constantly, 4 minutes or until vegetables are tender; remove from heat. Add parsley and next 6 ingredients, stirring well. Add breadcrumbs, and toss gently. Yield: 1½ cups.

Mississippi Reflections: A Collection of Recipes Seasoned with Memories
Hospice of Central Mississippi
Brookhaven, Mississippi

Charbroiled Albacore

Tuna steaks go Thai with a blending of fresh citrus and fiery jalapeño pepper to create a memorable spicy-sweet scenario.

8 (¾-inch-thick) albacore or
   yellowfin tuna steaks
2 tablespoons grated orange
   rind
1 cup fresh orange juice
1 cup olive oil
¾ cup minced green pepper
½ cup rice wine

¼ cup minced sweet red
   pepper
2 tablespoons sugar
2 tablespoons oriental chili-
   garlic sauce (we tested with
   A Taste of Thai)
1 jalapeño pepper, minced
1 large clove garlic

Place fish in a large heavy-duty, zip-top plastic bag. Combine orange rind and remaining 9 ingredients. Reserve 1 cup orange juice mixture. Pour remaining orange juice mixture over fish. Seal bag securely; marinate in refrigerator 1 hour, turning bag occasionally.

Remove fish from marinade, discarding marinade. Grill, uncovered, over medium-hot coals (350° to 400°) 4 to 5 minutes on each side or until fish flakes easily when tested with a fork, basting often with reserved orange juice mixture. Yield: 8 servings.

Classic Favorites
P.E.O., Chapter SB
Moraga, California

Sesame-Balsamic Tuna

½ cup balsamic vinegar
¼ cup dark sesame oil
2 tablespoons grated fresh
  ginger
2 tablespoons chopped fresh
  cilantro
2 green onions, chopped

1 tablespoon plus 1 teaspoon
  sugar
2 (½-inch-thick) tuna steaks
  (about 1 pound)
8 ounces fresh mushrooms,
  sliced
1½ teaspoons dark sesame oil

Combine first 6 ingredients in a large heavy-duty, zip-top plastic bag; add fish. Seal bag securely; turn bag to coat fish. Marinate in refrigerator 1 hour, turning occasionally. Drain, reserving marinade.

Cook mushrooms in 1½ teaspoons sesame oil in a large skillet over medium-high heat, stirring constantly, until tender. Stir in reserved marinade. Bring to a boil; cover and remove from heat. Set aside, and keep warm.

Grill fish, covered, over medium-hot coals (350° to 400°) 4 minutes on each side or until fish flakes easily when tested with a fork.

Arrange fish on a serving platter. Pour mushroom sauce over fish. Serve immediately. Yield: 2 servings.

Great Lake Effects
The Junior League of Buffalo, New York

Teriyaki Tuna with Asian Slaw

6 (¾-inch-thick) tuna steaks
  (about 3 pounds)
1 cup teriyaki sauce
2 tablespoons dry sherry
2 tablespoons fresh lemon
  juice

2 tablespoons minced fresh
  ginger
2 cloves garlic, minced
1 teaspoon pepper
Vegetable cooking spray
Asian Slaw

Place fish in a large heavy-duty, zip-top plastic bag. Combine teriyaki sauce and next 5 ingredients, stirring well. Pour teriyaki sauce mixture over fish; seal bag securely. Turn bag to coat fish. Marinate in refrigerator 1 hour, turning bag occasionally.

Remove fish from marinade, discarding marinade. Coat grill rack with cooking spray; place on grill over medium-hot coals (350° to 400°). Place fish on rack; grill, covered, 5 minutes on each side or until fish flakes easily when tested with a fork. Serve with Asian Slaw. Yield: 6 servings.

Asian Slaw

2 tablespoons fresh lime juice
2 tablespoons vegetable oil
1 tablespoon teriyaki sauce
1 tablespoon honey
1 teaspoon dark sesame oil
1 jalapeño pepper, minced
¼ teaspoon salt
2 small heads savoy cabbage, shredded (about 4 cups)

2 carrots, shredded (about ⅔ cup)
1 sweet red pepper, thinly sliced
¾ cup chopped fresh cilantro
¼ cup chopped roasted peanuts

Combine first 7 ingredients in a large bowl, stirring well. Add cabbage and remaining ingredients; toss gently. Yield: 6 cups.

Shalom on the Range
Shalom Park
Aurora, Colorado

Heavenly Crab

Serve this casserole on its own or spooned into puff pastry shells.

1 pound fresh crabmeat, drained and flaked
4 large hard-cooked eggs, finely chopped
3 cups soft breadcrumbs (homemade)
2 cups half-and-half

2 cups mayonnaise
1 onion, finely chopped
2 tablespoons finely chopped fresh parsley
1 tablespoon lemon juice
¼ teaspoon salt
¼ teaspoon pepper

Combine all ingredients. Cover and chill at least 3 hours or up to 8 hours. Transfer to an ungreased 3-quart casserole. Bake, uncovered, at 350° for 45 minutes. Yield: 8 servings.

Loving Spoonfuls
Covenant House of Texas
Houston, Texas

Mussels with Spaghettini

1½ pounds small fresh mussels
12 ounces spaghettini, uncooked
½ cup dry white wine
1 small onion, finely chopped
1 sprig fresh parsley
1 bay leaf
½ teaspoon dried thyme
2 cloves garlic, minced
½ cup minced fresh parsley, divided
¼ cup olive oil
1 (28-ounce) can plum tomatoes, undrained and chopped
1 teaspoon dried oregano
½ teaspoon salt
½ teaspoon pepper
⅓ cup freshly grated Parmesan cheese

Remove beards on mussels, and scrub shells with a brush. Discard opened, cracked, or heavy mussels (they're filled with sand). Set aside.

Cook spaghettini according to package directions. Drain well, and place in a large bowl. Set aside, and keep warm.

Combine wine and next 4 ingredients in a large skillet; bring to a boil. Add mussels; cover and simmer until mussels open. Remove mussels with a slotted spoon; set aside. Pour liquid through a double layer of cheesecloth into bowl, discarding solids; set liquid aside.

Cook garlic and ¼ cup parsley in oil in skillet over medium-low heat 2 minutes, stirring occasionally. Stir in reserved liquid, tomatoes, and next 3 ingredients; simmer, uncovered, 10 minutes or until sauce is slightly thickened. Remove from heat; add mussels, and toss gently to coat with sauce. Spoon mussels and sauce over pasta; sprinkle with remaining ¼ cup parsley and cheese. Serve immediately. Yield: 6 servings.

The Westmorelander

Country Recipes
Westmoreland United Church
Westmoreland, New Hampshire

Scalloped Oysters

1 pint fresh oysters
2 cups crumbled round buttery crackers, divided
½ cup butter or margarine, melted

2 cups fresh mushrooms, sliced
¼ cup half-and-half
¼ teaspoon Worcestershire sauce

Drain oysters, reserving ¼ cup liquid; set aside.

Combine 1¾ cups crumbs and butter. Add oysters, tossing to coat. Stir in reserved liquid, mushrooms, half-and-half, and Worcestershire sauce.

Spoon mixture into a greased 8-inch square or round baking dish; top with remaining ¼ cup crumbs. Bake, uncovered, at 325° for 50 minutes. Yield: 6 servings.

Becky Stone

Incredible Edibles
Missionary Temple CME Church
San Francisco, California

Penobscot Bay Scallops with Walnuts

Here's a quick but special scallop dish that takes on even more appeal when baked and served in shell-shaped dishes.

½ cup soft breadcrumbs (homemade)
¼ cup chopped walnuts
2 tablespoons butter
1 pound bay scallops
2 tablespoons minced green onions

2 tablespoons minced fresh parsley
2 tablespoons lemon juice
¼ teaspoon salt
⅛ teaspoon pepper

Combine first 3 ingredients in a medium-size ovenproof skillet. Bake, uncovered, at 425° for 3 minutes or until butter melts.

Add scallops and remaining ingredients; stir well. Bake an additional 6 minutes or until scallops are white. Yield: 4 servings.

Word of Mouth
Friends of the Humane Society of Knox County
Rockland, Maine

Scallops in White Wine

8 ounces sea scallops
⅓ cup milk
¼ cup all-purpose flour
1 tablespoon olive oil

¼ cup dry white wine
¼ cup chopped green onions
1 tablespoon fresh lemon juice
Lemon pepper to taste

Dip scallops in milk, and dredge in flour. Cook scallops in hot oil in a large skillet over medium-high heat 5 minutes on each side or until golden. Transfer to serving plates; keep warm. Add wine and green onions to skillet; cook 1 minute. Pour sauce over scallops; sprinkle with lemon juice. Season to taste with lemon pepper. Yield: 2 servings.

Our Sunrise Family Cookbook
Sunrise Drive Elementary School
Tucson, Arizona

Garlic-Skewered Grilled Shrimp

24 unpeeled large or jumbo
  fresh shrimp (2 pounds)
3 large cloves garlic, minced
⅓ cup olive oil
¼ cup tomato sauce

2 tablespoons chopped fresh
  basil
2 tablespoons red wine vinegar
½ teaspoon ground red pepper
18 large cloves garlic, peeled

Peel shrimp, and devein, if desired. Combine minced garlic and next 5 ingredients in a medium bowl. Add shrimp; stirring well. Cover and marinate in refrigerator 30 minutes.

Place 18 cloves garlic in a small saucepan; add water to cover, and bring to a boil. Boil 3 minutes; drain well, and set aside.

Remove shrimp from marinade; reserving marinade. Bring marinade to a boil in a small saucepan; set aside.

Thread shrimp and garlic cloves evenly onto six 10-inch metal skewers. Grill, covered, over medium-hot coals (350° to 400°) 3 to 4 minutes on each side or until shrimp turn pink, basting with reserved marinade. Yield: 6 servings.   The Wohlers Family

From Home Plate to Home Cooking
The Atlanta Braves
Atlanta, Georgia

Barbecued Shrimp

1 cup butter
1 cup olive oil
9 green onions, minced (about 1 cup)
½ cup chopped fresh parsley
1 lemon, cut into eighths
1 clove garlic, minced
1 teaspoon pepper
2 teaspoons hot sauce
2½ pounds unpeeled jumbo fresh shrimp

Melt butter in a large heavy skillet over medium-low heat; add olive oil and next 6 ingredients. Cook 2 minutes, stirring constantly. Add shrimp; cook over medium heat 12 minutes or until shrimp turn pink, stirring constantly. Yield: 4 servings.   Chantel Fouchi

Cooking from the Heart
Girl Scout Troop 669
Metairie, Louisiana

Grace's Broiled Shrimp

Serve this informal fare over toasted French bread to soak up the rich garlic-lemon sauce in which the shrimp are bathed.

2 pounds unpeeled large fresh shrimp
½ cup vegetable oil
¼ cup soy sauce
3 tablespoons chopped fresh parsley
1 tablespoon lemon juice
2 cloves garlic, minced
8 (1-inch) slices French bread, toasted

Peel shrimp, and devein, if desired, leaving tails intact. Place shrimp in the bottom of a large shallow roasting pan or broiler pan.

Combine oil and next 4 ingredients; pour over shrimp. Cover and marinate in refrigerator 2 hours.

Uncover and broil 5½ inches from heat (with electric oven door partially opened) 7 to 8 minutes or until shrimp turn pink, stirring once. Serve immediately over French bread. Yield: 4 servings.

Sterling Service
The Dothan Service League
Dothan, Alabama

Grilled Ginger Shrimp

Lots of grated fresh ginger and a measure of dry sherry add glorious flavor to these shrimp as they marinate.

4 pounds unpeeled medium-size fresh shrimp	½ cup soy sauce
1 cup minced green onions	½ cup vegetable oil
¼ cup grated fresh ginger	¼ cup lemon juice
½ cup dry sherry	1 tablespoon sugar
	Vegetable cooking spray

Peel shrimp, and devein, if desired. Set aside.

Combine green onions and next 6 ingredients in a large heavy-duty, zip-top plastic bag. Add shrimp; seal bag securely, and shake gently to coat shrimp. Marinate shrimp in refrigerator 2 to 3 hours, turning bag occasionally.

Meanwhile, soak 16 (10-inch) wooden skewers in water at least 30 minutes.

Remove shrimp from marinade; discard marinade. Thread shrimp evenly onto skewers. Coat grill rack with cooking spray; place on grill over medium-hot coals (350° to 400°). Place skewers on rack; grill, covered, 3 minutes on each side or until shrimp turn pink. Yield: 8 servings.   Jessica Kirk

The Kansas City Barbeque Society Cookbook
Kansas City Barbeque Society
Kansas City, Missouri

Shrimp and Veggie Oven Roast

Thirty-five whole cloves of garlic roasted to sweet perfection add mellow magic to this shrimp and vegetable medley.

18 unpeeled jumbo fresh
    shrimp
½ cup chopped fresh parsley
1 clove garlic, minced
1 tablespoon olive oil
1 teaspoon pepper
½ teaspoon dried rosemary
¼ teaspoon salt
6 medium-size red potatoes,
    unpeeled and cut into chunks
1 pound carrots, scraped and
    cut into chunks

2 onions, cut into chunks
35 cloves garlic, peeled
⅓ cup olive oil
1 tablespoon dried rosemary
1 teaspoon salt
1 pound kielbasa or other
    smoked sausage, cut into
    large chunks
1 large zucchini, cut into
    chunks
1 large sweet red pepper, cut
    into chunks

Peel shrimp, and devein, if desired. Place shrimp in a large shallow dish. Combine parsley and next 5 ingredients; drizzle marinade over shrimp. Cover and chill.

Place potato and next 3 ingredients in a shallow roasting pan; drizzle with ⅓ cup olive oil. Sprinkle with 1 tablespoon rosemary and 1 teaspoon salt; toss to coat.

Bake, uncovered, at 400° for 30 minutes. Add kielbasa, and bake 15 additional minutes, stirring once. Add zucchini and red pepper, and bake 10 additional minutes, stirring once. Add shrimp and marinade, and bake 10 additional minutes or until shrimp turn pink. Yield: 6 servings.

Dick and Ginger Howell

Specialties of the House
Ronald McDonald House
Rochester, New York

Étouffée

1 cup butter, melted
½ cup plus 2 tablespoons
  all-purpose flour
1¼ cups finely chopped celery
  (about 3 stalks)
1 cup chopped green pepper
  (about 1 medium)
½ cup chopped green onions
  (about 1 bunch)
1 (14½-ounce) can chicken
  broth
2 cups water
¼ cup chopped fresh parsley
1 tablespoon tomato paste
1 bay leaf
¼ teaspoon salt
¼ teaspoon black pepper
⅛ teaspoon ground red pepper
2 (1-pound) packages cooked,
  peeled, and deveined
  crawfish tail meat, drained
Hot cooked rice

Combine butter and flour in a large Dutch oven; cook over medium-high heat, stirring constantly, 5 minutes or until roux is caramel-colored. Add celery, green pepper, and green onions; cook 4 minutes. Add chicken broth and next 7 ingredients; bring to a boil. Cover, reduce heat, and simmer 30 minutes, stirring occasionally.

Add crawfish, and cook 5 minutes. Remove and discard bay leaf. Serve mixture over rice. Yield: 10 servings.   Lynda Huggins

Food for Thought
Northeast Louisiana Chapter, Autism Society of America
Monroe, Louisiana

Meats

Beef Fillets au Vin, page 189

Baked Corned Beef with Mustard Sauce

1 (4½-pound) corned beef
6 whole peppercorns
2 bay leaves
Vegetable cooking spray
1 tablespoon whole cloves
3 tablespoons butter

⅓ cup firmly packed brown sugar
⅓ cup ketchup
3 tablespoons white vinegar
3 tablespoons water
1 tablespoon prepared mustard

Place first 3 ingredients in a large Dutch oven; add cold water to cover. Bring to a boil; boil, uncovered, 5 minutes. Carefully skim off foam. Cover, reduce heat, and simmer 5 hours or until meat is tender.

Remove meat from pan, discarding water, peppercorns, and bay leaves. Place meat in a shallow baking pan coated with cooking spray. Insert cloves decoratively into top of meat.

Melt butter in a small saucepan over medium heat; add sugar and remaining 4 ingredients, stirring until smooth. Cook, uncovered, until thoroughly heated, stirring occasionally. Pour sauce over meat.

Bake, uncovered, at 350° for 30 minutes. To serve, slice meat diagonally across grain. Yield: 8 servings. Cindy Davis

Country Recipes
Westmoreland United Church
Westmoreland, New Hampshire

Foolproof Pot Roast

2 medium onions, thinly sliced
2 tablespoons vegetable oil
1 (3-pound) chuck roast

1 (16-ounce) can whole-berry cranberry sauce
1 (5-ounce) jar prepared horseradish

Cook onion in hot oil in a Dutch oven over medium-high heat, stirring constantly, until tender. Reduce heat to medium; add roast, and brown on both sides. Add cranberry sauce and horseradish. Cover and cook 3½ hours or until roast is tender. Yield: 8 servings.

Eat Your Dessert or You Won't Get Any Broccoli
The Sea Pines Montessori School
Hilton Head Island, South Carolina

Stuffed Tenderloin

Snuggled between tender slices of beef tenderloin lie fresh mushrooms, green onions, garlic, and parsley. The stuffing mixture is melded with melted crumbles of blue cheese.

1 (3-pound) beef tenderloin
2 tablespoons butter or margarine
½ pound fresh mushrooms, sliced
4 green onions, chopped
1 clove garlic, minced

2 tablespoons chopped fresh parsley
3 tablespoons crumbled blue cheese
1 tablespoon butter or margarine, melted
Vegetable cooking spray

Slice tenderloin lengthwise to, but not through, the center, leaving 1 long side connected; set aside.

Melt 2 tablespoons butter in a large skillet over medium-high heat. Add mushrooms and next 3 ingredients; cook 5 minutes or until tender, stirring often. Spoon mixture into opening of tenderloin, leaving a ½-inch border on all sides. Sprinkle cheese over mushroom mixture. Close tenderloin, and tie securely with heavy string at 2-inch intervals. Brush with melted butter.

Light gas grill on one side. Coat grill rack on opposite side with cooking spray. Place rack over cool lava rocks; let grill preheat 10 to 15 minutes. Place tenderloin on rack opposite hot coals; cover and grill 45 minutes or until meat thermometer inserted in thickest part of tenderloin registers 145° (medium-rare) to 160° (medium). Let stand 10 minutes before slicing. Yield: 8 servings.   Montgomery Ranch

Taste of the Territory, The Flair and Flavor of Oklahoma
The Service League of Bartlesville, Oklahoma

Peppered Chutney Roast Beef

Wonderfully succulent beef tenderloin is enhanced by a salty-sweet pineapple juice-steak sauce marinade. (We reserve a portion of the marinade to baste, preventing contamination with the raw meat juices.) Slices of smokey bacon and a mango chutney glaze complete this special-occasion entrée.

1 (4-pound) beef tenderloin, trimmed
1 (6-ounce) can unsweetened pineapple juice
½ cup steak sauce
⅓ cup Worcestershire sauce
⅓ cup port wine
¼ cup lemon juice

2 teaspoons seasoned salt
1 teaspoon lemon-pepper seasoning
1 teaspoon dry mustard
2 teaspoons cracked pepper
3 slices bacon
⅓ cup mango chutney

Place tenderloin in a large heavy-duty, zip-top plastic bag; set aside.

Combine pineapple juice and next 7 ingredients. Pour 1½ cups pineapple juice mixture over tenderloin. Set aside remaining pineapple juice mixture. Seal bag securely; turn to coat tenderloin. Marinate in refrigerator 8 hours, turning bag occasionally.

Remove tenderloin from marinade; discard marinade. Place tenderloin in a shallow roasting pan; rub with pepper. Insert meat thermometer into thickest part of tenderloin. Bake, uncovered, at 425° for 30 minutes, basting occasionally with reserved pineapple juice mixture. Arrange bacon slices over tenderloin. Bake 20 additional minutes, basting occasionally with reserved pineapple juice mixture. Spoon chutney over tenderloin; bake 5 to 10 additional minutes or until meat thermometer registers 145° (medium-rare) or 160° (medium). Let stand 15 minutes before slicing. Yield: 12 servings.

Food Fabulous Food
The Women's Board to Cooper Hospital/
University Medical Center
Camden, New Jersey

Beef Fillets au Vin

3 tablespoons butter or margarine, divided
4 (8-ounce) beef tenderloin steaks (1½ inches thick)
1 pound fresh mushrooms, thinly sliced
1 tablespoon minced shallot or green onions

½ cup dry red wine
1 teaspoon garlic powder
1 teaspoon butter or margarine, softened
1 teaspoon all-purpose flour
2 tablespoons dry red wine

Melt 1 tablespoon butter in a large skillet over medium heat. Add steaks; cook 9 minutes on each side or to desired degree of doneness. Remove from skillet; set aside, and keep warm.

Melt 1 tablespoon butter in skillet over medium-high heat; add mushrooms and shallot, and cook, stirring constantly, until tender. Stir in ½ cup wine and garlic powder; cook over high heat 6 minutes or until wine is reduced by half. Combine 1 teaspoon melted butter and flour; add to mushroom mixture, stirring well. Cook 30 seconds, stirring constantly. Add remaining 1 tablespoon butter and 2 tablespoons wine, stirring until butter melts. Serve steaks with mushroom-wine sauce. Yield: 4 servings.

Cooking on the Wild Side
Cincinnati Zoo and Botanical Garden Volunteer Program
Cincinnati, Ohio

Grilled Steak with Lime Marinade

⅓ cup fresh lime juice
¼ cup vegetable oil
¼ cup molasses
2 tablespoons prepared
  mustard

1 teaspoon grated lime rind
1 teaspoon garlic powder
½ teaspoon salt
2 pounds top sirloin steak
Vegetable cooking spray

Combine first 7 ingredients in a small bowl, mixing with a wire whisk; pour into a large heavy-duty, zip-top plastic bag. Add steak to bag; seal bag securely, and marinate in refrigerator 4 to 6 hours, turning once.

Remove steak from marinade, discarding marinade. Coat a grill rack with cooking spray; place on grill over medium-hot coals (350° to 400°). Grill steak, covered, 10 minutes on each side or to desired degree of doneness. Slice diagonally across grain into thin slices. Yield: 6 servings.

O Taste & Sing
St. Stephen's Episcopal Church Choir
Richmond, Virginia

Stroganoff Steak Sandwiches

Tender slices of dark beer-marinated flank steak are nestled atop crusty portions of French bread, and then capped with sautéed onions and an ample dollop of sour cream. This hearty fare requires a knife and a fork.

2 pounds flank steak
⅔ cup dark beer
⅓ cup vegetable oil
1 teaspoon garlic powder
1 teaspoon salt
¼ teaspoon pepper

4 medium onions, sliced
½ teaspoon paprika
2 tablespoons butter, melted
12 (1-inch-thick) slices French
  bread
1 (8-ounce) carton sour cream

Place flank steak in a large heavy-duty, zip-top plastic bag. Combine beer and next 4 ingredients; stir well. Pour marinade over steak. Seal bag securely; marinate in refrigerator 8 hours, turning occasionally.

Remove steak from marinade, discarding marinade. Place flank steak on a lightly greased rack of broiler pan; broil 3 inches from heat (with electric door partially opened) 10 minutes on each side or to desired degree of doneness. Cut steak diagonally across grain into thin strips.

Cook onions and paprika in butter in a large skillet over medium-high heat, stirring constantly, until tender.

To serve, place 2 slices French bread on serving plates; top with steak, onion, and sour cream. Yield: 6 servings.   Mary Shepley

Kimball Kub Grub
Kimball Elementary PTA
Kimball, Michigan

Mexican Beef Heros

4 slices bacon
½ pound ground chuck
½ cup chopped onion
1 (2.25-ounce) can chopped ripe olives
1 (4.5-ounce) can chopped green chiles, undrained
¼ cup ketchup
½ teaspoon salt
½ teaspoon chili powder
6 ounces Monterey Jack cheese, sliced
6 ounces mild Cheddar cheese, sliced
4 steak buns, split

Cook bacon in a large skillet until crisp; remove bacon, reserving 2 teaspoons drippings in skillet. Crumble bacon, and set aside.

Brown ground chuck and onion in drippings in skillet, stirring until meat crumbles. Add olives and next 4 ingredients; cook over medium heat 5 minutes, stirring occasionally.

Layer Monterey Jack cheese, meat mixture, reserved bacon, and Cheddar cheese on bottom halves of buns; top with remaining bun halves. Wrap each sandwich in aluminum foil, and bake at 375° for 10 minutes. Yield: 4 servings.   Willie Gentile

Dancers for Doernbecher Present Recipes from the Heart
Dancers for Doernbecher
Milwaukie, Oregon

Grilled Lemon-Herb Veal Chops

3 tablespoons fresh lemon
  juice
3 tablespoons olive oil
3 cloves garlic, quartered
2 teaspoons dried oregano

1 teaspoon freshly ground
  pepper
4 (1-inch-thick) veal loin chops
4 (¼-inch) slices firm ripe
  tomato

Combine first 5 ingredients in container of a food processor; process until well blended. Reserve 1 tablespoon marinade. Coat both sides of chops with marinade, and place in a shallow dish. Cover and marinate in refrigerator 2 hours.

Spread reserved marinade over 1 side of each tomato slice.

Grill chops, uncovered, over medium-hot coals (350° to 400°) 12 to 14 minutes, turning once. Cover and grill 10 to 12 minutes, turning once. Place tomato slices on grill during last 6 minutes of grilling time, turning once. Yield: 4 servings.

Beneath the Palms
The Brownsville Junior Service League
Brownsville, Texas

Veal Shanks with Capers

Rustic veal shanks become fall-off-the-bone tender when marinated and simmered with leeks, lemon, garlic, wine, and capers. Serve with rice, noodles, or mashed potatoes to complete the comfort food picture.

4 medium leeks
1½ cups buttermilk
¼ cup fresh lemon juice
3 cloves garlic, minced
1 tablespoon pepper
3 pounds (1-inch-thick) veal
  shanks

2 tablespoons olive oil
2 tablespoons butter
2 cups dry white wine
1 tablespoon capers, drained
½ teaspoon salt
¼ teaspoon pepper

Remove and discard root, tough outer leaves, and tops of leeks to where dark green begins to pale. Cut leeks in half lengthwise; rinse well, and cut lengthwise into ¼-inch strips. Set aside.

Combine buttermilk and next 3 ingredients in a heavy-duty, zip-top plastic bag; add veal shanks. Seal bag securely, and turn to coat veal.

Marinate in refrigerator 8 hours, turning occasionally. Drain, reserving marinade. Pat veal dry with paper towels.

Heat olive oil and butter in a heavy skillet. Cook veal, in batches, over medium heat until browned on both sides. Remove veal to a platter, reserving drippings in skillet.

Sauté leeks in pan drippings in skillet until tender. Stir in wine and reserved marinade. Return veal to pan; bring to a boil. Cover, reduce heat, and simmer 1 hour. Stir in capers; simmer 30 minutes or until very tender, stirring occasionally. Stir in salt and pepper. Yield: 6 servings.

Great Lake Effects
The Junior League of Buffalo, New York

Veal with Creamy Mustard Sauce

4 (4-ounce) veal cutlets
2 tablespoons all-purpose flour
½ teaspoon salt
Dash of pepper
2 tablespoons vegetable oil
3 tablespoons butter or
  margarine
1 cup sliced onion

1 cup sliced fresh mushrooms
½ cup half-and-half
2 tablespoons dried parsley
  flakes
2 tablespoons Dijon mustard
3 tablespoons fresh lemon
  juice

Place veal between two sheets of heavy-duty plastic wrap, and flatten to ¼-inch thickness, using a meat mallet or rolling pin.

Combine flour, salt, and pepper in a shallow dish; dredge veal in flour mixture. Heat oil in a large skillet over medium-high heat. Add veal; cook 2 minutes on each side or until done, reducing heat, if necessary. Remove veal to a serving platter; keep warm. Drain skillet.

Melt butter in skillet over medium-high heat. Add onion and mushrooms; cook 5 minutes or until tender, stirring occasionally. Reduce heat to medium-low; stir in half-and-half, parsley flakes, and mustard. Cook, stirring constantly, until sauce thickens (do not boil). Remove from heat, and stir in lemon juice. Spoon sauce over veal. Yield: 4 servings.

Barbara Reilly

Family Self Sufficiency International Cookbook
Central Falls Family Self Sufficiency Foundation
Central Falls, Rhode Island

Layered Veal

1 cup Italian-seasoned breadcrumbs
2 tablespoons chopped fresh parsley
½ teaspoon garlic powder
½ teaspoon dried oregano
1½ pounds veal, cut into 1-inch pieces
1 large egg, lightly beaten
½ cup olive or vegetable oil
8 ounces fresh mushrooms, sliced
1 (10-ounce) package frozen chopped spinach, thawed and drained
½ teaspoon salt
3 green onions, sliced (about ½ cup)
1 (15-ounce) can tomato sauce

Combine first 4 ingredients in a large heavy-duty, zip-top plastic bag. Dip veal in egg; place in bag with breadcrumb mixture. Seal bag securely, and shake until veal is coated. Remove veal from bag, reserving extra breadcrumb mixture.

Place oil in a large skillet over medium-high heat until hot; add veal, and cook until browned on all sides. Drain on paper towels. Add reserved crumb mixture to skillet, and cook until lightly browned, stirring often. Remove from skillet, and set aside.

Cook mushrooms in skillet until tender, stirring occasionally. Set aside.

Place spinach in a lightly greased 2-quart casserole; sprinkle with salt. Layer green onions over spinach layer and mushrooms over green onions. Top with veal. Pour tomato sauce evenly over veal mixture; top with reserved breadcrumbs. Bake, uncovered, at 325° for 1 hour. Yield: 6 servings.

Beyond Chicken Soup
Jewish Home of Rochester Auxiliary
Rochester, New York

Honey Mustard-Pecan Roasted Lamb

When company's coming, this rack of lamb is sure to impress. A pecan-breadcrumb mixture encrusts the elegant entrée, while Dijon mustard, molasses, garlic, and rosemary flatter the tender meat.

2 (1¼-pound) racks of lamb (8 chops each)
2 tablespoons olive oil
¼ cup Dijon mustard
1 tablespoon honey
1 tablespoon molasses
2 small cloves garlic, minced
½ cup pecan halves, toasted
3 tablespoons soft breadcrumbs (homemade)
1 teaspoon fresh rosemary

Trim exterior fat on lamb racks to ¼ inch; brown lamb racks, 1 rack at a time, in olive oil in a large skillet over medium-high heat. Place lamb racks, fat side up, on a rack in a roasting pan.

Combine mustard and next 3 ingredients in a small bowl, stirring well. Brush mustard mixture over both sides of lamb racks.

Position knife blade in food processor bowl. Add pecans, breadcrumbs, and rosemary; process until pecans are finely chopped. Sprinkle lamb racks with pecan mixture.

Insert a meat thermometer into thickest portion of 1 rack, making sure it does not touch fat or bone. Bake, uncovered, at 375° for 30 minutes or until thermometer registers 150° (medium-rare) or 160° (medium). Let stand 10 minutes before slicing. Yield: 8 servings.

Sweet Home Alabama
The Junior League of Huntsville, Alabama

Peach-Glazed Leg of Lamb

Garlic slices inserted in the leg of lamb add their sweet roasted good-ness. A peach-sherry glaze spiced with allspice and lemon rind is applied towards the end of roasting.

1 (8-pound) leg of lamb
2 cloves garlic, thinly sliced
2 tablespoons vegetable oil
2 (16-ounce) cans peach slices
   in juice, undrained
½ cup firmly packed brown
   sugar

½ cup dry sherry
¼ cup butter or margarine
2 tablespoons grated lemon
   rind
2 tablespoons cornstarch
1 teaspoon ground allspice
Ported Ginger Peaches

Cut small slits in surface of lamb; insert garlic slices into slits. Rub lamb with oil. Place lamb on a rack in a roasting pan. Insert a meat thermometer into thickest part of lamb, making sure it does not touch fat or bone. Bake at 450° for 15 minutes. Reduce oven temperature to 325°, and bake 2½ hours or until thermometer registers 150° (medium-rare) or 160° (medium).

Drain peach slices, reserving juice and peaches. Place juice in a medium saucepan. Add brown sugar and next 5 ingredients, stirring well. Cook over medium heat, stirring constantly, until thickened and smooth. Baste roast with glaze during last 20 minutes of cooking time. Let stand 20 minutes before serving. Serve with remaining glaze and Ported Ginger Peaches. Yield: 9 servings.

Ported Ginger Peaches

Reserved peach slices
1 (21-ounce) can cherry pie
   filling
2 tablespoons port or other
   sweet red wine

1 tablespoon chopped
   crystallized ginger
1 teaspoon grated orange rind

Place reserved peach slices in an ungreased 9-inch square baking dish. Combine pie filling and remaining 3 ingredients; spoon over peach slices. Bake, uncovered, at 350° for 15 minutes. Yield: 9 servings.

A Slice of Paradise
The Junior League of The Palm Beaches
West Palm Beach, Florida

Lamb Stuffed with Spinach and Chèvre

2 (10-ounce) packages frozen chopped spinach
2 tablespoons minced garlic
1 tablespoon olive oil
8 ounces chèvre (goat cheese)
½ teaspoon salt
1 teaspoon freshly ground pepper, divided

1 (5-pound) boneless leg of lamb, butterflied
2 cloves garlic, sliced
2 tablespoons fresh rosemary
½ teaspoon coarse salt

Cook spinach according to package directions; drain well. Press spinach between layers of paper towels to remove excess moisture. Set aside.

Cook minced garlic in hot oil in a large skillet over medium heat 1 minute, stirring constantly. Remove from heat; stir in spinach, chèvre, ½ teaspoon salt, and ½ teaspoon pepper.

Place lamb on a flat surface, opening to a single thickness. Trim excess fat from lamb. Spread chèvre mixture over lamb to within 1 inch of edges. Roll up lamb, jellyroll fashion, beginning with long side; tie securely with heavy string at 2-inch intervals. Make several small slits in lamb, and insert garlic slices. Sprinkle lamb evenly with remaining ½ teaspoon pepper, rosemary, and coarse salt.

Insert a meat thermometer into thickest part of lamb, making sure it does not touch stuffing. Place lamb in a lightly greased shallow roasting pan. Bake at 425° for 1½ hours or until meat thermometer registers 150° (medium-rare) or 160° (medium). Let stand 15 minutes before slicing. Remove string, and cut lamb into slices. Yield: 8 to 10 servings.

Barbara Law

Souvenirs of Mount Dora, Florida
GFWC Mount Dora Area Junior Woman's Club
Mount Dora, Florida

Rosemary-Marinated Lamb Kabobs

½ cup orange juice
¼ cup minced green onions
¼ cup soy sauce
2 tablespoons minced fresh rosemary
2 tablespoons teriyaki sauce
2 tablespoons lime juice
2 tablespoons lemon juice
1 clove garlic, crushed
6 black peppercorns, crushed

1 pound boneless leg of lamb or lamb loin, cut into 1-inch cubes
3 green peppers, cut into 1-inch pieces
1 large onion, cut into 1-inch wedges
Vegetable cooking spray
2 large navel oranges, cut into 4 slices each

Combine first 9 ingredients in a large heavy-duty, zip-top plastic bag; add lamb, green pepper, and onion. Seal bag securely; turn to coat lamb. Marinate in refrigerator 5 to 6 hours, turning bag occasionally; drain, discarding marinade. Thread lamb alternately with green pepper and onion onto 12-inch skewers.

Coat a grill rack with cooking spray; place on grill over medium-hot coals (350° to 400°). Place kabobs on rack, and grill, covered, 10 minutes or to desired degree of doneness, turning once. Place orange slices on grill rack; grill just until thoroughly heated, turning once. To serve, arrange 2 orange slices on each plate; top with 1 lamb kabob. Yield: 4 servings.

Ardie Davis

The Kansas City Barbeque Society Cookbook
Kansas City Barbeque Society
Kansas City, Missouri

Lamb Shanks with Rosemary Barbecue Sauce

Rosemary-infused barbecue sauce seeps into the shanks to give them a distinct character. They're delicious either served immediately or held over to develop even more intense flavor and then reheated.

6 lamb shanks (about 5½ pounds)
1 tablespoon vegetable oil
2 cups ketchup
1 cup orange juice
1 cup white vinegar
½ cup honey

1½ teaspoons dried rosemary
1 teaspoon dry mustard
1 teaspoon ground cloves
½ teaspoon salt
½ teaspoon pepper
½ teaspoon chili powder
1 teaspoon hot sauce

Brown lamb shanks, in batches, in hot oil in a large skillet over medium-high heat; remove shanks to a Dutch oven. Combine ketchup and remaining 10 ingredients in a large saucepan; bring to a boil. Reduce heat, and simmer, uncovered, 10 minutes. Pour sauce over shanks. Cover and bake at 350° for 2½ hours or until tender, basting once each hour. Skim excess fat from surface before serving, or cover and chill 8 hours. Remove and discard fat from surface before reheating. Yield: 6 servings.   Marian H. Morrow

Bully's Best Bites
The Junior Auxiliary of Starkville, Mississippi

Pork Loin Roast with Blueberry Sauce

1 (3½-pound) boneless pork
  loin roast, trimmed
½ cup dry sherry
½ cup soy sauce
1 tablespoon dry mustard
1 teaspoon minced garlic

1 teaspoon ground ginger
1 teaspoon dried thyme
1 (10-ounce) jar blueberry
  preserves
2 tablespoons dry sherry
1 tablespoon soy sauce

Place pork roast in a large heavy-duty, zip-top plastic bag. Combine ½ cup sherry and next 5 ingredients; pour over roast. Seal bag securely; marinate in refrigerator 2 to 3 hours, turning bag occasionally.

Remove roast from marinade, reserving marinade. Place marinade in a small saucepan; bring just to a boil. Set aside.

Place roast on a rack in a shallow roasting pan. Insert a meat thermometer into thickest portion of roast. Bake, uncovered, at 325° for 2½ hours or until thermometer registers 160°, basting occasionally with reserved marinade.

Combine blueberry preserves, 2 tablespoons sherry, and 1 tablespoon soy sauce in a small saucepan; bring to a simmer over medium-high heat. Cook, uncovered, 5 minutes or until thoroughly heated. Serve roast with blueberry sauce. Yield: 8 servings.

Apron Strings: Ties to the Southern Tradition of Cooking
The Junior League of Little Rock, Arkansas

Kitty's Barbecued Pork Tenderloin

½ cup soy sauce
2½ tablespoons dark
  sesame oil
2 teaspoons fresh lime juice
2 teaspoons rice wine
  vinegar
4 cloves garlic, minced

1½ teaspoons ground
  ginger
½ teaspoon sugar
3 (1-pound) pork tenderloins,
  trimmed
Vegetable cooking spray
Kitty's Barbecue Sauce

Combine first 7 ingredients in a large heavy-duty, zip-top plastic bag; add pork. Seal bag securely; turn bag to coat pork. Marinate in refrigerator 3 hours, turning bag occasionally.

Remove pork from marinade, reserving marinade. Bring marinade to a boil in a small saucepan. Remove from heat, and set aside.

Coat a grill rack with cooking spray; place over medium-hot coals (350° to 400°). Place pork on rack; grill, covered, 30 minutes or until a meat thermometer inserted in thickest portion of tenderloin registers 160°, turning once and basting occasionally with reserved marinade. Let stand 10 minutes before cutting into thin diagonal slices. Serve with Kitty's Barbecue Sauce. Yield: 12 servings.

Kitty's Barbecue Sauce

2 tablespoons vegetable oil
1 medium onion, chopped
4 cloves garlic, halved
1½ cups ketchup
1 cup fresh orange juice
½ cup water
¼ cup plus 2 tablespoons fresh lemon juice
¼ cup plus 2 tablespoons red wine vinegar
¼ cup firmly packed dark brown sugar
¼ cup honey
3 tablespoons finely chopped crystallized ginger
2 tablespoons chili powder
1 tablespoon ground coriander
1 tablespoon dry mustard
1 tablespoon Worcestershire sauce
2 tablespoons liquid smoke
2 tablespoons dark molasses
1 teaspoon salt
¼ teaspoon hot sauce

Heat oil in a large saucepan over medium heat; add onion, and cook 5 minutes or until golden, stirring occasionally. Add garlic; cook 1 minute. Stir in ketchup and remaining ingredients; bring to a boil. Reduce heat, and simmer, uncovered, 1 hour or until sauce is thickened, stirring often. Pour mixture through a wire-mesh strainer into a container, discarding onion, garlic, and ginger. Cool to room temperature; cover and store in the refrigerator up to 2 weeks. Yield: 3¾ cups.

Carolina Sunshine, Then & Now
The Charity League of Charlotte, North Carolina

Ric and Mickey's Jerk Pork

A make-your-own seasoning mix turns pork tenderloin into a spice explosion. Simply double the seasoning mix to grill a package of two 1-pound tenderloins–they often come prepackaged.

¼ cup lime juice
¼ cup soy sauce
1 teaspoon dried oregano
½ teaspoon dried thyme

1 (1-pound) pork tenderloin
Seasoning Mix
Vegetable cooking spray

Combine first 4 ingredients in a large heavy-duty, zip-top plastic bag; add pork. Seal bag securely, and turn to coat pork. Marinate in refrigerator at least 4 hours.

Remove pork from marinade, reserving marinade. Sprinkle pork with 2 tablespoons Seasoning Mix. Coat grill rack with cooking spray; place on grill over medium-hot coals (350° to 400°). Place pork on rack; grill, covered, about 25 to 30 minutes or until thermometer inserted in thickest portion of tenderloin registers 160°, turning once.

Place reserved marinade in a small saucepan; bring to a boil. Slice pork, and serve with marinade. Yield: 4 servings.

Seasoning Mix

1 tablespoon dried onion
  flakes
1 tablespoon onion powder
2 teaspoons salt
2 teaspoons sugar
2 teaspoons dried chives
2 teaspoons ground thyme

1 teaspoon ground allspice
1 teaspoon coarsely ground
  black pepper
1 teaspoon ground red pepper
¼ teaspoon ground nutmeg
¼ teaspoon ground cinnamon

Combine all ingredients in a bowl; stir well. Yield: ⅓ cup.

Project Open Hand Cookbook
Project Open Hand Atlanta
Atlanta, Georgia

Grilled Garlic-Lime Pork with Jalapeño-Onion Marmalade

½ cup olive oil
⅓ cup fresh lime juice
6 large cloves garlic, chopped
2 tablespoons soy sauce
2 tablespoons grated fresh ginger
2 teaspoons Dijon mustard

½ teaspoon salt
¼ teaspoon ground red pepper
4 (12-ounce) pork tenderloins, trimmed
Vegetable cooking spray
Jalapeño-Onion Marmalade

Position knife blade in food processor bowl; add first 8 ingredients. Process until well blended, stopping once to scrape down sides. Pour marinade mixture into a large heavy-duty, zip-top plastic bag; add pork. Seal bag securely, and turn to coat pork. Marinate in refrigerator 8 hours, turning bag occasionally. Remove pork from marinade, discarding marinade.

Coat grill rack with cooking spray; place on grill over medium-hot coals (350° to 400°). Place pork on rack; grill, covered, 22 minutes or until a meat thermometer inserted in thickest portion of each tenderloin registers 160°, turning once. Let stand 5 minutes before slicing. Serve with Jalapeño-Onion Marmalade. Yield: 9 servings.

Jalapeño-Onion Marmalade

3 tablespoons olive oil
1¼ pounds red or yellow onions, finely chopped
¼ teaspoon salt
¼ teaspoon pepper

2 jalapeño peppers, seeded and minced
2 tablespoons sugar or honey
¼ cup red wine vinegar
¼ cup water

Heat oil in a large skillet over medium-high heat. Add onion, salt, and pepper; cook until tender, stirring occasionally. Add jalapeño; cook 1 minute. Add sugar; cook 1 minute. Stir in vinegar; simmer, stirring constantly, until most of liquid evaporates. Stir in water; simmer 10 minutes or until mixture is slightly thickened and onion is very soft, stirring often. Yield: 1¾ cups.

Southern Settings
Decatur General Foundation
Decatur, Alabama

Pork with Pear Sauce

1 teaspoon rubbed sage
½ teaspoon salt
¼ teaspoon pepper
4 (½-inch-thick) boneless pork
  loin chops
½ cup all-purpose flour
2 tablespoons olive oil

3 large pears, peeled, cored,
  and thinly sliced
½ cup dry white wine
½ cup chicken broth
2 tablespoons sugar
¼ teaspoon salt
⅛ teaspoon pepper

Sprinkle sage, ½ teaspoon salt, and ¼ teaspoon pepper over pork chops. Dredge in flour. Cook pork chops in hot oil in a large skillet over medium-high heat 3 to 4 minutes on each side or until browned. Transfer pork chops to a plate, and keep warm.

Drain fat from skillet; add pear slices, and cook over medium-high heat 2 minutes. Add wine, broth, and sugar. Cook over high heat 8 minutes or until pear is tender and syrup is thickened. Return pork chops to skillet. Reduce heat, and simmer, uncovered, 5 minutes or until pork chops are tender. Sprinkle with ¼ teaspoon salt and ⅛ teaspoon pepper.

Arrange pork chops on a serving platter, and top with pear sauce. Serve immediately. Yield: 4 servings.

Capital Celebrations
The Junior League of Washington, DC

Smothered Pork Chops

Blanket thick center-cut chops with a honey-soy sauce blend that's warmly spiced with ginger and garlic.

6 (1-inch-thick) center-cut pork
  loin chops (about 2½ to 3
  pounds)
1 tablespoon vegetable oil
½ cup chicken broth
¼ cup honey

¼ cup soy sauce
2 tablespoons ketchup
¼ teaspoon ground
  ginger
1 clove garlic, crushed

Cook pork chops in hot oil in a large skillet over medium-high heat until browned on both sides. Arrange pork chops in an ungreased 13- x 9- x 2-inch baking dish, overlapping pork chops if necessary.

Combine chicken broth and remaining 5 ingredients; pour over pork chops. Cover and bake at 350° for 45 minutes or until pork chops are tender. Yield: 6 servings.　　　　　　　　　Linda Carlin

Recipes from Our Home to Yours
Hospice of North Central Florida
Gainesville, Florida

Asian Spareribs

Fresh ginger, garlic, oyster sauce, and soy sauce, a decidedly Asian combo, make these baby back pork ribs sizzle.

5 pounds baby back pork ribs	1 cup ketchup
2 (2-inch) pieces fresh ginger, peeled	¾ cup soy sauce
4 large cloves garlic, peeled	⅓ cup oyster sauce
1 cup firmly packed brown sugar	¼ cup white vinegar
	¼ teaspoon salt
	Vegetable cooking spray

Cut ribs into 5 or 6 sections. Place ribs, ginger, and garlic in a large Dutch oven; add water to cover. Bring to a boil over medium-high heat. Reduce heat, and simmer 45 minutes.

Meanwhile, combine brown sugar and next 5 ingredients in a large heavy-duty, zip-top plastic bag; turn bag to mix well. Drain ribs, and place in bag with marinade. Seal bag securely, and turn to coat ribs. Cover and marinate in refrigerator at least 8 hours, turning bag once.

Remove ribs from marinade, reserving marinade. Place marinade in a small saucepan; bring to a boil over medium-high heat, and cook until reduced to 1 cup.

Coat grill rack with cooking spray; place on grill over medium-hot coals (350° to 400°). Place ribs on rack; grill, covered, 14 minutes, turning once. Serve with sauce. Yield: 5 servings.　　　Penny Hermansader

60 Years of Serving
The Assistance League of San Pedro-Palos Verdes
San Pedro, California

Venison with Stout and Potatoes

Stout, a strong dark beer, boasts a deep color and bittersweet taste. It stands up well to the robust main-dish combination of venison, potato, and mushrooms teamed with mustard and bay leaf.

2 tablespoons butter or margarine
1 tablespoon vegetable oil
2 pounds venison or sirloin steak
1 teaspoon salt
1 teaspoon pepper
1 medium onion, chopped
1 tablespoon all-purpose flour
6 ounces stout beer (we tested with Guiness Extra Stout)

1¼ cups beef broth
½ teaspoon prepared mustard
1 bay leaf
1½ pounds red potatoes, unpeeled and cut into ½-inch slices
½ pound fresh mushrooms, sliced
Garnish: fresh thyme sprigs

Heat butter and oil in a Dutch oven over medium-high heat. Sprinkle venison with salt and pepper; add to pan. Brown meat on both sides; remove meat from pan, reserving drippings in pan. Set meat aside, and keep warm.

Cook onion in pan drippings 3 minutes or until lightly browned, stirring often. Stir in flour; add stout, broth, mustard, and bay leaf. Return meat to pan; add potato. Cover and simmer 30 minutes. Add mushrooms; cook 30 additional minutes. Remove and discard bay leaf. Garnish, if desired. Yield: 6 servings.   Daniel Wade Seeley

The Flavors of Mackinac
Mackinac Island Medical Center
Mackinac Island, Michigan

Pasta, Rice & Grains

Chicken Manicotti with Chive Cream Sauce, page 215

Bow Tie Pasta with Grilled Chicken

Fresh, full-bodied shiitake mushrooms team with vibrant slivers of dried tomatoes to lend pizzazz to this chicken and pasta mix. Choose shiitake mushrooms that are plump and have edges that turn under. The mushroom stems are tough and should be removed.

8 ounces bow tie pasta, uncooked
12 fresh asparagus spears
4 large skinned and boned chicken breast halves
¼ teaspoon salt
¼ teaspoon pepper
2 tablespoons olive oil
4 cloves garlic, crushed
4 plum tomatoes, diced (about 1½ cups)
8 oil-packed dried tomatoes, sliced
¼ cup sliced fresh shiitake mushrooms
½ cup chicken broth
1 tablespoon chopped fresh basil
1 tablespoon chopped fresh parsley
Salt and pepper to taste
Garnish: fresh basil sprigs

Cook pasta according to package directions; drain well. Set aside, and keep warm.

Snap off tough ends of asparagus. Remove scales with a vegetable peeler, if desired. Cut asparagus into 1-inch pieces; set aside.

Sprinkle chicken breasts with ¼ teaspoon salt and ¼ teaspoon pepper. Grill chicken, covered, over medium-hot coals (350° to 400°) 5 minutes on each side or until done. Let cool slightly, and dice. Set chicken aside.

Heat olive oil in a large skillet over medium-high heat until hot. Add garlic; cook 1 minute, stirring constantly. Add asparagus, plum tomato, dried tomato, and mushrooms; cook 3 minutes, stirring constantly. Add diced chicken, chicken broth, chopped basil, and parsley; cook 2 minutes or until thoroughly heated. Stir in salt and pepper to taste. To serve, spoon chicken mixture over pasta; toss, if desired. Garnish, if desired. Yield: 4 servings. The Club Pelican Bay

Compliments of the Chef
Friends of the Library of Collier County, Inc.
Naples, Florida

Farfalle with Mushrooms

5 shallots, chopped (about ¾ cup)
½ cup butter, melted
4 (8-ounce) packages sliced fresh mushrooms, coarsely chopped
½ to 1 cup chicken broth
1 teaspoon salt
½ teaspoon dried crushed red pepper
12 ounces farfalle (bow tie pasta), uncooked
½ cup freshly grated Romano cheese
Additional freshly grated Romano cheese

Cook shallot in melted butter in a large skillet over medium-high heat, stirring constantly, until tender. Add mushrooms and ½ cup broth; stir well. Bring to a boil; reduce heat, and simmer, uncovered, 45 minutes, stirring often. Add salt and pepper; cook 5 minutes, stirring often. Add additional broth, if needed, for desired consistency.

Meanwhile, cook pasta according to package directions; drain well. Place pasta in a serving bowl; add ½ cup cheese, and toss well. Pour mushroom sauce over pasta, and toss gently. Serve with additional cheese. Yield: 8 servings.
Holly Perkins

Mississippi Reflections: A Collection of Recipes Seasoned with Memories
Hospice of Central Mississippi
Brookhaven, Mississippi

Capellini with Bell Peppers and Snow Peas

This easy pasta side dish is a simple and colorful medley of ingredients. Turn it into satisfying main-dish fare by adding leftover cooked chicken or beef.

12 ounces dried capellini or angel hair pasta, uncooked
1 cup finely chopped onion
¼ cup butter or margarine, melted
1 medium-size sweet red pepper, thinly sliced lengthwise
1 medium-size sweet yellow pepper, thinly sliced lengthwise
¼ pound fresh snow pea pods, sliced diagonally into ¼-inch pieces
1 tablespoon chopped fresh parsley
½ teaspoon salt
½ teaspoon freshly ground pepper
½ cup freshly grated Parmesan cheese

Cook pasta according to package directions; drain well. Set aside, and keep warm.

Cook onion in butter in a medium skillet over medium-high heat 2 minutes, stirring constantly. Add red and yellow peppers and snow peas; cook 2 additional minutes or until snow peas are crisp-tender, stirring occasionally. Combine pasta, vegetable mixture, parsley, salt, and pepper; toss well. Sprinkle with cheese. Yield: 8 servings.

Women Who Can Dish It Out
The Junior League of Springfield, Missouri

Fettuccine with Smoked Salmon and Peas

1½ pounds refrigerated spinach fettuccine, uncooked
2 tablespoons olive oil, divided
1 (4-ounce) package smoked salmon, thinly sliced and cut into bite-size pieces
1 cup frozen English peas
2 cups whipping cream
1 tablespoon minced green onions
1 tablespoon grated Parmesan cheese
½ teaspoon salt
¼ teaspoon pepper

Cook pasta in a Dutch oven according to package directions; drain. Return pasta to Dutch oven. Toss lightly with 1 tablespoon olive oil; set aside.

Heat remaining 1 tablespoon olive oil in a skillet; add salmon, and cook over medium heat 1 minute. Stir in peas, and cook 1 to 2 minutes or until thoroughly heated.

Add whipping cream; cook 5 to 6 minutes or until mixture coats back of a metal spoon. Stir in green onions, cheese, salt, and pepper.

Pour cream sauce over pasta in Dutch oven; toss well. Serve immediately. Yield: 6 servings.   Tamalin Miner Christen

A Bite of the Best
The Relief Society Church of Jesus Christ of Latter Day Saints
Provo, Utah

Fettuccine with Shrimp and Artichokes

2 pounds unpeeled large fresh shrimp
1½ pounds fettuccine, uncooked
1 large onion, chopped
½ cup butter or margarine, melted
½ cup olive oil
1 cup dry white wine
6 to 8 cloves garlic, minced
½ teaspoon dried rosemary, crushed

⅛ teaspoon dried oregano
1 (28-ounce) can Italian-style tomatoes, drained and chopped
2 (14-ounce) cans artichoke hearts, drained and quartered
½ cup minced fresh parsley
¼ teaspoon salt
¼ teaspoon pepper

Peel shrimp, and devein, if desired; set aside.

Cook fettuccine according to package directions; drain well. Set aside, and keep warm.

Cook onion in butter and oil in a Dutch oven over medium heat, stirring constantly, until tender. Add wine and next 3 ingredients; cook 5 minutes. Add tomato and artichokes; bring to a boil. Reduce heat, and simmer, uncovered, 3 minutes. Add shrimp and parsley; cook 5 to 6 minutes or until shrimp turn pink. Add salt and pepper. Serve immediately over pasta. Yield: 8 servings.

Candlewood Classics
The Community Service Club of New Fairfield, Connecticut

Cajun Andouille Cream Sauce with Fettuccine

Spicy, heavily smoked andouille sausage reigns supreme in Cajun cooking and in this creamy pasta dish.

¼ cup butter
¼ cup all-purpose flour
½ cup finely chopped onion
½ cup finely chopped green pepper
½ cup finely chopped celery
1 pound andouille sausage, sliced and quartered
1 clove garlic, minced
1 teaspoon black pepper
1 teaspoon ground red pepper
1 teaspoon paprika
½ teaspoon salt
1 quart whipping cream
1 (8-ounce) package sliced fresh mushrooms
1 pound peeled, cooked medium-size fresh shrimp or crawfish (optional)
1 (16-ounce) package fettuccine

Melt butter in a Dutch oven over medium-low heat; stir in flour. Cook until mixture is caramel-colored, stirring constantly. Add onion, green pepper, and celery; cook over medium heat 2 minutes, stirring constantly. Add sausage and next 5 ingredients, and cook 1 minute. Slowly stir in whipping cream; add mushrooms and shrimp, if desired; cook, uncovered, 15 minutes or until mixture is thickened and thoroughly heated.

Cook fettuccine according to package directions; drain well. Spoon sauce over pasta, and toss gently. Yield: 8 servings.   Laura Hebert

Somethin' to Smile About
St. Martin, Iberia, Lafayette Community Action Agency
Lafayette, Louisiana

Clam Lasagna

If you're a clam fan, you'll want to dive into this very different, but divine, recipe for spinach lasagna.

1 (8-ounce) package lasagna noodles
2 (6½-ounce) cans minced clams, undrained
¼ cup butter or margarine
¼ cup all-purpose flour
1 (8-ounce) bottle clam juice
2 cloves garlic, minced
¼ cup finely chopped fresh parsley
3 tablespoons fresh lemon juice

1 teaspoon dried Italian seasoning
1 (15-ounce) carton ricotta cheese
1 (10-ounce) package frozen chopped spinach, thawed and drained
8 ounces sliced Monterey Jack cheese
¼ cup grated Parmesan cheese

Cook lasagna noodles according to package directions; drain well. Set aside.

Drain clams, reserving liquid; set clams and liquid aside.

Melt butter in a heavy saucepan over low heat; add flour, stirring until smooth. Cook 1 minute, stirring constantly. Gradually add reserved clam liquid and clam juice; cook over medium heat, stirring constantly, until mixture is thickened and bubbly. Stir in clams, garlic, and next 3 ingredients.

Layer one-third of lasagna noodles in bottom of a greased 13- x 9- x 2-inch baking dish; spread ricotta cheese evenly over noodles. Spoon one-third of clam sauce evenly over ricotta cheese; place half of remaining noodles over clam sauce. Press spinach between paper towels to remove excess moisture; sprinkle evenly over lasagna noodles, and top with half of Monterey Jack cheese slices.

Spoon half of remaining clam sauce over cheese slices, and top with remaining lasagna noodles, cheese slices, and clam sauce. Sprinkle with Parmesan cheese. Bake, uncovered, at 350° for 30 minutes or until bubbly. Let stand 10 minutes before serving. Yield: 8 servings.

Gladys Daniels Johnston

Curtain Calls
The Arts Society of the Norris Cultural Arts Center
St. Charles, Illinois

Ranchero Macaroni Bake

This lively casserole is definitely a family affair. It boasts lots of familiar ingredients, including macaroni, cream of chicken soup, tortilla chips, and salsa. It's sure to be a hit!

2½ cups elbow macaroni, uncooked
1 (26-ounce) can cream of chicken soup
1 cup milk
3 cups (12 ounces) shredded Cheddar or Monterey Jack cheese

1½ cups salsa (we tested with Taco Bell Thick 'n Chunky)
1 cup coarsely crushed tortilla chips (about 3 cups chips)

Cook macaroni according to package directions; drain well.

While macaroni cooks, combine soup and milk in a large bowl, stirring well with a wire whisk. Add macaroni, cheese, and salsa; stir well. Pour mixture into a lightly greased 13- x 9- x 2-inch baking dish.

Bake, uncovered, at 400° for 20 minutes; stir carefully, and sprinkle with crushed chips. Bake 5 additional minutes or until bubbly. Yield: 10 servings.   Linda Farmer

A Collection of Favorite Recipes of the Congregation and Friends of White Clay Creek Presbyterian Church
White Clay Creek Presbyterian Church
Newark, Delaware

Chicken Manicotti with Chive Cream Sauce

Streamlined is the word for this manicotti—a tub of chive cream cheese is used in the sauce, while frozen diced chicken and broccoli comprise the filling. We discovered a trick in our Test Kitchens that enabled us to fill the shells quickly and cleanly. Simply put the filling in a zip-top plastic bag, seal it, and cut a hole in one corner to "pipe" the filling into the shells.

1 (1-pound) package manicotti shells
2 (8-ounce) containers cream cheese with chives and onion
⅔ cup milk
¼ cup grated Parmesan cheese
2 cups diced cooked chicken (we tested with Tyson frozen diced cooked chicken)
1 (10-ounce) package frozen chopped broccoli, thawed and drained
1 (4-ounce) jar diced pimiento, drained
¼ teaspoon pepper
Paprika

Cook pasta according to package directions; drain well.

While pasta cooks, place cream cheese in a saucepan, and cook over medium-low heat until cheese melts. Slowly add milk, stirring until smooth. Add Parmesan cheese, stirring well.

Combine ¾ cup cream sauce, chicken, and next 3 ingredients in a large bowl. Carefully stuff about ⅓ cup filling into 12 manicotti shells, discarding any shells that split. Arrange shells in an ungreased 13- x 9- x 2-inch baking dish. Pour remaining cream sauce over shells. Sprinkle with paprika. Cover and bake at 350° for 30 minutes. Yield: 6 servings.

Raynae Hammond

Just Peachey, Cooking Up a Cure
Catherine Peachey Fund, Inc.
Warsaw, Indiana

Shrimp with Orzo and Sun-Dried Tomatoes

2 tablespoons butter
3 tablespoons olive oil, divided
1½ tablespoons minced shallots
¾ cup canned diced tomatoes, drained
1 to 2 tablespoons minced garlic (3 to 6 cloves)
2 teaspoons chopped fresh oregano
1 pound unpeeled large fresh shrimp, peeled and deveined

6 oil-packed dried tomatoes, drained and chopped
1½ cups crumbled feta cheese
½ cup pitted kalamata olives
½ teaspoon freshly ground pepper
1½ cups orzo, uncooked
3 tablespoons chopped fresh basil

Melt butter in a large skillet over medium-high heat; add 2 tablespoons olive oil. Add shallot, and cook, stirring constantly, until tender. Stir in tomatoes, garlic, and oregano. Add shrimp and dried tomato; cook 3 to 5 minutes or until shrimp turn pink. Sprinkle with feta cheese, olives, and pepper.

Meanwhile, cook orzo according to package directions; drain well. Transfer orzo to a large serving bowl. Add remaining 1 tablespoon olive oil and basil; toss well. Spoon shrimp mixture over orzo. Serve immediately. Yield: 4 servings.

Savoring San Diego: An Evolving Regional Cuisine
University of California, San Diego Medical Center Auxiliary
San Diego, California

Creamy Artichoke and Mushroom Penne

Tender artichoke hearts, plump slices of fresh mushrooms, and a luscious cream sauce make this pasta entrée the perfect choice for a romantic dinner. If you prefer, serve it as a sublime side dish to partner with your favorite steak.

12 ounces penne pasta, uncooked
½ small onion, minced (about ¼ cup)
1 clove garlic, crushed
3 tablespoons butter, melted
1 (8-ounce) package sliced fresh mushrooms
1 (15-ounce) can artichoke hearts, drained and chopped
1 cup whipping cream
2 tablespoons capers, drained
¼ teaspoon salt
¼ teaspoon freshly ground pepper
¼ cup freshly grated Parmesan cheese
2 tablespoons chopped fresh parsley

Cook pasta according to package directions; drain well.

While pasta is cooking, cook onion and garlic in butter in a medium skillet over medium-high heat, stirring constantly, until tender. Add mushrooms, and cook 5 minutes. Add artichokes, and cook 2 minutes or until thoroughly heated. Remove vegetables from skillet; set aside, and keep warm.

Add whipping cream to skillet; bring to a boil, and cook, stirring constantly, until whipping cream is reduced by half. Add artichoke mixture, capers, salt, and pepper, stirring well. Toss artichoke mixture with pasta. Sprinkle with cheese and parsley. Serve immediately. Yield: 6 servings.

Stop and Smell the Rosemary: Recipes and Traditions to Remember
The Junior League of Houston, Texas

Vegetable Kugel

This captivating noodle dish is packed to the brim with chunky vegetables and cheese. Tarragon and dry mustard give it personality to spare. Serve it as a meatless main dish for 8 or as a side dish for 16.

8 ounces medium egg noodles, uncooked
2 cups coarsely chopped fresh broccoli
2 cups coarsely chopped fresh cauliflower
1 (8-ounce) package sliced fresh mushrooms
1½ cups diced onion (about 1 large)
1 clove garlic, minced
2 tablespoons butter or margarine, melted
2 cups low-fat cottage cheese
1½ cups (6 ounces) shredded Cheddar cheese, divided
1½ teaspoons dried tarragon
½ teaspoon dry mustard
½ teaspoon salt
½ teaspoon pepper

Cook noodles according to package directions; drain well. Combine noodles, broccoli, and cauliflower in a large bowl; set aside.

Cook mushrooms, onion, and garlic in butter in a large skillet over medium-high heat, stirring constantly, until tender. Add to noodle mixture. Stir in cottage cheese, ¾ cup Cheddar cheese, tarragon, and remaining 3 ingredients. Spoon into a greased 13- x 9- x 2-inch baking dish. Sprinkle with remaining ¾ cup Cheddar cheese.

Bake, uncovered, at 350° for 30 minutes or until set and golden. Yield: 16 servings.

Beyond Chicken Soup
Jewish Home of Rochester Auxiliary
Rochester, New York

Summer Risotto

Serve this incredibly light entrée with a crusty loaf of bread and a freshly tossed green salad. The blue cheese adds a distinctive, but subtle, note to the risotto-vegetable blend.

4½ cups reduced-sodium chicken broth
2 tablespoons butter, divided
2 cloves garlic, minced
2 shallots, minced
1¼ cups Arborio rice, uncooked
¼ teaspoon salt
¼ teaspoon pepper
¼ cup thinly sliced purple onion
¼ cup julienne-sliced carrot

¼ cup thinly sliced zucchini
¼ cup thinly sliced yellow squash
¼ cup chopped arugula
3 tablespoons chopped fresh basil
2 tablespoons chopped fresh oregano
⅓ cup crumbled blue cheese
3 tablespoons chopped walnuts, toasted
Garnish: fresh oregano sprigs

Bring chicken broth to a simmer in a saucepan, and keep warm over low heat.

Melt 1 tablespoon butter in a 3-quart saucepan over medium-high heat. Add garlic and shallot; cook 2 minutes, stirring constantly. Reduce heat to medium; add rice, and continue to cook 5 additional minutes or until rice is translucent, stirring constantly.

Add warm chicken broth to rice mixture, ½ cup at a time, stirring constantly. Allow liquid to be absorbed after each addition before adding more chicken broth. Stir in salt and pepper; set aside.

Melt remaining 1 tablespoon butter in a large skillet over medium-high heat. Add onion and carrot; cook 2 minutes, stirring constantly. Reduce heat to medium; add zucchini and squash, and cook 2 minutes or until vegetables are tender, stirring often. Stir in arugula. Add vegetable mixture to rice mixture; stir gently. Stir in basil and oregano; sprinkle with blue cheese and walnuts. Garnish, if desired. Serve immediately. Yield: 8 servings.

Call to Post
Lexington Hearing and Speech Center
Lexington, Kentucky

Wild Rice with Grapes

2 tablespoons butter or
  margarine, divided
2 tablespoons sliced almonds
¼ cup chopped green onions
1 (14½-ounce) can chicken
  broth
3 tablespoons water

½ teaspoon salt
¼ teaspoon pepper
⅔ cup wild rice, uncooked
½ cup seedless green grapes,
  halved
½ cup seedless red grapes,
  halved

Melt 1 tablespoon butter in a large saucepan over medium heat; add almonds, and cook 2 minutes, stirring constantly, until golden. Remove almonds from pan; set almonds aside.

Melt remaining 1 tablespoon butter in pan. Add green onions; cook, stirring constantly, until tender. Add broth and next 3 ingredients; bring to a boil. Stir in rice; return to a boil. Cover, reduce heat, and simmer 1 hour or until rice is tender. Drain any liquid. Stir in grapes. Sprinkle with almonds. Yield: 4 servings.   Linda Norton

With Love from the Shepherd's Center of North Little Rock
The Shepherd's Center of North Little Rock, Arkansas

Wild Rice and Orzo

2 (6-ounce) packages wild rice,
  uncooked
1 cup orzo, uncooked
2 medium onions, chopped
2 cloves garlic, minced
2 tablespoons butter, melted

¼ cup honey
1 tablespoon chopped fresh
  parsley
2 teaspoons reduced-sodium
  soy sauce
2 teaspoons fresh lemon juice

Cook wild rice and orzo separately according to package directions; drain well.

While rice and orzo are cooking, cook onion and garlic in butter in a Dutch oven until tender. Add rice, orzo, honey, and remaining ingredients; stir mixture well. Cook until thoroughly heated. Yield: 10 servings.

Main Line Classics II, Cooking Up a Little History
The Junior Saturday Club of Wayne, Pennsylvania

Mixed Grain and Mushroom Casserole

1 large onion, thinly sliced
4 cloves garlic, minced
¼ cup vegetable oil
½ cup wild rice, uncooked
½ cup brown rice, uncooked
½ cup pearl barley, uncooked
¼ cup unsalted butter

1 (8-ounce) package sliced fresh mushrooms
2 (14½-ounce) cans beef broth
¼ cup chopped fresh parsley
1 teaspoon salt
¼ teaspoon pepper
½ to 1 teaspoon dried thyme
¼ to ½ teaspoon dried oregano

Cook onion and garlic in oil in a large Dutch oven over medium-high heat 5 minutes or until tender, stirring often. Add wild rice, brown rice, and barley; cook 1 minute, stirring constantly. Set aside.

Melt butter in a skillet over medium-high heat. Add mushrooms, and cook 1 minute, stirring constantly. Remove from heat. Add mushrooms, beef broth, and remaining 5 ingredients to mixture in Dutch oven; bring to a boil. Pour mixture into a lightly greased 13- x 9- x 2-inch baking dish. Cover and bake at 350° for 1 hour. Yield: 6 servings.

Praiseworthy
Foundation for Historic Christ Church
Irvington, Virginia

Barley-Lentil Pilaf

2½ cups chicken broth
½ cup pearl barley, uncooked
½ cup dried lentils
1 cup sliced fresh mushrooms
½ small onion, finely chopped
1 stalk celery, diced

4 cloves garlic, minced
2 teaspoons soy sauce
½ teaspoon dried dillweed
Dash of pepper
1 tablespoon chopped fresh parsley

Bring chicken broth to a boil in a large saucepan; add barley and next 8 ingredients, stirring well. Cover, reduce heat to medium-low, and cook 30 minutes or until barley and lentils are tender. Sprinkle with parsley. Serve immediately. Yield: 4 servings.   Millie Becker

Expressions
National League of American Pen Women, Chester County
Coatesville, Pennsylvania

Barley with Smoked Ham and Peas

3 cups water
1 cup pearl barley, uncooked
½ teaspoon salt
2 slices bacon
3 ounces smoked ham, cut into very thin strips
1 medium onion, finely chopped

1 (10-ounce) package frozen English peas
2 tablespoons chicken broth
4 fresh sage leaves, minced, or ¼ teaspoon dried sage
½ teaspoon fresh marjoram, minced, or ⅛ teaspoon dried marjoram

Bring water to a boil in a medium saucepan; add barley and salt. Reduce heat, and simmer, uncovered, 40 minutes or until liquid is absorbed. Set aside.

Cook bacon in a large skillet until crisp; remove bacon, reserving drippings in skillet. Crumble bacon, and set aside.

Cook ham in drippings in skillet over medium heat until edges of ham are lightly browned, stirring often. Remove ham from skillet, reserving drippings in skillet; set ham aside.

Cook onion in drippings in skillet 2 minutes, stirring often. Add peas; cook, stirring constantly, 2 to 3 minutes or until peas are thoroughly heated. Add reserved barley, ham, and chicken broth; cook over medium-low heat until thoroughly heated, stirring occasionally. Stir in sage and marjoram. Sprinkle with crumbled bacon. Yield: 6 servings.

Special Selections of Ocala
Ocala Royal Dames for Cancer Research, Inc.
Ocala, Florida

Apple Couscous

¾ cup unsweetened apple juice
¾ cup water
1 cup couscous, uncooked
1½ cups peeled, chopped cooking apple

2 tablespoons raisins
2 tablespoons chopped dates
¼ teaspoon apple pie spice

Combine apple juice and water in a saucepan; bring to a boil. Remove from heat; stir in couscous and remaining ingredients. Cover tightly; let stand 5 minutes or until liquid is absorbed. Fluff with a fork before serving. Yield: 6 servings.

A Cookbook
Life Education Department of the Cheshire Center of
Applied Science & Technology at Keene High School
Keene, New Hampshire

Sunny's Portobello Grits

¼ cup butter, divided
4 fresh portobello mushrooms,
  sliced and cut into 1-inch
  pieces
6 ounces fresh mushrooms,
  sliced
1 clove garlic, minced
¾ cup quick-cooking grits,
  uncooked

2 cups whipping cream
½ cup (2 ounces) shredded
  Swiss cheese
½ (8-ounce) package cream
  cheese, softened
½ teaspoon salt
¼ teaspoon freshly ground
  pepper

Melt 2 tablespoons butter in a large skillet over medium-high heat; add mushrooms and garlic, and cook 5 minutes, stirring constantly, or until mushrooms are tender.

Meanwhile, cook grits according to package directions, substituting 2 cups whipping cream for the water. Add remaining 2 tablespoons butter, mushroom mixture, cheeses, salt, and pepper, stirring just until blended. Serve immediately. Yield: 8 servings.

Eat Your Dessert or You Won't Get Any Broccoli
The Sea Pines Montessori School
Hilton Head Island, South Carolina

Mexican Polenta Casserole

Polenta is basically a mush made from cornmeal. Our version goes south-of-the-border for flavor impact. Plenty of cheese and beans plus salsa, chili powder, green onions, and fresh cilantro set the scene. We suggest topping each serving with a dollop of sour cream to cool the palate.

2 cups (8 ounces) shredded Monterey Jack cheese, divided
1 (15-ounce) can black beans, drained
1 cup mild salsa
½ cup chopped fresh cilantro
½ teaspoon chili powder
Basic Polenta
1 cup sliced green onions
Vegetable cooking spray
Sour cream (optional)

Combine 1 cup cheese, beans, and next 3 ingredients in a bowl. Stir well, and set aside.

Combine hot cooked Basic Polenta, remaining 1 cup cheese, and green onions in a bowl, stirring until cheese melts.

Coat a 13- x 9- x 2-inch baking dish with cooking spray. Spread half of polenta mixture in baking dish. Spread bean mixture over polenta layer. Top with remaining polenta mixture. Bake, uncovered, at 350° for 35 minutes or until lightly browned. Let stand 15 minutes before serving. Top each serving with sour cream, if desired. Yield: 6 servings.

Basic Polenta

1¼ cups yellow cornmeal
½ teaspoon salt
4 cups water

Combine cornmeal and salt in a large saucepan. Gradually add water, stirring constantly with a wire whisk. Bring to a boil, stirring constantly. Reduce heat to medium; cook, uncovered, 15 minutes, stirring often. Yield: 3¾ cups.

Maggie Hinkley

Bartlett Memorial Hospital's 25th Anniversary Cookbook
Bartlett Memorial Hospital
Juneau, Alaska

Pies & Pastries

Mocha Profiteroles, page 238

Apple Pie with Rum-Butter Sauce

Our crustless homespun pie is served up warm and cozy under a blanket of Rum-Butter Sauce. This delightful dessert has a texture like bread pudding.

¼ cup butter, softened
1 cup sugar
1 large egg
1 cup all-purpose flour
1 teaspoon salt
1 teaspoon ground cinnamon
2 tablespoons water

1 teaspoon vanilla extract
3 cups peeled, chopped
   Granny Smith apple (about 3
   medium)
½ cup chopped pecans
Rum-Butter Sauce

Beat butter at medium speed of an electric mixer until creamy; gradually add sugar, beating well. Add egg, and beat well.

Combine flour, salt, and cinnamon; add to butter mixture, beating until blended. Add water and vanilla; beat well. Stir in apple and pecans. Pour into a greased and floured 9-inch pieplate.

Bake at 350° for 45 minutes or until a wooden pick inserted in center comes out clean. Serve warm with warm Rum-Butter Sauce. Yield: one 9-inch pie.

Rum-Butter Sauce

½ cup sugar
½ cup firmly packed brown
   sugar

½ cup whipping cream
¼ cup butter
1 tablespoon dark rum

Combine first 4 ingredients in a small saucepan. Bring to a boil; cook 1 minute, stirring constantly. Remove from heat, and stir in rum. Yield: 1¼ cups.

Landmark Entertaining
The Junior League of Abilene, Texas

Dutch Apple Pie

1 cup sugar
2 tablespoons plus 1 teaspoon
  all-purpose flour
½ teaspoon ground cinnamon
⅛ teaspoon salt
6 cups peeled, sliced Granny
  Smith apple (about 6 to 8
  medium)

1 unbaked 9-inch pastry shell
2 tablespoons butter
¼ cup whipping cream
1 egg yolk, lightly beaten

Combine first 4 ingredients in a large bowl; add apple slices, and toss until evenly coated. Spoon apple mixture into pastry shell; dot with butter. Bake at 400° for 30 minutes or until apple is tender. Remove pie from oven. Reduce oven temperature to 350°.

Combine whipping cream and egg yolk, stirring well. Pour over apple slices, lightly pressing apple with a fork to allow whipping cream mixture to seep in between apple slices. Cover pie with aluminum foil to prevent excessive browning. Bake 15 additional minutes or until crust is browned and filling is bubbly. Let cool completely on a wire rack. Yield: one 9-inch pie.
Georgette Menster

Quad City Cookin'
Queen of Heaven Circle of OLV Ladies Council
Davenport, Iowa

Carrot Pie

Versatile carrots make the culinary leap from good-for-you vegetable to stellar dessert in this pumpkin pielike recipe. Serve it at room temperature or chilled.

1 pound carrots, scraped and sliced
1½ cups water
1 teaspoon salt, divided
4 large eggs
1 (5-ounce) can evaporated milk
1 cup sugar
1 tablespoon all-purpose flour
1 teaspoon ground ginger
1 teaspoon ground cinnamon
½ teaspoon ground nutmeg
⅛ teaspoon ground cloves
1 unbaked 9-inch pastry shell
Whipped cream (optional)

Combine carrot, water, and ½ teaspoon salt in a medium saucepan; bring to a boil. Cover, reduce heat, and simmer 20 minutes or until carrot is very tender. Drain well, and let cool.

Combine cooked carrot, remaining ½ teaspoon salt, eggs, and next 7 ingredients in container of an electric blender; process until smooth, stopping once to scrape down sides. Pour carrot mixture into pastry shell.

Bake at 425° for 12 minutes; cover pie with aluminum foil to prevent excessive browning. Reduce oven temperature to 350°; bake 30 additional minutes or until a knife inserted in center comes out clean. Let cool completely on a wire rack. Serve with whipped cream, if desired. Yield: one 9-inch pie.

The Best of Mayberry
The Foothills Lions Club of Mount Airy, North Carolina

Cranberry Festival Cranberry Pie

This easy-to-make recipe boasts a delightfully chewy texture and scarlet color, courtesy of plenty of fresh cranberries.

1½ cups fresh cranberries
¼ cup firmly packed brown sugar
¼ cup chopped pecans or walnuts
1 unbaked 9-inch pastry shell
1 large egg, lightly beaten
½ cup sugar
½ cup all-purpose flour
⅓ cup butter, melted

Combine first 3 ingredients in a bowl; stir gently. Spoon cranberry mixture into pastry shell.

Combine egg and remaining 3 ingredients, stirring with a wire whisk until blended; pour over cranberry mixture. Bake at 350° for 35 to 40 minutes or until golden and bubbly. Let cool completely on a wire rack. Yield: one 9-inch pie.   Agnes Weinberg

A Taste of Greene
Playground Committee
Greene, Iowa

White Chocolate-Berry Pie

5 (1-ounce) squares white chocolate, divided (we tested with Baker's premium white chocolate baking squares)
2 tablespoons milk
½ (8-ounce) package cream cheese, softened

⅓ cup sifted powdered sugar
1 teaspoon grated orange rind
1 cup whipping cream, whipped
1 baked 9-inch pastry shell
2 cups fresh raspberries or strawberries, hulled

Combine 4 (1-ounce) squares white chocolate and milk in a 2-cup liquid measuring cup; microwave at HIGH 1 to 2 minutes or until chocolate is almost melted, stirring once halfway through cooking time. Remove from microwave, and stir until smooth. Let cool.

Combine cream cheese, powdered sugar, and orange rind in a mixing bowl; beat at medium speed of an electric mixer until blended. Add melted white chocolate, and beat at high speed until smooth. Fold whipped cream into white chocolate mixture; pour filling into pastry shell. Arrange raspberries on top of filling.

Place remaining 1-ounce square white chocolate in a 1-cup liquid measuring cup; microwave at HIGH 1 to 2 minutes or until chocolate is almost melted, stirring once halfway through cooking time. Remove from microwave, and stir until smooth. Drizzle chocolate over raspberries. Cover and chill at least 1 hour. Yield: one 9-inch pie.

Swap Around Recipes
Delmarva Square Dance Federation
Salisbury, Maryland

Raspberry Mountain Pie

This "pie" is like a cobbler incognito. The edges are brown and crusty, while the center remains gloriously gooey. Vanilla ice cream or whipped cream are ideal toppers.

2½ cups fresh raspberries	¾ cup sugar
¼ cup sugar	1½ teaspoons baking powder
3 tablespoons butter	½ teaspoon salt
1 cup all-purpose flour	¾ cup milk

Combine raspberries and ¼ cup sugar in a bowl, and set aside.

Place butter in a 9½-inch deep-dish pieplate. Bake at 350° for 3 minutes or until butter is melted. Remove pieplate from oven.

Combine flour, ¾ cup sugar, baking powder, and salt; stir well. Add milk, stirring until smooth. Pour batter over melted butter (do not stir). Spoon raspberry mixture over batter (do not stir).

Bake at 350° for 25 minutes or until edges are browned (center will not be browned or set). Cool slightly on a wire rack. Serve warm, at room temperature, or chilled. Yield: one 9½-inch pie.   Fran Clapp

Country Recipes
Westmoreland United Church
Westmoreland, New Hampshire

Pumpkin Pecan Pie

No need trying to choose between pumpkin and pecan pie at your next holiday meal. When you prepare this Test Kitchens favorite, you'll have the best of both worlds because a crunchy pecan topping sits atop a creamy pumpkin filling.

3 large eggs, lightly beaten	½ teaspoon ground cinnamon
1 cup sugar	¼ teaspoon salt
1 cup canned pumpkin	1 unbaked 9-inch pastry shell
½ cup dark corn syrup	1 cup chopped pecans
1 teaspoon vanilla extract	Whipped cream

Combine first 7 ingredients in a large bowl, stirring well with a wire whisk until blended. Pour mixture into pastry shell; sprinkle evenly with pecans.

Bake at 350° for 50 to 55 minutes or until a knife inserted in center comes out clean. (Cover with aluminum foil to prevent excessive browning, if necessary.) Let cool completely on a wire rack. Serve with whipped cream. Yield: one 9-inch pie.   Charlotte Nelson

Our Sunrise Family Cookbook
Sunrise Drive Elementary School
Tucson, Arizona

Honey-Crunch Pecan Pie

A splash of bourbon and a measure of golden honey enhance this impressive nut-filled dessert. Chopped pecans flavor the filling, while glazed pecan halves crown the surface.

4 large eggs, lightly beaten
1 cup light corn syrup
¼ cup sugar
¼ cup firmly packed brown
   sugar
2 tablespoons butter or
   margarine, melted
1 tablespoon bourbon
1 teaspoon vanilla extract

½ teaspoon salt
1 cup chopped pecans
1 unbaked 10-inch pastry shell
¼ cup plus 3 tablespoons
   firmly packed brown sugar
¼ cup butter or margarine
⅓ cup honey
2 cups pecan halves

Combine first 8 ingredients in a large bowl; stir well with a wire whisk until blended. Stir in chopped pecans. Spoon pecan mixture into pastry shell.

Bake at 350° for 35 minutes. (Cover with aluminum foil after 25 minutes to prevent excessive browning, if necessary.)

Meanwhile, combine ¼ cup plus 3 tablespoons brown sugar, ¼ cup butter, and honey in a medium saucepan; cook mixture over medium heat 2 minutes or until sugar dissolves and butter melts, stirring mixture often. Add pecan halves, and stir gently until pecan halves are coated. Spoon pecan mixture evenly over pie. Bake 10 additional minutes or until topping is bubbly. Let cool completely on a wire rack. Yield: one 10-inch pie.   April Kopin

Love for Others
Our Shepherd Lutheran Church
Birmingham, Michigan

Mincemeat-Cheese Pie

1 (9-ounce) package mincemeat
  (2 cups prepared)
1 baked 9-inch pastry shell
1½ (8-ounce) packages cream
  cheese, softened
2 large eggs

½ cup sugar
1 teaspoon grated lemon rind
1 teaspoon fresh lemon juice
1 (8-ounce) carton sour cream
1 teaspoon sugar
½ teaspoon vanilla extract

Prepare mincemeat according to package directions; let cool slightly, and spoon into pastry shell. Combine cream cheese and next 4 ingredients in a large mixing bowl; beat at medium speed of an electric mixer until smooth. Pour cream cheese mixture over mincemeat. Bake at 375° for 20 minutes.

Combine sour cream, 1 teaspoon sugar, and vanilla, stirring until smooth. Spread evenly over baked cream cheese mixture. Bake 10 additional minutes. Let cool completely on a wire rack; cover and chill thoroughly. Yield: one 9-inch pie.

Exchanging Tastes
The Depot
Midland Park, New Jersey

Persian Lime Pie with Chocolate-Coconut Crust

Melted chocolate morsels and flaked coconut form this pie's unique crust. It becomes very hard when frozen, so use a warm knife to carefully cut the pie into wedges. You can substitute a commercial chocolate-flavored crumb crust if you're pressed for time. Persian lime is the larger size variety of lime.

2 tablespoons butter, softened
1 cup (6 ounces) semisweet
  chocolate morsels
1¼ cups flaked coconut, lightly
  toasted and chopped

1 cup whipping cream
1 (14-ounce) can sweetened
  condensed milk
Zest and juice of 4 limes

Lightly butter a 9-inch pieplate with 2 tablespoons softened butter; set aside.

Place chocolate morsels in a small saucepan; cook over low heat until melted, stirring constantly. Combine chocolate and coconut; pat in bottom and up sides of pieplate, forming a thin shell. Cover and chill until firm.

Beat cream at high speed of an electric mixer until soft peaks form. Combine condensed milk, lime zest, and lime juice in large a bowl, stirring well; fold in whipped cream. Pour mixture into prepared pieplate; cover and freeze at least 8 hours. To serve, cut carefully with a warm knife. Yield: one 9-inch pie.   Glenview at Pelican Bay

Compliments of the Chef
Friends of the Library of Collier County
Naples, Florida

Frozen Strawberry Margarita Pie

This frozen refresher stars a salty pretzel crust and all the makings of a cool strawberry margarita. It's a slice of paradise.

1¼ cups finely crushed pretzels (we tested with 3½ cups whole Rold Gold Tiny Twists, crushed)
¼ cup sugar
½ cup plus 2 tablespoons butter or margarine, melted
1 (14-ounce) can sweetened condensed milk
1½ cups chopped fresh strawberries
⅓ cup lime juice
¼ cup tequila
2 tablespoons Triple Sec or other orange-flavored liqueur
3 drops of red food coloring (optional)
1½ cups whipping cream, whipped

Combine first 3 ingredients in a medium bowl; stir well. Press mixture firmly in bottom and up sides of a lightly buttered 10-inch pieplate.

Combine condensed milk and next 5 ingredients, stirring well. Fold in whipped cream; pour into prepared pieplate. Cover and freeze at least 4 hours or until firm. Let stand at room temperature 10 minutes before serving. Yield: one 10-inch pie.

Sweet Home Alabama
The Junior League of Huntsville, Alabama

Chocolate-Macadamia Nut Pie

This simple sweet looks smashing, in part because it's shaped in a springform pan. A chocolate-cream cheese mixture is softened with whipped cream before it's frozen. We liked it chilled, too.

1 cup (6 ounces) semisweet
chocolate morsels
1⅔ cups crushed chocolate
wafers (6 ounces)
¼ cup butter or margarine,
melted
½ (8-ounce) package cream
cheese, softened

¾ cup sugar
1½ teaspoons vanilla extract
1 (3½-ounce) jar macadamia
nuts, coarsely chopped
2 cups whipping cream

Place chocolate morsels in top of a double boiler; bring water to a boil. Reduce heat to low; cook until chocolate melts, stirring often. Remove from heat, and set aside.

Combine crushed wafers and butter. Firmly press mixture in bottom of a lightly buttered 9-inch springform pan.

Combine melted chocolate, cream cheese, sugar, and vanilla in a mixing bowl; beat at medium speed of an electric mixer until smooth. Fold in macadamia nuts.

Beat whipping cream at high speed of an electric mixer until soft peaks form. Add about one-fourth of whipped cream to chocolate mixture, and beat until blended. Fold remaining whipped cream into chocolate mixture. Pour into crust. Cover and freeze 4 hours or until firm.

To serve, carefully remove sides of springform pan; let pie stand 10 minutes before serving. Yield: one 9-inch pie.

Azaleas to Zucchini
Smith County Medical Society Alliance
Tyler, Texas

Five-Nut Caramel Tart

This dessert is picture-perfect: A tender pastry crust contains the buttery honey-kissed filling of cashews, macadamia nuts, almonds, pistachios, and pine nuts. Serve rich wedges of tart with a complementary cupful of an extra-special coffee or tea.

1½ cups all-purpose flour
½ cup unsalted butter, cut into 1-inch pieces
¼ cup plus 1 tablespoon sugar, divided
2 egg yolks, lightly beaten
1 tablespoon cold water
½ cup unsalted butter
½ cup firmly packed dark brown sugar

¼ cup honey
1 cup salted roasted whole cashews
⅔ cup macadamia nuts
½ cup whole blanched almonds
⅓ cup pistachio nuts
¼ cup pine nuts
2 tablespoons whipping cream
¼ cup (1½ ounces) semisweet chocolate morsels (optional)

Position knife blade in food processor bowl; add flour, ½ cup butter pieces, and 3 tablespoons sugar. Pulse 12 times or until mixture is crumbly. Combine egg yolks and water; add to flour mixture, and process just until dough begins to leave sides of bowl and forms a ball. Cover and chill 30 minutes.

Roll dough to ⅛-inch thickness on a lightly floured surface. Fit pastry into a 9-inch tart pan; trim off excess pastry along edges. Cover and chill thoroughly.

Line pastry shell with aluminum foil; fill with pie weights or dried beans. Bake at 375° for 10 minutes. Remove pie weights and aluminum foil; bake 10 additional minutes.

Combine remaining 2 tablespoons sugar, ½ cup butter, brown sugar, and honey in a medium-size heavy saucepan. Cook over medium heat, stirring constantly, until mixture comes to a boil. Remove from heat. Stir in nuts and whipping cream. Pour mixture into prepared tart pan.

Bake at 350° for 20 minutes or until lightly browned and bubbly. If desired, sprinkle with chocolate morsels; let stand until softened enough to spread. Let cool completely on a wire rack. Yield: one 9-inch tart.

Special Selections of Ocala
Ocala Royal Dames for Cancer Research, Inc.
Ocala, Florida

Blueberry Tart

There's a double dose of plump blueberries hidden in this tart. A plentiful amount is sugared and baked in the filling; then more berries are sprinkled willy-nilly over the top. It's a blueberry bonanza!

1 cup all-purpose flour
2 tablespoons sugar
⅛ teaspoon salt
½ cup butter, cut into 1-inch pieces
1 tablespoon white vinegar
5 cups fresh blueberries, divided

⅔ cup sugar
3 tablespoons all-purpose flour
⅛ teaspoon ground cinnamon
½ cup whipping cream
2 teaspoons powdered sugar

Position knife blade in food processor bowl; add 1 cup flour, 2 tablespoons sugar, and salt, and process until combined. Add butter; process until mixture is crumbly. Sprinkle vinegar evenly over mixture; process just until dough begins to leave sides of bowl and forms a ball. Press mixture in bottom and 1¼ inches up sides of a buttered 9-inch springform pan.

Sprinkle 3 cups blueberries into prepared crust. Combine ⅔ cup sugar, 3 tablespoons flour, and cinnamon; sprinkle sugar mixture evenly over blueberries in crust. Bake on lowest rack of oven at 400° for 25 minutes. Remove from oven; gently stir sugar mixture into berries. Reduce oven temperature to 350°, and bake 15 additional minutes or until crust is lightly browned and filling is bubbly.

Remove pan to a wire rack. Sprinkle remaining 2 cups berries on top of filling; let cool completely on wire rack.

Beat whipping cream until foamy; gradually add powdered sugar, beating until soft peaks form. Serve tart with sweetened whipped cream. Yield: one 9-inch tart.

Albertina's Exceptional Recipes
Albertina's
Portland, Oregon

Apple Chimichangas

This rebel chimichanga takes a turn from its traditional savory filling and contains a sweet apple filling. It's also baked instead of fried. Top each serving with some ice cream, caramel sauce, and toasted pecans.

1 (6-ounce) package dried
  apples, coarsely chopped
1½ cups water
½ cup sugar
3 tablespoons butter or
  margarine
2 tablespoons lemon juice
1 teaspoon ground cinnamon

¼ teaspoon ground nutmeg
6 (8-inch) flour tortillas
Butter-flavored vegetable
  cooking spray
Vanilla ice cream
Caramel sauce (we tested with
  Smucker's)
Toasted chopped pecans

Combine apple and water in a large saucepan. Bring to a boil; reduce heat, and simmer, uncovered, 20 minutes or until apple is tender and most of liquid is absorbed.

Add sugar and next 4 ingredients; cook until butter melts, stirring often; set aside.

Heat tortillas according to package directions; coat both sides of each tortilla with cooking spray.

Spoon about ½ cup apple mixture down center of each tortilla. Fold in sides of each tortilla, forming a rectangle, and secure with wooden picks. Place tortillas, seam side down, on a baking sheet coated with cooking spray.

Bake at 450° for 10 minutes or until golden. Remove wooden picks before serving. Serve with ice cream, caramel sauce, and pecans. Serve immediately. Yield: 6 servings.

Moments, Memories & Manna
Restoration Village
Rogers, Arkansas

Mocha Profiteroles

These miniature cream puffs are filled from the bottom with mocha magic. If you prefer, remove the tops of the puffs to pipe in the filling. Either way, they demand a drizzle of the coffee-kissed chocolate sauce.

1 cup water
¾ cup unsalted butter, divided
1 cup all-purpose flour
¼ teaspoon salt
4 large eggs
1 large egg
1½ tablespoons instant coffee granules
¼ cup hot water

9 ounces milk chocolate, chopped (we tested with Ghirardelli)
1 tablespoon Kahlùa
2½ cups whipping cream, divided
1 cup sugar
¾ cup Dutch process cocoa
1 teaspoon instant coffee granules

Combine 1 cup water and ¼ cup butter in a medium saucepan; bring to a boil. Reduce heat to medium-high; add flour and salt, all at once, stirring vigorously until mixture leaves sides of pan and forms a smooth ball. Remove from heat, and let cool 5 minutes.

Add 4 eggs, one at a time, beating thoroughly with a wooden spoon after each addition; beat until dough is smooth.

Spoon dough into a pastry bag fitted with a medium-size round tip. Pipe dough into 1½-inch rounds on lightly greased baking sheets.

Beat remaining egg well. Brush rounds lightly with beaten egg. Bake at 400° for 30 minutes or until puffed and browned. Let cool completely on wire racks away from drafts.

Dissolve 1½ tablespoons coffee granules in ¼ cup hot water. Combine coffee mixture, chocolate, and Kahlùa in top of a double boiler; bring water to a boil. Reduce heat to low; cook until chocolate melts. Remove from heat, and let cool to room temperature.

Beat 1½ cups whipping cream until soft peaks form. Gently fold whipped cream into chocolate mixture. Spoon chocolate mixture into a large pastry bag fitted with a small round tip. Quickly make a hole in bottom of pastries with piping tip, and pipe in filling.

Combine sugar, cocoa, and 1 teaspoon coffee granules in a heavy saucepan. Stir in remaining 1 cup whipping cream. Cook over medium heat until sugar and cocoa dissolve. Add remaining ½ cup butter; cook 5 minutes, stirring constantly, or until cocoa mixture is smooth.

To serve, spoon about 2 tablespoons sauce onto each individual dessert plate. Set 2 or 3 profiteroles on top of sauce, and drizzle with additional sauce. Serve any leftover sauce over ice cream or pound cake. Yield: 22 profiteroles.

Malibu's Cooking Again
Malibu's Cooking Again
Malibu, California

Puff Pastry Pears

Cascade caramel sauce over these pastry-encrusted pears for a divine dessert experience. Substitute your favorite chocolate or raspberry sauce for equal pleasure.

1 (17¼-ounce) package frozen puff pastry sheets
8 small ripe pears
½ cup (3 ounces) semisweet chocolate morsels
¼ cup all-purpose flour, divided

1 large egg, beaten
1 tablespoon water
Caramel sauce (we tested with Smucker's)

Thaw puff pastry according to package directions.

Peel pears, leaving stems intact. Make a large scoop from the bottom of each pear, using the large side of a melon baller ; reserve. Scoop out core and seeds, using the small side of melon baller; discard. Fill each pear cavity with 1 tablespoon chocolate morsels. Replace large scoop from bottom of each pear to seal cavity.

Dust work surface with 2 tablespoons flour. Unfold each puff pastry sheet, and roll out with a rolling pin to smooth. Sprinkle pastry sheets with remaining 2 tablespoons flour to prevent sticking.

Cut each pastry sheet into quarters; place a pear in center of each pastry square. Bring up edges of pastry, wrapping around pear; leave stem exposed at top. Combine egg and water, and brush over pastry.

Place pears on ungreased baking sheets. Bake at 425° for 15 minutes. Reduce oven temperature to 375°; bake 5 additional minutes or until pastry is puffed and golden. Serve immediately with warm caramel sauce. Yield: 8 servings.

Capital Celebrations
The Junior League of Washington, DC

Arant Clan's Cobbler

2 cups sugar
2 cups water
½ cup shortening
1½ cups self-rising flour
⅓ cup milk

2 cups finely chopped Granny
  Smith apple
1 teaspoon ground cinnamon
½ cup butter, melted
Vanilla ice cream (optional)

Combine sugar and water in a small saucepan; cook over medium heat until sugar dissolves, stirring occasionally. Set aside.

Cut shortening into flour with a pastry blender until mixture is crumbly. Sprinkle milk over dry ingredients, stirring just until dry ingredients are moistened. Turn out dough onto a floured surface; knead 4 or 5 times. Roll dough into an 8- x 10-inch rectangle.

Sprinkle apple evenly over dough; sprinkle cinnamon over apple. Roll up dough, jellyroll fashion, starting at long side; dampen edges of dough, and press together to seal. Cut into 16 slices.

Pour butter into an ungreased 13- x 9- x 2-inch baking dish. Place dough slices in pan, cut side down; pour reserved sugar syrup carefully around slices. Bake at 350° for 55 minutes. Let cool 5 minutes before serving. Serve with ice cream, if desired. Yield: 8 servings.

Food for Thought
Northeast Louisiana Chapter, Autism Society of America
Monroe, Louisiana

Poultry

A Few Good Hens with Orange Sauce, page 258

Tarragon and Garlic Roasted Chicken

Roasting chicken in a tightly covered casserole keeps it moist and tasty. A fresh tarragon- and garlic-infused butter tucked under the skin deliciously permeates the meat.

1 (3½-pound) roasting chicken	½ teaspoon salt
6 cloves garlic, divided	¼ teaspoon freshly ground
¾ cup unsalted butter,	pepper
softened	¼ teaspoon salt
2 tablespoons minced fresh	¼ teaspoon pepper
tarragon	Garnish: fresh tarragon leaves
1 tablespoon grated lemon rind	

Remove giblets and neck from chicken; reserve for another use. Rinse chicken thoroughly under cold water, and pat dry with paper towels.

Crush 4 cloves garlic. Combine crushed garlic, butter, and next 4 ingredients. Cut remaining 2 cloves garlic in half. Place 4 garlic halves into cavity of chicken. Loosen skin from chicken breast by running fingers between the two; do not totally detach skin. Spread butter mixture under skin on chicken. Spread any remaining butter mixture over outside of skin. Sprinkle with ¼ teaspoon salt and ¼ teaspoon pepper.

Place chicken in a lightly greased 3-quart casserole or Dutch oven. Insert meat thermometer into meaty portion of thigh, making sure it does not touch bone. Cover and bake at 425° for 1 hour or until thermometer registers 180°. Garnish, if desired. Yield: 4 to 6 servings.

Treasures of the Great Midwest
The Junior League of Wyandotte and Johnson Counties
Kansas City, Kansas

Spicy Roast Chicken

Zippy lime juice, pungent fresh ginger, and nutty cumin, along with feisty red and black pepper, form the mélange of flavor that infuses this bird.

1 (3-pound) broiler-fryer	2 teaspoons grated fresh ginger
1 (8-ounce) carton plain yogurt	1 teaspoon ground cumin
⅓ cup lime juice	½ teaspoon ground red pepper
3 cloves garlic, minced	¼ teaspoon black pepper

Remove giblets and neck from chicken; reserve for another use. Rinse chicken thoroughly under cold water, and pat dry with paper towels. Place chicken in a large heavy-duty, zip-top plastic bag.

Combine yogurt and remaining 6 ingredients; pour into cavity of chicken. Seal bag securely. Turn bag to allow marinade to flow out of cavity and coat chicken. Marinate in refrigerator 8 hours, turning bag occasionally.

Remove chicken from marinade, reserving ½ cup marinade. Bring reserved marinade to a boil in a small saucepan; set aside.

Place chicken on a lightly greased rack in broiler pan. Insert meat thermometer into meaty portion of thigh, making sure it does not touch bone. Bake, uncovered, at 375° for 1 hour and 10 minutes or until thermometer registers 180°, basting with reserved marinade after 30 minutes. Let chicken stand 15 minutes before carving. Yield: 4 servings.   Suzanne Sharron

A Cookbook
Life Education Department of the Cheshire Center of
Applied Science & Technology at Keene High School
Keene, New Hampshire

Thai Barbecue Chicken

A leisurely soak in an Asian blend of curry and coconut milk bathes this chicken with signature flavors of Thai cuisine. Chile paste adds subtle warmth to the accompanying apricot sauce.

½ cup coconut milk
1 tablespoon sugar
2 teaspoons curry powder
1 teaspoon salt
1 teaspoon ground turmeric
¼ teaspoon pepper
3 tablespoons minced fresh
 cilantro

3 tablespoons minced garlic
1 tablespoon minced onion
1 (4-pound) broiler-fryer,
 quartered
Apricot Sauce

Combine first 9 ingredients in a large heavy-duty, zip-top plastic bag; seal bag securely, and shake until blended. Add chicken; reseal bag securely, and turn to coat chicken. Marinate in refrigerator 8 hours, turning bag occasionally.

Remove chicken from marinade, discarding marinade. Place chicken, skin side up, on a lightly greased rack in broiler pan. Bake, uncovered, at 350° for 1 hour or until done. Serve with warm Apricot Sauce. Yield: 4 servings.

Apricot Sauce

½ cup apricot preserves or jam
¼ cup apricot nectar

1 teaspoon Thai chile paste (we
 tested with Dynasty)

Combine all ingredients in a small saucepan. Cook over medium-high heat, stirring constantly, until mixture comes to a boil. Remove from heat; let cool slightly. Yield: ¾ cup.   Mickey Harris Chapter

60 Years of Serving
The Assistance League of San Pedro-Palos Verdes
San Pedro, California

Lemon-Kissed Chicken

1 cup all-purpose flour
2 teaspoons salt
2 teaspoons paprika
1 large egg, beaten
2 cloves garlic, minced
1 tablespoon grated lemon rind
¼ cup fresh lemon juice
¼ cup butter or margarine
2½ to 3½ pounds assorted
   chicken pieces

Combine first 3 ingredients; set aside. Combine egg and next 3 ingredients; set aside. Melt butter in a roasting pan in a 400° oven. Dip chicken in egg mixture; dredge in flour mixture. Place chicken, skin side down, in pan. Bake at 400° for 1 hour or until done, turning chicken after 30 minutes. Yield: 4 to 6 servings.   Tricia Yee

Incredible Edibles
Missionary Temple CME Church
San Francisco, California

Chicken and Peaches Polynesian

3 pounds assorted chicken
   pieces
1 (29-ounce) can sliced peaches
   in lite syrup, undrained
1 (16-ounce) can whole
   tomatoes, undrained
1 small onion, chopped
⅔ cup chopped green pepper
1 clove garlic, minced
2 tablespoons butter, melted
¼ cup apple cider vinegar
2 tablespoons prepared
   mustard
2 tablespoons steak sauce
1½ teaspoons salt
¼ teaspoon pepper

Place chicken on a greased rack in broiler pan. Broil 5½ inches from heat (with electric oven door partially opened) 15 minutes.

Position knife blade in food processor bowl; add peaches and tomatoes, and process until smooth. Cook onion, green pepper, and garlic in butter in a large Dutch oven over medium heat, stirring constantly, until tender. Add chicken, peach mixture, vinegar, and remaining ingredients. Simmer, uncovered, 50 minutes or until done. Yield: 4 to 6 servings.   Sandra Jordin

Recipes & Remembrances
Women of Opportunity Presbyterian Church
Spokane, Washington

Maple Syrup Chicken

A savory tomato sauce is sweetened with maple syrup and plump raisins for an entrée reminiscent of Country Captain Chicken.

1 cup real maple syrup
1 (8-ounce) can tomato sauce
4 cloves garlic, crushed
2 tablespoons red wine vinegar
1 tablespoon vegetable oil
1 tablespoon soy sauce
2 teaspoons curry powder
1 teaspoon dried marjoram
½ teaspoon salt
½ teaspoon pepper

3 pounds assorted chicken
  pieces
2 stalks celery, diced
1 green pepper, diced
1 medium onion, diced
¼ cup diced fresh mushrooms
¼ cup raisins
¼ cup slivered almonds
Hot cooked rice

Combine first 10 ingredients in a large heavy-duty, zip-top plastic bag; add chicken. Seal bag securely; turn to coat chicken. Marinate in refrigerator 4 hours, turning bag occasionally.

Place chicken and marinade in a Dutch oven; bring to a boil. Reduce heat to low; cover and simmer 30 minutes. Add celery and next 5 ingredients; cover and simmer 30 additional minutes. Serve over rice. Yield: 4 to 6 servings.   Kathleen Thompson

Our Favorite Recipes
The Claremont Society for the Prevention of Cruelty to Animals
Claremont, New Hampshire

Mexican Chicken

The mystery ingredient lending authenticity to this Mexican main dish is unsweetened chocolate. It provides a traditional touch to the spicy tomato sauce.

3 pounds assorted chicken
  pieces
1 green pepper, chopped
1 medium onion, chopped
1 tablespoon vegetable oil
2 (8-ounce) cans tomato sauce
1 clove garlic, minced

½ (1-ounce) square
  unsweetened chocolate
½ teaspoon salt
2 teaspoons chili powder
Dash of ground cloves
¼ to ½ teaspoon hot sauce

Arrange chicken in an ungreased 13- x 9- x 2-inch pan; broil 5½ inches from heat (with electric oven door partially opened) until browned, turning once. Remove from oven; set aside, and keep warm.

Cook green pepper and onion in oil in a large skillet over medium heat, stirring constantly until tender. Reduce heat; stir in tomato sauce and remaining 6 ingredients. Cook, stirring constantly, until chocolate melts. Pour over chicken. Cover and bake at 350° for 30 minutes or until done. Yield: 4 to 6 servings.   Isabel Sobol

A Gardener Cooks
Danbury Garden Club
New Milford, Connecticut

Pollo à la Catalona

Chicken pieces simmer to tenderness in an intense mixture that includes tomatoes, olives, peppers, and zucchini.

3 pounds assorted chicken pieces	1 clove garlic, chopped
½ teaspoon salt	4 tomatoes, peeled, seeded, and chopped
½ teaspoon pepper	1 cup fresh mushrooms, chopped
¼ cup olive oil	½ cup chopped prosciutto or smoked ham
3 medium zucchini, sliced	
2 large onions, sliced	6 pitted green olives, halved
2 green peppers, cut into strips	6 pitted ripe olives, halved
1 sweet red pepper, cut into strips	

Sprinkle chicken with salt and pepper; cook in oil in a large Dutch oven over medium-high heat until browned, turning once. Remove from pan, reserving drippings in pan; set aside. Add zucchini and next 4 ingredients to pan; cook 8 minutes or until tender, stirring often. Add tomato, mushrooms, and prosciutto; cook until thickened, stirring often. Return chicken to pan; spoon sauce over chicken. Cover and simmer 20 minutes or until done. Stir in olives. Yield: 4 to 6 servings.   Andrea Sparenberg

Howey Cook
Howey-in-the-Hills Garden and Civic Club
Howey-in-the-Hills, Florida

East-West Chicken

6 whole chicken breasts, boned and butterflied
½ cup teriyaki sauce
½ pound lean ground pork
⅓ cup fine, dry breadcrumbs (store-bought)
¼ cup milk
2 tablespoons chopped green onions
2 tablespoons chopped water chestnuts
2 tablespoons soy sauce
1 large egg, lightly beaten
¼ teaspoon ground ginger
2 tablespoons butter, melted

Place chicken breasts and teriyaki sauce in a large heavy-duty, zip-top plastic bag; seal bag securely, and turn to coat chicken. Marinate in refrigerator 1 hour.

Combine pork and next 7 ingredients in a medium bowl, stirring well. Remove chicken from marinade, reserving 2 tablespoons marinade. Place chicken breasts, skin side down, on a flat surface; divide pork mixture evenly among chicken breasts. Roll up chicken, jellyroll fashion, starting with short side; secure with wooden picks. Place chicken, skin side up, in a greased 13- x 9- x 2-inch pan. Combine butter and reserved marinade; set aside. Bake, uncovered, at 350° for 1 hour or until done, basting often with butter mixture and pan drippings. Yield: 6 servings.   Sara Jones

Blue Stocking Club Forget-Me-Not Recipes
Blue Stocking Club
Bristol, Tennessee

Squash Stuffed Chicken

A moist breadcrumb stuffing is laced with shreds of zucchini and Swiss cheese, and then plumped like a pillow under the chicken breast skin.

½ cup chopped onion
1 tablespoon chopped fresh parsley
½ teaspoon dried basil
3 tablespoons butter, melted
2 medium zucchini, shredded (about 3 cups)
2¼ cups soft breadcrumbs
1 large egg, lightly beaten
¾ cup (3 ounces) shredded Swiss cheese
½ teaspoon salt
⅛ teaspoon pepper
4 chicken breast halves

Cook onion, parsley, and basil in butter in a skillet over medium heat, stirring constantly, until tender. Add zucchini; cook 2 minutes, stirring often. Stir in breadcrumbs and next 4 ingredients.

Loosen skin from chicken breast by running fingers between the two; do not totally detach skin. Stuff zucchini mixture under skin. Place stuffed chicken breast halves, skin side up, in a lightly greased 13- x 9- x 2-inch baking dish. Bake, uncovered, at 375° for 50 minutes or until done. Yield: 4 servings.   Ruth Lightner

Memorial Hospital Associates Favorites
Memorial Hospital Activities Committee
York, Pennsylvania

Pistachio Chicken with Fresh Peaches

This company-worthy fare features a swirl of prosciutto tucked inside pistachio-encrusted rolls of chicken breast.

4 **skinned and boned chicken breast halves**
2 **tablespoons Dijon mustard**
¾ **cup chopped pistachio nuts, divided**
4 **(1-ounce) slices prosciutto**
2 **tablespoons all-purpose flour**
1 **teaspoon chopped fresh tarragon**

1 **large egg, lightly beaten**
¼ **cup plus 2 tablespoons butter or margarine, melted**
3 **medium-size fresh ripe peaches, peeled and sliced**
¼ **cup dry white wine**

Place each chicken breast half between two sheets of wax paper, and flatten to ¼-inch thickness, using a meat mallet or rolling pin. Spread mustard on 1 side of each breast half. Sprinkle with half of nuts.

Place 1 slice prosciutto over nuts. Roll up, jellyroll fashion, starting with short side; secure with wooden picks. Combine remaining nuts, flour, and tarragon. Dip chicken in egg; dredge in nut mixture. Pour butter in a 13- x 9- x 2-inch baking dish. Place chicken, seam side down, in dish. Bake, uncovered, at 375° for 20 minutes. Add peaches and wine; bake 15 additional minutes or until done. Yield: 4 servings.

Call to Post
Lexington Hearing and Speech Center
Lexington, Kentucky

Grilled Chicken with Corn Salsa

Sprinkle these sizzling beer-lime-jalapeño marinated chicken breasts with some kicky corn salsa as they come off the grill.

4 skinned and boned chicken breast halves
½ cup light beer
1 tablespoon chopped fresh cilantro
1 tablespoon low-sodium soy sauce
2 teaspoons seeded, minced jalapeño pepper
2 teaspoons fresh lime juice
¼ teaspoon salt

¼ teaspoon pepper
1¼ cups frozen whole kernel corn, thawed
¼ cup chopped purple onion
¼ cup chopped sweet red pepper
¼ cup chopped fresh cilantro
1½ tablespoons fresh lime juice
2 teaspoons seeded, minced jalapeño pepper

Place chicken in a large heavy-duty, zip-top plastic bag. Combine beer and next 6 ingredients; pour over chicken. Seal bag securely; turn to coat chicken. Marinate in refrigerator at least 1 hour, turning bag occasionally.

Meanwhile, combine corn and remaining 5 ingredients; stir well. Cover and chill.

Remove chicken from marinade, discarding marinade. Grill chicken, covered, over medium-hot coals (350° to 400°) 5 minutes on each side or until done. Cut chicken diagonally into thin slices. Top evenly with salsa mixture. Yield: 4 servings.

Women Who Can Dish It Out
The Junior League of Springfield, Missouri

Three-Citrus Grilled Chicken

Three citrus stars—lemon, lime, and orange—add their refreshing essence to this chicken combo. Honey, cumin, cinnamon, and fresh mint tame the tanginess.

¼ cup olive oil
¼ cup honey
3 tablespoons chopped fresh mint or 3 teaspoons dried mint
2 tablespoons grated lemon rind
1 tablespoon grated orange rind
1¼ teaspoons grated lime rind
½ cup fresh lemon juice
⅓ cup fresh orange juice
3 tablespoons fresh lime juice
¼ teaspoon ground cumin
¼ teaspoon ground cinnamon
⅛ teaspoon salt
⅛ teaspoon pepper
4 chicken breast halves
½ cup vertically sliced purple onion

Combine first 13 ingredients in a large bowl, stirring well. Reserve ½ cup marinade; cover and chill. Add chicken and onion to remaining marinade in bowl. Cover and marinate in refrigerator 8 hours, turning chicken occasionally.

Remove chicken from marinade; pour marinade into a medium saucepan. Bring to a boil; reduce heat, and simmer, uncovered, 5 minutes. Remove from heat.

Grill chicken, covered, over medium-hot coals (350° to 400°) 30 minutes or until chicken is done, turning occasionally and basting often with marinade.

Pour reserved ½ cup marinade into a small saucepan; cook over medium heat until thoroughly heated. Serve chicken with warm marinade. Yield: 4 servings.

Exchanging Tastes
The Depot
Midland Park, New Jersey

Chicken Taj Mahal

¾ cup apple juice
½ cup long-grain rice, uncooked
¼ cup dried fruit mix
1 stalk celery, chopped
2 tablespoons chopped onion

2 teaspoons curry powder, divided
4 skinned chicken breast halves
2 tablespoons plain yogurt
1 tablespoon tamari
½ teaspoon salt

Combine first 5 ingredients in a 13- x 9- x 2-inch baking dish; stir well. Sprinkle with 1 teaspoon curry powder. Place chicken breast halves over rice mixture.

Combine remaining 1 teaspoon curry powder, yogurt, tamari, and salt; spread evenly over chicken. Bake, uncovered, at 350° for 45 minutes. Uncover and bake 30 additional minutes or until chicken is done. Yield: 4 servings.   Sarah Winters

H.E.A.L. of Michiana Cookbook: A Collection of
Health Conscious Recipes
The Human Ecology Action League of Michiana
Stevensville, Michigan

Kiva Chicken with Red Chile Glaze

Slather these southwestern-inspired chicken breast halves with a fiery-sweet red jalapeño pepper jelly glaze, and then scatter tangy crumbles of goat cheese atop.

⅓ cup all-purpose flour
½ teaspoon salt
½ teaspoon freshly ground pepper
6 skinned and boned chicken breast halves
½ cup finely chopped celery
¼ cup finely chopped onion
2 tablespoons chopped fresh parsley

¼ cup olive oil
2 tablespoons butter, melted
2 tablespoons chicken broth or water
2 tablespoons dry vermouth
¾ cup red jalapeño pepper jelly
1 (3.5-ounce) package goat cheese, crumbled

Combine first 3 ingredients. Dredge chicken in flour mixture, and set aside.

Cook celery, onion, and parsley in oil and butter in a medium skillet over medium-high heat, stirring constantly, 5 minutes or until tender. Remove from skillet with a slotted spoon; set aside.

Add chicken to pan drippings, and cook 6 minutes on each side or until browned. Sprinkle celery mixture evenly over each chicken breast. Add chicken broth and vermouth. Bring to a boil; cover, reduce heat, and simmer 5 minutes or until chicken is done. Remove chicken to a serving platter; top with vegetable mixture.

Melt jelly in a small saucepan over medium heat. Spoon jelly over chicken and vegetables; sprinkle with cheese. Yield: 6 servings.

Colorado Collage
The Junior League of Denver, Colorado

Margarita Chicken

Peak inside the aluminum foil packets and you'll find succulent chicken breast halves soaking in the must-have elements of a classic margarita–tequila and lime juice.

4 **skinned and boned chicken breast halves**
2 **tablespoons finely chopped poblano chile pepper**
4 **teaspoons tequila**
1 **teaspoon grated lime rind**
1 **tablespoon fresh lime juice**
1 **tablespoon vegetable oil**

2 **teaspoons chopped fresh parsley**
1 **teaspoon chopped fresh tarragon**
1 **teaspoon honey**
½ **teaspoon salt**
¼ **teaspoon freshly ground pepper**

Place chicken in a large heavy-duty, zip-top plastic bag. Combine poblano chile pepper and remaining 9 ingredients; pour over chicken. Seal bag securely; turn to coat chicken. Marinate in refrigerator 8 hours, turning bag occasionally.

Remove chicken from marinade, discarding marinade. Place each chicken breast half on a piece of aluminum foil. Fold foil edges over to seal securely. Place packets on an ungreased baking sheet. Bake at 450° for 20 minutes or until chicken is done. Yield: 4 servings.

Celebrate Chicago! A Taste of Our Town
The Junior League of Chicago, Illinois

Crispy Potato Chicken

Golden shreds of russet potato cuddle up against mustard-garlic coated chicken to create a crispy coating.

1 (8-ounce) russet potato, peeled and coarsely shredded
4 skinned chicken breast halves
3 to 4 tablespoons Dijon mustard
2 cloves garlic, minced
1 teaspoon olive oil
½ teaspoon salt
½ teaspoon freshly ground pepper
2 tablespoons chopped fresh parsley, cilantro, rosemary, or thyme

Place shredded potato in a bowl of ice water; set aside.

Place chicken, breast side up, in an aluminum foil-lined 13- x 9- x 2-inch pan. Combine mustard and garlic; spread evenly over meaty side of chicken.

Drain potato, and pat dry with paper towels. Combine potato and oil in a bowl; toss well. Top each piece of chicken evenly with potato mixture; sprinkle with salt and pepper.

Bake, uncovered, at 425° for 45 minutes or until chicken is done and potato is golden. If desired, broil 5½ inches from heat (with electric oven door partially opened) 5 minutes or until browned. Sprinkle with parsley. Yield: 4 servings.

Beyond Burlap, Idaho's Famous Potato Recipes
The Junior League of Boise, Idaho

Chicken Scampi

½ cup olive oil
¼ cup lemon juice
2 cloves garlic, minced
1 teaspoon salt
1 teaspoon dry mustard
½ teaspoon pepper
¼ cup chopped fresh parsley
¼ teaspoon dried basil
¼ teaspoon dried oregano
1½ pounds skinned and boned chicken breast halves, cut into bite-size pieces
½ cup Italian-seasoned breadcrumbs
Hot cooked rice

Combine first 9 ingredients in a large heavy-duty, zip-top plastic bag; add chicken pieces. Seal bag securely, and turn to coat chicken pieces with marinade. Marinate chicken in refrigerator 1½ hours, turning bag occasionally.

Place chicken and marinade in an ungreased 9-inch square pan; sprinkle with breadcrumbs. Bake, uncovered, at 350° for 25 minutes or until chicken is done. Serve chicken and pan juices over rice. Yield: 4 servings.

Alberta Picozzi

Newport Cooks & Collects
The Preservation Society of Newport County
Newport, Rhode Island

Chicken and Sausages

4 mild link Italian sausages, cut into ½-inch pieces
3 cloves garlic, minced
2 tablespoons olive oil
½ teaspoon salt
6 skinned and boned chicken breast halves
½ cup dry white wine
1 green pepper, cut into strips
1 sweet red pepper, cut into strips

1 cup sliced mushrooms
1 medium onion, coarsely chopped
½ cup chopped ripe olives
¼ cup minced fresh basil
2 tablespoons minced fresh tarragon
⅛ teaspoon pepper
Hot cooked rice

Brown sausage in a Dutch oven, stirring occasionally. Add garlic and olive oil, and cook over medium-high heat 2 minutes, stirring often; remove and discard garlic. Sprinkle salt over chicken, and add chicken to pan; cook 5 minutes on each side or until browned. Remove chicken and sausage, reserving drippings in pan. Set chicken and sausage aside, and keep warm.

Add wine to drippings; cook 2 minutes, scraping particles that cling to bottom of pan. Add chicken, sausage, green pepper, and next 7 ingredients. Cover, reduce heat, and simmer 20 minutes or until chicken is done. Serve over rice. Yield: 6 servings.   Barbara Bundy

Tasty Temptations
Our Lady of the Mountains Church
Sierra Vista, Arizona

Cobb Sandwiches

4 skinned and boned chicken breast halves
½ teaspoon salt
½ teaspoon pepper
¼ cup olive oil
¼ cup balsamic vinegar
1 tablespoon Dijon mustard
Vegetable cooking spray
1 ripe avocado
1 teaspoon fresh lemon juice
⅓ cup mayonnaise
8 slices challah or other egg bread, toasted
4 Boston lettuce leaves
1 tomato, thinly sliced
8 ounces blue cheese, thinly sliced
8 slices bacon, cooked and crumbled

Sprinkle chicken with salt and pepper; place in a shallow dish.

Combine oil, vinegar, and mustard; pour over chicken. Cover chicken, and marinate in refrigerator at least 30 minutes, turning occasionally. Drain, discarding marinade.

Coat grill rack with cooking spray; place on grill over medium-hot coals (350° to 400°). Grill chicken, covered, 5 minutes on each side or until done. Let chicken stand until cool to touch; cut chicken diagonally into thin slices.

Slice avocado, and sprinkle with lemon juice. Spread mayonnaise evenly on 1 side of each bread slice. Layer 4 slices of bread with lettuce, tomato, avocado, cheese, bacon, and chicken; top with remaining bread slices. Yield: 4 servings.

Landmark Entertaining
The Junior League of Abilene, Texas

Oyster Chicken

Fried chicken wings benefit from a generous dose of Asian oyster sauce. Thighs work well in this recipe, too. Simply fry as directed 14 minutes or until they're done.

2 pounds chicken wings
¼ cup all-purpose flour
Vegetable oil
½ cup oyster sauce
⅓ cup water
2 tablespoons sugar
½ teaspoon salt
½ teaspoon pepper
Garnishes: green onions, fresh cilantro sprigs

Cut off and discard chicken wingtips; cut wings in half at joint. Dredge in flour.

Pour oil to depth of ½ inch into a large heavy skillet; heat to 350°. Fry chicken in hot oil 14 minutes or until done. Drain and place in a serving dish.

Combine oyster sauce and next 4 ingredients in a small saucepan. Cook over low heat until sugar dissolves, stirring occasionally. Pour sauce over chicken, and toss to coat. Garnish, if desired. Yield: 4 servings.   Doris Harada

From ANNA's Kitchen
Adams-Normandie Neighborhood Association (ANNA)
Los Angeles, California

Chicken Liver Stroganoff

½ cup all-purpose flour
1 teaspoon salt
1 pound chicken livers
½ cup vegetable oil
2 medium onions, thinly sliced
  and separated into rings
½ cup water

1 teaspoon lemon-pepper
  seasoning
1 teaspoon dried parsley flakes
1 teaspoon pepper
1 (8-ounce) carton sour cream
Toast points or hot cooked egg
  noodles

Combine flour and salt; dredge chicken livers in flour mixture. Fry livers in hot oil in a large skillet over medium-high heat until browned, turning occasionally. Remove livers from skillet; add onion, and cook, stirring constantly, until tender and browned. Remove onion, and carefully drain excess oil from skillet.

Return livers and onion to skillet. Add water and next 3 ingredients. Bring to a boil; reduce heat, and simmer, uncovered, 5 minutes. Stir in sour cream, and cook until thoroughly heated (do not boil). Serve immediately over toast points or noodles. Yield: 4 servings.

Have You Heard . . . A Tasteful Medley of Memphis
Subsidium, Inc.
Memphis, Tennessee

A Few Good Hens with Orange Sauce

We love this title and this recipe. The gingery-orange glaze elevates these birds to special-occasion status.

4 (1½- to 2-pound) Cornish hens
1 teaspoon salt
2 tablespoons butter, melted
⅔ cup orange marmalade, divided

2 tablespoons butter
2 tablespoons all-purpose flour
¼ teaspoon ground ginger
1 cup milk
Hot cooked rice pilaf
Garnish: orange slices

Remove giblets from hens; reserve for another use. Rinse hens thoroughly under cold water, and pat dry with paper towels. Rub salt inside cavity of each hen. Place hens, breast side up, on a lightly greased rack in a shallow roasting pan; tie ends of legs together with string. Brush with 2 tablespoons melted butter. Bake, uncovered, at 350° for 1 hour. Brush hens with ⅓ cup orange marmalade, and bake 15 additional minutes or until done.

Melt 2 tablespoons butter in a small heavy saucepan over low heat; add flour and ginger, stirring until smooth. Cook 1 minute, stirring constantly. Gradually add milk; cook over medium heat, stirring constantly, until thickened and bubbly. Stir in remaining ⅓ cup marmalade. Serve Cornish hens over rice pilaf with sauce. Garnish, if desired. Yield: 4 servings.

Waiting to Inhale
Pacific Coast Mothers Club
Huntington Beach, California

Roasted Duck with Hot-and-Sour Chutney

2 (5-pound) dressed ducklings
½ lemon
1 teaspoon salt

½ teaspoon freshly ground
    pepper
Hot-and-Sour Chutney

Remove giblets and neck from ducklings; reserve for another use. Rinse ducklings thoroughly under cold water, and pat dry with paper towels. Rub ducklings with lemon half, squeezing juice over ducklings and into cavities; sprinkle cavities and skin with salt and pepper.

Place ducklings, breast side up, on a lightly greased rack in broiler pan. Insert meat thermometer into meaty portion of thigh, making sure it does not touch fat or bone. Bake, uncovered, at 350° for 2 hours or until thermometer registers 180°. Transfer ducklings to a serving platter; let stand 10 minutes before carving. Serve with warm Hot-and-Sour Chutney. Yield: 6 servings.

Hot-and-Sour Chutney

¾ cup minced purple onion
½ cup minced sweet red pepper
1 tablespoon minced fresh
    ginger
1 jalapeño pepper, minced
1 clove garlic, minced
1 tablespoon olive oil
½ cup currants
¼ cup firmly packed brown
    sugar
¼ cup white wine vinegar
1 teaspoon grated lemon rind

½ teaspoon salt
½ teaspoon ground red pepper
¼ teaspoon ground turmeric
¼ teaspoon dry mustard
2 medium Granny Smith
    apples, peeled and chopped
    (about 2 cups)
2 medium peaches, peeled and
    chopped (about ¾ cup)
1 medium-size ripe pear,
    peeled and chopped (about 1
    cup)

Cook first 5 ingredients in oil in a saucepan over medium-high heat, stirring constantly, 6 minutes or until tender. Add currants and next 7 ingredients. Reduce heat to medium; cook 10 minutes, stirring occasionally. Stir in apple, peach, and pear; cover, reduce heat to low, and cook 15 minutes, stirring often. Yield: 4 cups.

Texas Ties
The Junior League of North Harris County
Spring, Texas

Barbecued Duck Breasts on Sweet Corn Pancakes

This recipe is a Test Kitchens' favorite. Brush the sweet-sour barbecue sauce over the duck, and then grill to add just the right amount of smoky nuance. Serve the breasts atop corn-studded cornmeal pancakes to qualify this dish as four-star fare.

1 tablespoon minced garlic
1 tablespoon minced shallot
1 tablespoon minced fresh ginger
1 tablespoon dark sesame oil
½ cup soy sauce
½ cup barbecue sauce
¼ cup firmly packed brown sugar
¼ cup hoisin sauce
¼ cup rice wine vinegar
4 skinned and boned duck breast halves
Sweet Corn Pancakes

Cook first 3 ingredients in hot oil in a saucepan over medium-high heat, stirring constantly, until tender. Add soy sauce and next 4 ingredients; stir well. Reduce heat, and simmer, uncovered, 10 minutes, stirring occasionally. Let cool. Reserve ½ cup sauce.

Brush duck breasts with half of remaining 1 cup sauce. Grill duck, covered, over medium-hot coals (350° to 400°) 8 to 10 minutes or until done, turning once and basting often with remaining half of sauce. Let stand 5 minutes.

Cut duck diagonally across grain into thin slices. Arrange over Sweet Corn Pancakes; serve with reserved ½ cup sauce. Yield: 4 servings.

Sweet Corn Pancakes

1 (16-ounce) package frozen whole kernel corn, thawed and divided
2 large eggs, lightly beaten
¼ cup finely chopped onion
¼ cup finely chopped green onions
1 clove garlic, minced
¾ cup all-purpose flour
¼ cup yellow cornmeal
1 tablespoon baking powder
1½ teaspoons sugar
1½ teaspoons dried crushed red pepper
1 teaspoon salt

Position knife blade in food processor bowl; add half of corn. Process until pureed, stopping once to scrape down sides. Combine pureed corn, remaining whole kernel corn, eggs, and next 3 ingredients.

Combine flour and remaining 5 ingredients; stir well. Add corn mixture, stirring well. Cover and chill 2 hours.

Pour about ¼ cup batter for each pancake into a hot, lightly oiled skillet. Cook pancakes until tops are covered with bubbles and edges look cooked; turn and cook other side. Yield: 8 (4-inch) pancakes.

Great Lake Effects
The Junior League of Buffalo, New York

Turkey Scaloppine

1 **large onion, thinly sliced**
¼ **pound fresh mushrooms,**
   sliced
¼ **cup olive oil**
1 **(1½-pound) turkey breast**
⅓ **cup all-purpose flour**
1 **teaspoon salt**
¼ **teaspoon pepper**

1 **cup chicken broth**
3 **tablespoons lemon juice**
1 **large clove garlic, minced**
¼ **cup grated Parmesan cheese**
Hot cooked rice
2 **tablespoons chopped fresh**
   parsley

Cook onion and mushrooms in oil in a large nonstick skillet over medium-high heat, stirring constantly, until tender. Drain vegetables on paper towels, reserving drippings in skillet.

Cut turkey breast across grain into ¼-inch-thick strips. Combine flour, salt, and pepper in a large heavy-duty, zip-top plastic bag. Add turkey; seal bag securely, and shake to coat turkey.

Place skillet with reserved drippings over medium-high heat. Add turkey, and cook until browned on both sides. Transfer turkey and vegetables to a lightly greased 2-quart casserole, reserving drippings in skillet. Add chicken broth, lemon juice, and garlic to skillet; stir well, scraping particles that cling to bottom of skillet. Pour broth mixture over turkey mixture; sprinkle with cheese.

Bake, uncovered, at 350° for 20 minutes. Serve over rice, and sprinkle with parsley. Yield: 6 servings.

Albertina's Exceptional Recipes
Albertina's
Portland, Oregon

Miners' Turkey Burgers with Black Bean Salsa

These hefty burgers are miner-appetite worthy. If you aren't that famished, try serving the burgers atop lettuce leaves instead of a bun.

3 tablespoons olive oil, divided
½ small purple onion, minced
1 carrot, scraped and finely chopped
1 stalk celery, finely chopped
1 pound ground turkey
1 slice white bread, crumbled

1 (4.5-ounce) can chopped green chiles, drained
½ teaspoon salt
6 Boston lettuce leaves
6 (8-inch) hamburger buns, flour tortillas, or pita bread rounds, warmed
Black Bean Salsa

Heat 1 tablespoon oil in a skillet over medium heat; add onion. Cook 2 minutes, stirring often. Add 1 tablespoon oil, carrot, and celery; cook 10 minutes or until very tender, stirring often. Remove mixture to a large bowl; add turkey, bread, chiles, and salt; stir and shape into 6 (¾-inch-thick) patties.

Heat remaining 1 tablespoon oil in skillet over medium-high heat. Add patties; reduce heat, and cook 6 minutes on each side or until done.

Place lettuce leaves on bottom halves of buns; top with burgers, Black Bean Salsa, and top halves of buns. Yield: 6 servings.

Black Bean Salsa

2 tablespoons lime juice
1 tablespoon olive oil
½ teaspoon salt
¼ teaspoon coarsely ground pepper
1 (15-ounce) can black beans, rinsed and drained

1 (8¾-ounce) can whole kernel corn, drained
1 large tomato, seeded and diced
1 ripe avocado, diced
1 tablespoon minced purple onion

Combine first 4 ingredients in a bowl; stir in beans and remaining ingredients. Yield: 4 cups.

Shalom on the Range
Shalom Park
Aurora, Colorado

Salads

Cranberry-Eggnog Salad, page 265

Italian Ambrosia

Five fresh fruits mingle in a sweet blend of peach nectar and honey balanced with pungent balsamic vinegar and lemon juice. This blissful salad is special enough to serve as a light dessert.

1 medium cantaloupe, peeled, seeded, and cut into chunks
2 navel oranges, sectioned
2 cups fresh pineapple chunks
2 fresh plums, sliced
1 cup seedless green grapes
¾ cup peach nectar
¼ cup honey
2 tablespoons balsamic vinegar
2 tablespoons lemon juice

Combine first 5 ingredients in a large bowl. Combine peach nectar and remaining 3 ingredients, stirring with a wire whisk until blended. Pour dressing over fruit mixture, stirring gently to coat fruit. Cover and chill at least 1 hour, stirring occasionally. Yield: 8 servings.

Women Who Can Dish It Out
The Junior League of Springfield, Missouri

Banana Split Salad

1 (8-ounce) package cream cheese, softened
½ cup sugar
1 (20-ounce) can crushed pineapple in juice, drained
1 (10-ounce) package frozen strawberries in syrup, thawed and undrained
2 medium bananas, coarsely chopped
1 (12-ounce) carton frozen whipped topping, thawed
1 cup chopped walnuts

Combine cream cheese and sugar in a mixing bowl; beat at medium speed of an electric mixer until blended. Stir in pineapple, strawberries, and bananas. Gently fold in whipped topping and walnuts. Pour mixture into an ungreased 13- x 9- x 2-inch dish. Cover and freeze 8 hours. Let stand at room temperature 30 minutes before serving. Yield: 15 servings.   Ruby Pitman

The Great Delights Cookbook
Genoa Serbart United Methodist Churches
Genoa, Colorado

Champagne Fruit Salad

¾ cup white grape juice
4 (3-inch) sticks cinnamon
1 tablespoon honey
1 teaspoon grated orange rind
3 medium nectarines, sliced
3 kiwifruit, peeled and sliced

2 cups fresh strawberries, hulled, halved, and divided
1 cup seedless green grapes
1 cup seedless red grapes
½ cup champagne, chilled

Combine first 4 ingredients in a saucepan. Bring to a boil. Reduce heat; simmer, uncovered, 5 minutes, stirring occasionally. Discard cinnamon sticks; chill. Combine nectarine and next 4 ingredients. Combine grape juice mixture and champagne; pour over fruit. Yield: 12 servings.

Low-Fat Favorites
Tri-Valley Haven for Women
Livermore, California

Cranberry-Eggnog Salad

1 (8-ounce) can crushed pineapple, undrained
3 tablespoons lime juice
1 envelope unflavored gelatin
1½ cups eggnog
1½ cups cranberry juice drink
1 (3-ounce) package raspberry-flavored gelatin

1 (12-ounce) container cranberry-orange relish (we tested with Ocean Spray)
½ cup finely chopped celery
Garnishes: lettuce and celery leaves

Combine pineapple and lime juice in a saucepan. Sprinkle unflavored gelatin over mixture; let stand 1 minute. Cook over low heat, stirring 2 minutes or until gelatin dissolves; cool. Stir in eggnog. Pour into an ungreased 11- x 7- x 1½-inch dish. Cover and chill until firm.

Pour juice drink into a saucepan; bring to a boil. Place raspberry gelatin in a bowl; add juice drink, stirring 2 minutes or until gelatin dissolves. Chill until consistency of unbeaten egg white. Fold in relish and chopped celery. Carefully spoon over eggnog mixture. Chill until firm. Cut into squares. Garnish, if desired. Yield: 8 servings.

The Best of Mayberry
The Foothills Lions Club of Mount Airy, North Carolina

Mainline Marinated Asparagus

A hint of cinnamon, clove, and celery seed spices these tender asparagus spears with a flavor reminiscent of bread-and-butter pickles.

1 pound fresh asparagus
⅓ cup white vinegar
¼ cup sugar
¼ cup water

3 whole cloves
1 (3-inch) stick cinnamon
¼ teaspoon celery seeds
½ teaspoon salt

Snap off tough ends of asparagus. Remove scales from stalks with a vegetable peeler, if desired. Cook asparagus in boiling water to cover 10 seconds; drain and plunge into ice water to stop the cooking process. Drain well, and place in a large shallow dish.

Combine vinegar and remaining 6 ingredients in a small saucepan. Bring to a boil; reduce heat, and simmer, uncovered, 5 minutes, stirring occasionally. Remove and discard cloves and cinnamon stick. Pour hot vinegar mixture over asparagus. Cover and chill 8 hours. Yield: 6 servings.

Take the Tour
St. Paul's Episcopal Church Women
Edenton, North Carolina

Chutney-Broccoli Salad

1 (10-ounce) package fresh
  broccoli flowerets
5 cups seedless red grapes
  (about 1½ pounds)
1 cup slivered almonds,
  toasted

¾ cup chopped purple onion
2 cups mayonnaise
1 (9-ounce) jar mango chutney
2 tablespoons curry powder

Combine first 4 ingredients in a large bowl. Combine mayonnaise, chutney, and curry powder in a small bowl, stirring well.

Gently stir mayonnaise mixture into broccoli mixture. Cover and chill thoroughly. Yield: 12 servings.   Charlene Jones

Barnard 'Beary' Best Cookbook
Barnard United Methodist Youth Department
Barnard, Kansas

Piccalilli Corn Salad

This colorful corn combo is the perfect picnic companion. It makes enough for a crowd, but can easily be cut in half if you're planning a more intimate outing.

6 cups fresh whole kernel corn (about 12 ears)
1 cup peeled, diced cucumber
1 medium-size green pepper, finely chopped
1 medium tomato, finely chopped
¼ cup chopped purple onion
1 green onion, thinly sliced
3 tablespoons olive oil
2 tablespoons apple cider vinegar
1 teaspoon salt
½ teaspoon Dijon mustard
½ teaspoon minced garlic
½ teaspoon sugar
½ teaspoon pepper
⅛ teaspoon curry powder
2 tablespoons chopped fresh parsley

Cook corn in boiling salted water 2 to 3 minutes; drain and plunge into ice water to stop the cooking process. Drain well. Place corn in a large bowl; add cucumber and next 4 ingredients.

Combine oil and next 7 ingredients in a small bowl; stir well with a wire whisk. Pour over corn mixture; stir well. Serve immediately or cover and chill. Sprinkle with parsley just before serving, and toss well. Yield: 16 servings.

Bobbi Trombley

Exclusively Corn Cookbook
Coventry Historical Society
Coventry, Connecticut

French Potato Salad

Roquefort, the king of highly flavored cheeses, and crunchy toasted walnuts dominate this oil- and vinegar-dressed potato salad. Pair it with grilled chicken or steak, and give your guests the royal treatment.

⅔ cup chopped shallots
¼ cup Dijon mustard
3 tablespoons white wine vinegar
2 tablespoons chopped fresh rosemary
2 teaspoons chopped fresh sage
¾ teaspoon salt
½ teaspoon pepper
¾ cup olive oil
4 pounds small red potatoes, unpeeled and quartered
1½ pounds fresh green beans
1⅓ cups crumbled Roquefort cheese, divided
1 cup chopped walnuts, toasted

Combine first 7 ingredients in a bowl; gradually add oil, stirring well with a wire whisk. Set dressing aside.

Place potato in an ungreased 13- x 9- x 2-inch baking dish. Pour ½ cup dressing over potato; stir to coat. Bake, uncovered, at 450° for 20 minutes; reduce oven temperature to 375°, and bake 45 additional minutes or until potato is tender, stirring occasionally.

While potato bakes, wash beans, trim ends, and remove strings. Cook beans in a small amount of boiling water 4 minutes or until crisp-tender. Drain beans, and plunge into ice water to stop the cooking process. Let stand until completely cool; drain well. Place beans in a large bowl. Add ½ cup dressing, ⅓ cup cheese, and walnuts; toss well. Remove beans from bowl with a slotted spoon or tongs, reserving dressing mixture in bowl. Arrange beans on a serving platter.

Add potato to reserved dressing mixture in bowl, and let cool slightly. Pour remaining ½ cup dressing over potato, and sprinkle with ⅔ cup cheese; toss well. Mound potato mixture on top of beans, using a slotted spoon. Drizzle any remaining dressing over potato salad, and sprinkle with remaining ⅓ cup cheese. Serve immediately. Yield: 10 servings.

Neil Weiler

Rotary Wheel of Recipes
The Rotary Club of Cooperstown, New York

Stuffed Lettuce Salad

A creamy blue cheese blend sparked with bright bits of pimiento and chives nestles within an iceberg lettuce shell. Cut the stuffed head of lettuce into crescent-shaped wedges, and drizzle with your favorite salad dressing.

1 head iceberg lettuce
1 (3-ounce) package cream
   cheese, softened
2 ounces blue cheese, softened
1 (2-ounce) jar diced pimiento,
   drained

¼ cup milk
½ teaspoon chopped fresh
   chives
French salad dressing or other
   salad dressing

Cut a thin slice off top of head of lettuce; hollow out center of head, leaving a 2-inch shell.

Combine cream cheese and next 4 ingredients in a mixing bowl. Beat at medium speed of an electric mixer until smooth; spoon into lettuce shell. Wrap loosely in a damp towel, and place in a large heavy-duty, zip-top plastic bag; chill at least 1 hour.

To serve, unwrap lettuce, and cut into 6 wedges. Serve with French salad dressing. Yield: 6 servings.

Flavor of Nashville
Home Economists in Home and Community
Nashville, Tennessee

Field Greens, Crumbled Blue Cheese, and Spicy Pecans

This salad is crisp, tangy, and terrific with spicy-hot pecans. As a bonus, you'll have spiced pecans left over to serve as an appetizer or snack. When preparing the nuts, we suggest using a disposable aluminum baking sheet for easy cleanup.

⅔ cup sugar
⅔ cup white vinegar
3 tablespoons apple cider vinegar
2 tablespoons Worcestershire sauce
1½ tablespoons onion juice
1 teaspoon salt
1 teaspoon dry mustard

1 cup vegetable oil
4 cups loosely packed mixed greens
1 Granny Smith apple, unpeeled, cored, and chopped
4 ounces blue cheese, crumbled
¼ cup coarsely chopped Spicy Pecans
2 green onions, chopped

Combine first 7 ingredients, stirring until sugar dissolves. Slowly add oil, stirring constantly with a wire whisk until blended.

Combine greens and remaining 4 ingredients in a large bowl. Add desired amount of dressing, and toss gently. Serve immediately. Store any remaining dressing in refrigerator. Yield: 8 servings.

Spicy Pecans

2 egg whites
1½ teaspoons salt
¾ cup sugar
2 tablespoons Hungarian paprika
1½ teaspoons ground red pepper

2 teaspoons Worcestershire sauce
4½ cups pecan halves
¼ cup plus 2 tablespoons unsalted butter, melted

Beat egg whites and salt with a wire whisk until foamy. Add sugar and next 3 ingredients, beating well. Stir in pecans and butter. Spread mixture evenly on a heavily greased large baking sheet.

Bake at 325° for 30 minutes or until pecans are crisp and browned, stirring every 10 minutes. Remove from pan; let cool completely. Store pecans in an airtight container. Yield: 5½ cups.

Stop and Smell the Rosemary: Recipes and Traditions to Remember
The Junior League of Houston, Texas

Mixed Salad Greens with Warm Goat Cheese

Pecan-encrusted slices of creamy goat cheese crown a fresh mix of five salad greens. Buy bags of washed, torn salad greens to save preparation time and effort.

2 heads Boston lettuce, torn
2 heads Bibb lettuce, torn
2 heads romaine lettuce, torn
3 bunches arugula, torn
2 bunches watercress, torn
3 cups seedless red grapes
1 (1-pound) log goat cheese
1⅔ cups chicken broth, divided
1 to 1½ cups ground pecans
½ cup chopped fresh parsley
⅓ cup red wine vinegar

3 tablespoons fresh lemon juice
3 tablespoons walnut oil
2 tablespoons safflower oil
1 tablespoon Dijon mustard
2 green onions, chopped
1 clove garlic, minced
1 tablespoon sugar
¼ teaspoon salt
¼ teaspoon freshly ground pepper

Combine first 6 ingredients in a large bowl, tossing gently; cover and chill thoroughly.

Cut goat cheese into ¼-inch rounds. Dip each round in 1 cup broth; roll in pecans, and then in parsley. Place on a lightly greased baking sheet. Bake, uncovered, at 325° for 5 minutes or until toasted.

Combine remaining ⅔ cup broth, vinegar, and remaining 9 ingredients in container of an electric blender; process 1 minute. Drizzle over salad greens, and toss gently; place cheese on top of salad. Serve immediately. Yield: 8 servings.

Call to Post
Lexington Hearing and Speech Center
Lexington, Kentucky

Greens Julius

Crunchy homemade croutons frolic among the salad greens, while a lovely lemon dressing enlivens the spirited mix.

1 head romaine lettuce, torn
½ (10-ounce) package fresh
  spinach, torn
½ cup freshly grated Parmesan
  cheese
Croutons
⅓ cup vegetable oil
3 tablespoons fresh lemon
  juice
2 tablespoons olive oil

2 tablespoons white wine
  vinegar
2 teaspoons minced fresh
  chives
1 teaspoon Dijon mustard
1 clove garlic, minced
¾ teaspoon salt
½ teaspoon Maggi seasoning
¼ teaspoon freshly ground
  pepper

Combine first 4 ingredients in a large bowl; toss gently, and set aside.

Combine vegetable oil and remaining 9 ingredients, stirring well with a wire whisk. Pour desired amount of dressing over salad, and toss gently. Serve immediately. Yield: 6 servings.

Croutons

5 slices Italian bread
¼ cup butter, melted

⅛ teaspoon garlic powder
2 drops of Maggi seasoning

Remove crust from bread; cut bread into ½-inch cubes, and place in a bowl. Combine butter, garlic powder, and seasoning; drizzle over bread cubes, and toss gently. Place bread cubes on an ungreased baking sheet; bake at 350° for 22 minutes or until golden, stirring often. Yield: 2 cups.

Albertina's Exceptional Recipes
Albertina's
Portland, Oregon

Wilted Greens with Sweet-and-Sour Sauce

4 slices bacon, cut into 1-inch
  pieces
½ cup chopped onion
½ cup sugar

⅓ cup white vinegar
12 cups torn fresh Swiss chard
  or spinach
1 hard-cooked egg, chopped

Cook bacon in a large Dutch oven until crisp; remove bacon, reserving drippings in pan. Set bacon aside. Add onion to drippings, and cook over medium heat 5 minutes, stirring occasionally. Add sugar and vinegar, and cook over high heat until sugar dissolves, stirring often. Add greens, and cook, stirring constantly, 3 minutes or until greens wilt. Sprinkle with bacon and egg. Serve immediately. Yield: 4 servings.

Tita Eberly

Past Receipts, Present Recipes
Cumberland County Historical Society
Carlisle, Pennsylvania

Tangy Slaw

4 cups shredded cabbage
½ cup diced green pepper
½ cup shredded carrot
½ cup sliced radish
½ cup peeled, diced jícama
½ cup finely chopped
  onion

3 tablespoons brown sugar
3 tablespoons water
2 tablespoons red wine
  vinegar
1 tablespoon vegetable oil
½ teaspoon salt
1 clove garlic, minced

Combine first 6 ingredients in a large bowl; cover and chill.
Combine brown sugar and remaining 5 ingredients in a bowl, stirring with a wire whisk. Pour over cabbage mixture, and toss gently. Yield: 4 servings.

Misty Browne

A Cookbook
Life Education Department of the Cheshire Center of
Applied Science & Technology at Keene High School
Keene, New Hampshire

Thai Cabbage Salad

20 cups shredded cabbage
  (about 2½ pounds)
2 cups shredded carrot
1 small purple onion, slivered
½ cup chopped fresh cilantro

½ cup chopped fresh mint
¼ cup vegetable oil
¼ cup lemon juice
1 tablespoon sugar
2 teaspoons salt

Combine first 5 ingredients in a large bowl; toss well.

Combine oil and remaining 3 ingredients; stir well with a wire whisk. Pour over salad; toss. Yield: 12 servings.   Patti Litman

a la Park
Park School Parent-Teachers Association
Mill Valley, California

Chicken Tabbouleh

This trendy tabbouleh builds upon the traditional bulgur base with the fashionable addition of roasted chicken, feta cheese, kalamata olives, and fresh basil.

1 cup bulgur wheat, uncooked
4 cups boiling water
4 cups cubed deli-roasted
  chicken (about 2 chickens)
3 medium tomatoes, seeded
  and chopped (about 3 cups)
1 cup crumbled feta cheese
½ cup sliced purple onion

¼ cup pitted, chopped kalamata
  olives
¼ cup thinly sliced fresh basil
  leaves
¼ cup chopped fresh parsley
⅓ cup fresh lemon juice
3 tablespoons olive oil
¾ teaspoon salt

Place bulgur in a large bowl. Add boiling water; stir well. Cover and let stand 30 minutes. Drain well, and return bulgur to bowl. Add chicken and remaining ingredients; toss well. Serve immediately or cover and chill. Yield: 6 servings.

Mediterranean Delights
St. Elias Orthodox Theotokos Society/Philoptochos Society
St. Elias Orthodox Church
New Castle, Pennsylvania

Tortellini Salad with Chicken and Artichokes

1 (9-ounce) package refrigerated cheese-filled tortellini, uncooked
1 (14-ounce) can quartered artichokes, drained
1 (5-ounce) can chicken breast meat, undrained
1 (2¼-ounce) can sliced ripe olives, drained
2 tablespoons olive oil
2 tablespoons white wine vinegar
1 to 2 teaspoons dried Italian seasoning
1 teaspoon salt
⅛ teaspoon pepper
1 teaspoon Dijon mustard
¼ cup freshly grated Parmesan cheese
4 leaf lettuce leaves
1 tomato, cut into 8 wedges

Cook tortellini according to package directions; drain. Rinse with cold water; drain. Place pasta in a large bowl; add artichokes, chicken, and olives.

Combine olive oil and next 5 ingredients, stirring well. Pour dressing over pasta mixture; sprinkle with Parmesan cheese, and toss gently. Cover and chill thoroughly.

To serve, line individual salad plates with lettuce leaves. Spoon pasta mixture evenly over lettuce; arrange 2 tomato wedges on each salad. Yield: 4 servings.

Carol L. Hoffman

Nothing But the Best!
College of Human Environmental Sciences/University of Alabama
Tuscaloosa, Alabama

Turkey, Black Bean, and Orzo Salad

2 large cloves garlic, minced
½ teaspoon salt
3 tablespoons fresh lime juice
1½ tablespoons white wine vinegar
1 jalapeño pepper, seeded and minced
1½ teaspoons ground cumin
¼ teaspoon salt
¼ teaspoon pepper
⅔ cup olive oil
1¼ cups orzo, uncooked

8 ounces smoked turkey breast, cut into ½-inch pieces
1 (15-ounce) can black beans, rinsed and drained
1 cup chopped sweet red pepper
1 cup chopped sweet yellow pepper
1 cup chopped purple onion
½ cup finely chopped fresh cilantro
2 avocados, chopped (optional)

Place garlic and salt on work surface; mash with a fork or side of knife until paste forms. Combine mashed garlic mixture, lime juice, and next 5 ingredients in container of an electric blender; process until smooth. With blender running, add oil in a slow, steady stream, processing until smooth. Set aside.

Cook orzo according to package directions; drain. Combine orzo, turkey, and next 5 ingredients in a large bowl. Add dressing mixture, and toss well. Cover and chill. Sprinkle with avocado, if desired. Yield: 5 servings.

Celebrate Chicago! A Taste of Our Town
The Junior League of Chicago, Illinois

Grilled Salmon Louis

⅓ cup olive oil
6 cloves garlic, minced
3 anchovies
3 tablespoons red wine-garlic vinegar
2 tablespoons water
1 tablespoon fresh lemon juice
1 teaspoon Worcestershire sauce
⅛ teaspoon hot sauce
1 (6-ounce) salmon fillet (about 1 inch thick)

¼ teaspoon salt
¼ teaspoon pepper
Vegetable cooking spray
2 large heads romaine lettuce, torn
1 cup garlic- or Caesar-flavored croutons
½ cup freshly grated Parmesan cheese

Combine first 8 ingredients in container of an electric blender; process until blended, stopping once to scrape down sides. Set aside.

Sprinkle salmon with salt and pepper. Coat grill rack with cooking spray; place fish on grill rack. Grill, covered, over medium-hot coals (350° to 400°) 5 minutes on each side or until fish flakes easily when tested with a fork. Let salmon cool slightly; flake.

Place lettuce in a large bowl; add croutons and cheese, and toss gently. Drizzle dressing over salad. Top with flaked salmon. Serve immediately. Yield: 6 servings.

Beautiful, Bountiful Oregon
The Assistance League of Corvallis, Oregon

Garlic Shrimp, Tropical Fruit, and Baby Lettuce

1½ pounds unpeeled large fresh shrimp	6 cups tightly packed mixed baby lettuces
1½ cups extra-virgin olive oil, divided	1 ripe papaya, peeled, seeded, and cubed
⅓ cup champagne vinegar	1 ripe mango, peeled, seeded, and cubed
½ teaspoon salt	1 kiwifruit, peeled and cubed
¼ teaspoon pepper	Garnish: edible flowers
1 tablespoon crushed garlic	
1 teaspoon kosher salt	

Peel shrimp, and devein, if desired.

Combine ¾ cup oil, vinegar, ½ teaspoon salt, and pepper in a bowl. Place remaining ¾ olive oil and garlic in a large heavy-duty, zip-top plastic bag; add shrimp, and seal bag securely. Turn bag to coat shrimp. Marinate in refrigerator 45 minutes, turning bag occasionally.

Remove shrimp from marinade, discarding marinade. Sprinkle shrimp with 1 teaspoon kosher salt. Grill, covered, over medium-hot coals (350° to 400°) 8 to 10 minutes or until shrimp turn pink.

Combine lettuce, shrimp, papaya, mango, and kiwifruit in a large bowl. Add half of dressing, and toss gently. Serve with remaining dressing. Garnish, if desired. Yield: 6 servings.

Colorado Collage
The Junior League of Denver, Colorado

Shrimp-Pasta Caesar Salad

6 cups water
2 pounds unpeeled medium-size fresh shrimp
7 ounces rotini, uncooked (about 2½ cups)
1 cup fresh snow pea pods, trimmed and cut in half
½ cup sliced green onions
1 (2¼-ounce) can sliced ripe olives, drained
Lemon Caesar Dressing
1½ cups seasoned croutons
½ cup freshly grated Parmesan cheese
6 cups torn romaine lettuce

Bring water to a boil; add shrimp, and cook 3 to 5 minutes or until shrimp turn pink. Drain well; rinse with cold water. Chill. Peel shrimp, and devein, if desired.

Cook pasta according to package directions; drain and rinse with cold water.

Cook pea pods in boiling water to cover 1 minute; drain and immediately plunge into ice water to stop the cooking process.

Combine shrimp, pasta, pea pods, green onions, and olives. Pour Lemon Caesar Dressing over salad, and toss gently. Cover and chill 1 to 2 hours. To serve, add croutons and cheese; toss. Place ¾ cup lettuce on each of eight salad plates. Top with pasta mixture. Yield: 8 servings.

Lemon Caesar Dressing

1 teaspoon grated lemon rind
3 tablespoons fresh lemon juice
1 teaspoon Dijon mustard
1 teaspoon anchovy paste
1 teaspoon dry white wine
2 cloves garlic, minced
¼ teaspoon salt
⅛ teaspoon pepper
½ cup olive oil
1 tablespoon sour cream

Combine first 8 ingredients in a bowl; gradually add oil, stirring constantly with a wire whisk until smooth. Add sour cream, stirring until blended. Yield: ¾ cup.

Simply Cape Cod
The Sandwich Junior Women's Club
Sandwich, Massachusetts

Grapefruit-Raspberry Vinaigrette

Fresh tarragon reigns supreme in this supereasy salad topper.

3 tablespoons grapefruit or
  orange juice
1 tablespoon raspberry vinegar
¼ cup olive oil
2 teaspoons chopped fresh
  tarragon

⅛ teaspoon salt
⅛ teaspoon freshly ground
  pepper

Combine grapefruit juice and vinegar in a small bowl. Gradually add oil, stirring with a wire whisk until blended. Stir in tarragon, salt, and pepper. Cover and chill. Yield: ½ cup.

Azaleas to Zucchini
Smith County Medical Society Alliance
Tyler, Texas

Lemon-Ginger Dressing

Fresh ginger and lemon juice add spice and sparkle to this dressing, while sunflower kernels and tamari lend body and balance. The dressing keeps its character up to a week stored in the refrigerator.

¾ cup olive oil
½ cup fresh lemon juice
⅓ cup tamari
¼ cup water
2 cloves garlic

2 tablespoons sunflower
  kernels
1½ tablespoons minced fresh
  ginger
1½ teaspoons dry mustard

Combine all ingredients in container of an electric blender or food processor; process until smooth, stopping once to scrape down sides. Cover and chill. Yield: 2 cups.   Jim Jansen and Charles Mizelle

From ANNA's Kitchen
Adams-Normandie Neighborhood Association (ANNA)
Los Angeles, California

Honey-Poppy Seed Dressing

This delectable dressing is a crowd-pleaser—think church supper or family reunion. It can be halved easily, if you like.

1½ cups honey
½ cup boiling water
4 cups olive oil
2 cups safflower oil
1½ cups champagne vinegar

1 cup prepared mustard
½ cup poppy seeds
½ cup coarse-grained Dijon mustard
½ cup Dijon mustard

Combine honey and water in a large bowl, stirring with a wire whisk until blended. Stir in olive oil and remaining ingredients. Cover and chill 4 hours. Serve dressing over salad greens or fresh fruit. Store in refrigerator up to 1 week. Yield: 12 cups.   Winnie Sandifer

Mississippi Reflections: A Collection of Recipes Seasoned with Memories
Hospice of Central Mississippi
Brookhaven, Mississippi

Sauces & Condiments

Vegetable Sauce, page 283

Hot Fresh Peach Sauce

Succulent summer peaches form the base of this fragrant fruit sauce. A touch of orange liqueur and brandy brings out the intoxicating peach essence. Offer it as a sweet treat over ice cream or pound cake.

3 medium-size fresh peaches, peeled and pitted
¼ cup sugar
3 tablespoons orange juice concentrate, thawed
1 tablespoon peach jam
1 cup peeled, sliced fresh peaches
1½ tablespoons Triple Sec or other orange-flavored liqueur
1½ tablespoons brandy

Place pitted peaches in container of an electric blender; process until smooth, stopping once to scrape down sides. Pour puree into a saucepan. Stir in sugar, orange juice, and jam; bring just to a boil over medium heat, stirring constantly. Stir in peach slices, Triple Sec, and brandy. Serve warm over ice cream. Yield: 2½ cups.   Joyce Aiken

The Parkway Palate
San Joaquin River Parkway & Conservation Trust
Fresno, California

Spicy Fruit Sauce

Ginger and cinnamon warm this raisin-studded sauce with spicy goodness. You can store it in the refrigerator up to one week.

1⅓ cups apple jelly
1 cup raisins
2 tablespoons cornstarch
1 tablespoon apple cider vinegar
¼ teaspoon ground cinnamon
⅛ teaspoon ground ginger

Combine all ingredients in a small saucepan; cook over medium heat 10 minutes or until thickened, stirring often. Serve warm as a topping for ham or pork. Yield: 2 cups.

Savoring Cape Cod
Massachusetts Audubon Society/Wellfleet Bay Wildlife Sanctuary
South Wellfleet, Massachusetts

Pecan Tartar Sauce

Toasted pecans make this fish and seafood flatterer thick and chunky.

½ cup coarsely chopped
   pecans, toasted
½ cup mayonnaise
1 tablespoon minced fresh
   parsley
1 tablespoon minced gherkin
   pickle

1 tablespoon apple cider
   vinegar
1 teaspoon grated lemon rind
½ teaspoon dry mustard
¼ teaspoon salt

Combine all ingredients in a small bowl, stirring well; cover and chill thoroughly. Serve with fish, crab cakes, or shrimp. Yield: about 1 cup.

The Cook's Canvas
St. John's Museum of Art
Wilmington, North Carolina

Vegetable Sauce

A mere three ingredients makes up this luxuriously rich cheese sauce that's ideal for ladling over vegetables.

½ cup shredded process
   American cheese

½ cup mayonnaise
⅓ cup milk

Combine all ingredients in a heavy saucepan; cook over low heat, stirring constantly, until cheese melts and mixture is smooth. Serve warm as a topping for steamed broccoli, asparagus, or cauliflower. Yield: 1 cup.

Zoe Wetzsteon

A Recipe Runs Through It
Sula Country Life Club
Sula, Montana

Two Great Pestos

These two fabulous pestos move beyond the basil-pine nut basics. The first features fresh dill and walnuts, while the second scores high marks with garlic, chives, and spinach plus walnuts. These pestos shine over hot cooked pasta, pizza, or vegetables.

Dill Pesto

1½ cups loosely packed fresh
    dill
½ cup loosely packed fresh
    parsley sprigs
2 large cloves garlic, halved

2 tablespoons walnut pieces
3 to 4 tablespoons olive oil
2 tablespoons freshly grated
    Parmesan cheese

Position knife blade in food processor bowl; add first 4 ingredients, and pulse 15 times. Gradually add 3 tablespoons olive oil and cheese, pulsing until mixture is blended. Add remaining 1 tablespoon oil, if necessary, to reach desired consistency. Store in an airtight container in refrigerator. Yield: ¾ cup.

Garlic-Chive Pesto

1 cup loosely packed fresh
    parsley sprigs
½ cup loosely packed fresh
    garlic-chives or chives
½ cup tightly packed fresh
    spinach leaves

1 large clove garlic, halved
2 tablespoons walnut pieces
3 to 4 tablespoons olive oil
2 tablespoons freshly grated
    Parmesan cheese

Position knife blade in food processor bowl; add first 5 ingredients, and pulse 15 times. Gradually add 3 tablespoons olive oil and cheese, pulsing until mixture is blended. Add remaining 1 tablespoon oil, if necessary, to reach desired consistency. Store in an airtight container in refrigerator. Yield: ¾ cup.   Barbara Gordon

Vermont Children's Aid Society Cookbook
Vermont Children's Aid Society
Winooski, Vermont

Grilled Tomato Sauce

Grill thick slices of yellow and plum tomatoes to create the smoky foundation of this distinctive sauce. Dried crushed red pepper sparks a bit of heat, while marjoram, basil, and thyme lend their herbed freshness.

8 large yellow tomatoes, cut into ½-inch slices
8 large plum tomatoes, cut into ½-inch slices
¼ cup olive oil, divided
Vegetable cooking spray
1 onion, chopped
3 cloves garlic, minced
2 cups dry red wine
2½ tablespoons chopped fresh marjoram

2 tablespoons chopped fresh basil
1 tablespoon chopped fresh thyme
1 tablespoon dried crushed red pepper
2 tablespoons balsamic vinegar
1 teaspoon salt

Brush tomato slices evenly with 2 tablespoons olive oil. Coat grill rack with cooking spray; place tomato slices on grill rack. Grill, covered, over medium-hot coals (350° to 400°) 10 minutes, turning once. Coarsely chop tomato; set aside.

Cook onion in remaining 2 tablespoons olive oil in a large Dutch oven over medium-high heat, stirring constantly, 5 minutes or until tender. Add tomato, garlic, and remaining ingredients; simmer, uncovered, 20 minutes or to desired consistency. Serve warm over pasta. Yield: 8 cups.

Under the Canopy
GFWC Tallahassee Junior Woman's Club
Tallahassee, Florida

Kiwi Salsa

Sweet-tart morsels of kiwifruit and tangerine team with crunchy cubes of jícama and sweet peppers in this unusual take on salsa. You can pulse the mixture in a food processor for a smoother, more dippable version of this distinctive sauce.

4 kiwifruit, peeled and diced
2 medium tangerines, peeled, seeded, and chopped
1 cup peeled, diced jícama
¼ cup diced sweet red pepper
¼ cup diced sweet yellow pepper

¼ cup chopped fresh cilantro
1 jalapeño pepper, seeded and chopped
1 tablespoon lime juice
1 tablespoon vegetable oil
¼ teaspoon salt

Combine all ingredients in a medium bowl, stirring well. Serve immediately or cover and chill. Serve as a dip for tortilla chips or as a topping for fish, pork, or chicken. Yield: 3¾ cups.   Laura Keslick

Cooking with Legal Ease
Chester County Paralegal Association
West Chester, Pennsylvania

Pineapple Salsa

The generous yield of this robust salsa shouts party. Though it keeps its racy character up to one week when stored in the refrigerator, it can be halved easily. Be sure to wear rubber gloves to protect your hands when working with the habanero pepper–it's superhot!

1 large pineapple, peeled, cored and diced (about 5½ cups)
1 papaya, peeled, seeded, and diced (about 1¾ cups)
1 sweet red pepper, diced (about 1 cup)
1 cup minced purple onion
½ green pepper, diced (about ½ cup)

3 green onions, finely chopped
1 habanero chile pepper, minced
3 tablespoons minced fresh cilantro
2 tablespoons fresh lime juice
1½ teaspoons seasoned rice vinegar
⅛ teaspoon ground red pepper

Combine all ingredients in a large bowl. Cover and chill. Serve as a dip for tortilla chips or as a topping for grilled chicken, pork, or fish. Yield: 8 cups.   Barbara Pool Fenzl

The Phoenix Zoo Auxiliary Cookbook
The Phoenix Zoo Auxiliary
Phoenix, Arizona

Cherry-Honey Relish

Tart red cherries, raisins, and pecans glisten in a coat of spiced honey. Serve this pretty accompaniment as the crowning glory atop turkey, pork, or ham.

1 (14.5-ounce) can pitted tart cherries, undrained	¼ cup apple cider vinegar
½ cup raisins	½ teaspoon ground cinnamon
½ cup honey	⅛ teaspoon ground cloves
¼ cup firmly packed brown sugar	½ cup chopped pecans
	1 tablespoon cornstarch
	1 tablespoon cold water

Combine first 7 ingredients in a large saucepan, stirring well. Cook, uncovered, over medium heat 30 minutes, stirring occasionally. Stir in chopped pecans. Combine cornstarch and water, stirring until smooth. Gradually stir cornstarch mixture into cherry mixture; cook, stirring constantly, 1 minute or until mixture thickens and comes to a boil. Serve relish warm or cover and chill. Serve with turkey, pork, or ham. Yield: 2¼ cups.   New York Cherry Growers Association

Specialties of the House
Ronald McDonald House
Rochester, New York

Mission Inn's Peach and Ginger Relish

Curry and ginger season sweet slices of peaches, onion, and sweet red pepper. Apple cider vinegar and lemon juice provide tangy balance to this uncommon relish.

2 medium-size sweet red peppers, chopped
1 small onion, chopped
12 medium-size fresh peaches, peeled and sliced
½ cup coarsely chopped fresh cilantro
½ cup firmly packed brown sugar

½ cup apple cider vinegar
2 tablespoons curry powder
1½ ounces grated fresh ginger or 1½ teaspoons ground ginger
2 tablespoons lemon juice
½ teaspoon ground red pepper

Cook sweet red pepper and onion in a large nonstick skillet over medium-high heat, stirring constantly, until vegetables are tender. Add peaches and remaining ingredients, stirring well; cook until mixture is thoroughly heated. Serve relish warm as a topping for grilled chicken. Yield: 10 cups.

Howey Cook
Howey-in-the-Hills Garden and Civic Club
Howey-in-the-Hills, Florida

Ruby Relish

Gloriously red tomatoes and sweet peppers give this hot and spicy relish a regal air. It partners well with pork or chicken. In addition, try serving this crimson concoction over cream cheese with crackers as an appetizer.

16 large tomatoes, peeled, seeded, and chopped
4 large sweet red peppers, chopped
2 cups chopped celery
1 large onion, chopped
1 small jalapeño pepper, seeded and chopped

2 cups sugar
2 cups apple cider vinegar (5% acidity)
1 tablespoon salt
1 tablespoon dry mustard
1 tablespoon celery seeds

Combine all ingredients in a large Dutch oven, stirring well; bring to a boil over medium-high heat. Reduce heat, and simmer, uncovered, 2½ hours, stirring occasionally.

Pack hot mixture into hot jars, filling ½ inch from top. Remove air bubbles; wipe jar rims. Cover at once with metal lids, and screw on bands. Process in boiling water bath 15 minutes. Serve with beef, pork, or chicken. Yield: 8 half-pints.   Carol Scherbarth

Love for Others
Our Shepherd Lutheran Church
Birmingham, Michigan

Apricot Chutney

1 **cooking apple, peeled and chopped**	¼ **cup raisins**
1 **cup sugar**	¼ **cup fresh lemon juice**
1 **cup water**	1 **tablespoon chopped fresh ginger**
¾ **cup chopped dried apricot halves**	1 **teaspoon grated lemon rind**
½ **cup chopped onion**	½ **teaspoon dry mustard**
½ **cup apple cider vinegar**	¼ **teaspoon ground cinnamon**
	¼ **teaspoon ground cloves**

Combine all ingredients in a large saucepan; bring to a boil over high heat. Reduce heat, and simmer, uncovered, 30 minutes or to desired consistency, stirring occasionally. Cover and chill. Serve with ham or cheese and crackers. Yield: 3 cups.

Delta Informal Gardeners Cook
Delta Informal Gardeners
Brentwood, California

Pear Mincemeat

5 pounds Bartlett pears, unpeeled, cored, and cut into eighths (about 10)
1 medium-size orange, seeded and cut into eighths
1 (16-ounce) package raisins
4 cups sugar
¾ cup apple cider vinegar
2 teaspoons ground allspice
2 teaspoons ground cinnamon
1 teaspoon ground ginger
1 teaspoon ground cloves

Position knife blade in food processor bowl; add pear and orange, and process until fruit is coarsely chopped, stopping once to scrape down sides.

Combine chopped fruit, raisins, and remaining ingredients in a large Dutch oven. Bring mixture to a boil; reduce heat, and simmer, uncovered, 1 hour and 30 minutes or until mixture is very thick, stirring occasionally. Cover and chill or freeze for pies, tarts, or cookies. Yield: 10 cups.   Norma Jean Butts

Crossroads Cookbook
New Albany-Plain Township Historical Society
New Albany, Ohio

Cranberry Ketchup

Spread this spiced berry blend on your next turkey or ham sandwich for a sweet-sour surprise.

1 (16-ounce) can whole-berry cranberry sauce
½ cup sugar
¼ cup plus 2 tablespoons apple cider vinegar
¾ teaspoon ground cinnamon
½ teaspoon ground allspice
½ teaspoon ground cloves
¼ teaspoon salt
¼ teaspoon pepper

Combine all ingredients in a medium saucepan, stirring well. Bring to a boil; reduce heat, and simmer, uncovered, 5 minutes or until slightly thickened, stirring occasionally. Store in an airtight container in refrigerator up to 2 weeks. Yield: 2 cups.   Lil England

Bone Appetit: A Second Helping
Operation Kindness
Carrollton, Texas

Soups & Stews

Cream of Roasted Tomato Soup with Parsley Croutons, page 298

Fresh Blueberry Soup

A hint of cardamom and cinnamon imbues this fresh blueberry soup with fragrance and spice. For extra presence, float a dollop of whipped cream in each beautiful bowlful and crown it with a few plump blueberries.

1½ cups fresh blueberries
1¼ cups unsweetened grape
  juice
1 cup water
2 to 3 teaspoons sugar

1 (3-inch) stick cinnamon
2 tablespoons cornstarch
¼ cup cold water
⅛ teaspoon ground cardamom

Combine first 5 ingredients in a medium saucepan; bring to a boil. Cover, reduce heat, and simmer 5 minutes.

Combine cornstarch and water, stirring until smooth. Add cornstarch mixture and cardamom to blueberry mixture, stirring until blended. Cook, stirring constantly, 8 minutes or until mixture is thickened and bubbly. Remove from heat, and let cool completely. Cover and chill thoroughly. Remove and discard cinnamon stick before serving. Yield: 3 cups.

Sweet Home Alabama
The Junior League of Huntsville, Alabama

Cantaloupe-Amaretto Soup

Exquisitely ripened cantaloupe and peaches sweeten this soup flawlessly. If your fruit isn't fully ripened or purchased at its peak, simply add a tablespoon or two of powdered sugar to coax the sweet fruit juices.

1 large ripe cantaloupe,
  cubed
2 fresh peaches, peeled and
  sliced
¼ cup amaretto
2 tablespoons fresh lemon
  juice

1 teaspoon almond extract
2 cups whipping cream or
  half-and-half, divided
Ground nutmeg or ground
  cinnamon

Combine first 5 ingredients in container of an electric blender; process until smooth, stopping once to scrape down sides. Add 1 cup whipping cream, and pulse just until blended. Transfer mixture to a large bowl; stir in remaining 1 cup whipping cream. Cover and chill thoroughly. Sprinkle with nutmeg just before serving. Yield: 6 cups.

O Taste & Sing
St. Stephen's Episcopal Church Choir
Richmond, Virginia

Spicy Guacamole Bisque

If you're a fan of the popular green dip, you'll love this chilly bisque. Satiny smooth avocado is spiced with cumin and chili powder, while splashes of lime juice and lemon juice plus cilantro add tartness and zip. Chill the soup before serving to blend the fiesta of flavors.

3 ripe avocados, coarsely
  chopped
½ cup finely chopped fresh
  cilantro
¼ cup finely chopped onion
¼ cup chopped green onions
¼ cup finely chopped fresh
  parsley
¼ cup lemon juice
1 to 3 tablespoons lime juice

1 teaspoon chili powder
½ teaspoon salt
¼ teaspoon pepper
¼ teaspoon ground cumin
½ teaspoon hot sauce
4 cups chicken broth
1 (16-ounce) carton sour cream
Garnish: sweet orange pepper
  strips

Position knife blade in food processor bowl. Add avocado; process until smooth, stopping once to scrape down sides.

Add cilantro and next 10 ingredients to processor bowl; process until smooth, stopping once to scrape down sides. Pour avocado mixture into a large bowl. Stir in chicken broth and sour cream. Cover and chill 3 to 4 hours.

To serve, ladle soup into individual bowls. Garnish, if desired. Yield: 8 cups.

Betty Petersen

Savoring Cape Cod
Massachusetts Audubon Society/Wellfleet Bay Wildlife Sanctuary
South Wellfleet, Massachusetts

Shaker Fresh Herb Soup

Visit your herb garden and gather fresh chives, chervil, sorrel, and tarragon to create this simple pleasure. The herbed broth is poured over toasted bread and sprinkled with nutmeg and Cheddar cheese. The result is comforting and satisfying.

1 cup minced celery
2 tablespoons minced fresh
  chervil
2 tablespoons chopped fresh
  chives
2 tablespoons minced fresh
  sorrel
1½ teaspoons minced fresh
  tarragon

1 tablespoon butter, melted
4 cups chicken broth
½ teaspoon sugar
Salt and pepper to taste
6 slices white bread, toasted
⅛ teaspoon ground nutmeg
⅓ cup (1.3 ounces) shredded
  Cheddar cheese

Cook first 5 ingredients in butter in a large saucepan over medium-high heat 3 minutes, stirring constantly. Add broth, sugar, and salt and pepper to taste. Bring to a boil; reduce heat, and simmer, uncovered, 20 minutes. Place toast in a soup tureen; pour soup over toast. Sprinkle with nutmeg and cheese. Serve immediately. Yield: 4 cups.

Simply Cape Cod
The Sandwich Junior Women's Club
Sandwich, Massachusetts

Curried Asparagus Soup

Pureed asparagus and potato thicken this distinctive soup. Accent each colorful serving with tender tips of spring green asparagus.

1 pound fresh asparagus
1 small onion, finely chopped
3 tablespoons unsalted butter,
  melted
3 tablespoons all-purpose flour
1 tablespoon curry powder

4 cups chicken broth
1 medium-size red potato,
  peeled and diced
½ teaspoon salt
¼ teaspoon pepper
1 (8-ounce) carton sour cream

Snap off tough ends of asparagus. Remove scales from stalks with a vegetable peeler, if desired. Cut asparagus into 1-inch pieces;

set stem pieces aside. Cook asparagus tips in boiling salted water to cover 3 to 5 minutes or until crisp-tender; drain and set aside.

Cook onion in melted butter in a saucepan over medium-high heat, stirring constantly, until tender. Reduce heat to medium-low. Stir in flour and curry powder; cook 1 minute, stirring constantly. Gradually add chicken broth; cook, stirring constantly, until mixture is slightly thickened. Add reserved asparagus stem pieces, potato, salt, and pepper; simmer, uncovered, 20 minutes or until vegetables are tender, stirring occasionally. Transfer mixture to container of an electric blender; process until smooth, stopping once to scrape down sides.

Return mixture to saucepan; stir in sour cream, and cook over medium heat until thoroughly heated, stirring often.

To serve, ladle soup into individual bowls; top each serving with reserved asparagus tips. Yield: 7 cups.

Music, Menus & Magnolias
The Charleston Symphony Orchestra League
Charleston, South Carolina

Autumn Butternut Squash Soup

2 **medium butternut squash**
  (about 3 pounds)
4 **cups chicken broth**
4 **cups whipping cream**
½ **cup firmly packed brown**
  sugar

1 **tablespoon ground cinnamon**
¼ **teaspoon ground nutmeg**
Salt and ground white pepper
  to taste

Cut each squash in half lengthwise; remove and discard seeds and membranes. Place squash halves, cut side down, in two lightly greased jellyroll pans. Bake, uncovered, at 350° for 1 hour. Let cool to touch; scrape out pulp, discarding rind. Position knife blade in processor bowl; add pulp, and process 2 minutes or until smooth.

Combine 4 cups pureed squash (reserve any remaining pureed squash for another use), chicken broth, and remaining ingredients in a large Dutch oven; stir well. Cook, uncovered, over low heat 10 minutes or until mixture is thoroughly heated, stirring occasionally. Yield: 11 cups.

Dawn to Dusk, A Taste of Holland
The Junior Welfare League of Holland, Michigan

Brie and Roasted Garlic Soup

Roasting the garlic makes it a sweet and mellow base for this soup. Buttery Brie melts into the broth, making it rich, creamy, and in a class by itself. Grab a spoon and indulge.

2 large heads garlic
2 tablespoons olive oil
7 ounces Brie
2 stalks celery, finely chopped
1 medium onion, finely chopped
1 medium carrot, scraped and finely chopped
¼ cup olive oil
¼ cup all-purpose flour
6 cups chicken broth
1 teaspoon chopped fresh oregano
1 teaspoon chopped fresh parsley
½ teaspoon chopped fresh thyme
⅛ teaspoon ground white pepper

Peel outer skin from each garlic head, and discard. Cut off top one-third of each garlic head. Place garlic, cut side up, on an aluminum foil-lined baking sheet. Drizzle garlic with 2 tablespoons olive oil. Bake, uncovered, at 350° for 1 hour or until garlic is soft. Remove from oven; cool 10 minutes. Squeeze pulp from each clove; set pulp aside.

Remove and discard rind from cheese; coarsely chop cheese, and set aside.

Cook celery, onion, and carrot in ¼ cup olive oil in a large saucepan over medium-high heat, stirring constantly, 10 minutes or until tender. Add flour, stirring until smooth. Cook 1 minute, stirring constantly. Gradually add chicken broth; bring to a boil, stirring often. Reduce heat, and simmer, uncovered, 15 minutes or until vegetables are tender, stirring often.

Position knife blade in food processor bowl. Add garlic pulp and 1 cup soup mixture; process until smooth. Stir pureed mixture into remaining soup mixture; add oregano, parsley, and thyme. Bring to a simmer over medium-low heat. Add cheese, and cook, stirring constantly, until cheese melts. Stir in pepper. Yield: 6½ cups.

Apron Strings: Ties to the Southern Tradition of Cooking
The Junior League of Little Rock, Arkansas

Mushroom and Potato Soup

2 large red potatoes, peeled and cubed (about 3 cups)
1 large onion, finely chopped (about 1½ cups)
2 stalks celery, finely chopped
2¾ cups water
3 slices bacon
2 tablespoons butter or margarine
2 tablespoons all-purpose flour
5 cups chicken broth or vegetable broth
8 ounces fresh mushrooms, chopped
½ teaspoon caraway seeds
½ teaspoon salt
¼ teaspoon pepper

Combine first 4 ingredients in a large saucepan; bring to a boil. Cover, reduce heat, and simmer 15 minutes or until vegetables are tender.

Meanwhile, cook bacon in a large skillet until crisp; remove bacon from skillet, discarding drippings. Crumble bacon, and set aside. Wipe skillet with a paper towel.

Melt butter in skillet over medium heat; add flour, stirring until smooth. Cook, stirring constantly, until flour browns. Stir in vegetables and cooking liquid.

Bring chicken broth to a boil in a large Dutch oven; add vegetable mixture, bacon, mushrooms, and remaining ingredients, stirring well. Cover, reduce heat, and simmer 20 minutes, stirring occasionally. Yield: 11 cups.

Marjorie Allen

West Virginia DAR at Work for Our Schools
School Committee, West Virginia State Society
Daughters of the American Revolution
Peterstown, West Virginia

Cream of Roasted Tomato Soup
With Parsley Croutons

Thin, crunchy slices of French baguettes topped with garlic, Muenster cheese, and parsley grace each serving of this creamy tomato soup. Roasting the tomatoes brings out the sweet, intense flavor of the vine-ripened fruit.

3 pounds tomatoes, cut in half crosswise and seeded
3 tablespoons olive oil
1 small head fennel
3 tablespoons unsalted butter
3 small shallots, coarsely chopped
1 small carrot, scraped and coarsely chopped
3 cups chicken broth, divided
5 fresh tarragon sprigs
5 fresh parsley sprigs
1 cup whipping cream
¼ teaspoon salt
¼ teaspoon pepper
Parsley Croutons

Brush tomato halves with olive oil; place tomato halves, cut side down, in an aluminum foil-lined shallow baking dish. Bake, uncovered, at 400° for 45 minutes or until tomato is soft and skins are dark. Let cool to touch; remove skins.

Rinse fennel thoroughly. Trim and discard bulb base. Trim stalks from bulb; discard stalks. Coarsely chop fennel bulb.

Melt butter in a large saucepan over medium heat; add fennel, shallot, and carrot, and cook 12 minutes or until vegetables are tender. Add 2 cups chicken broth, tarragon, and parsley. Reduce heat, and simmer, uncovered, 30 minutes. Remove from heat. Remove and discard herb sprigs, and add tomato. Let cool slightly.

Pour mixture into container of an electric blender; process until smooth, stopping once to scrape down sides. Return puree to saucepan; stir in whipping cream. Bring just to a simmer; stir in remaining 1 cup chicken broth, salt, and pepper.

To serve, ladle soup into individual bowls; top each serving with Parsley Croutons. Yield: 7 cups.

Parsley Croutons

12 thin slices French baguette
3 tablespoons olive oil
2 cloves garlic, halved
½ cup (2 ounces) shredded Muenster cheese
¼ cup chopped fresh parsley

Brush both sides of baguette slices with olive oil; rub garlic halves over slices. Place slices on an ungreased baking sheet, and sprinkle evenly with cheese and parsley. Bake, uncovered, at 400° for 5 minutes or until golden. Yield: 1 dozen croutons.

Savour St. Louis
Barnes-Jewish Hospital Auxiliary Plaza Chapter
St. Louis, Missouri

Italian Zucchini Soup

⅓ cup orzo, uncooked
2 medium zucchini, shredded (about 2¾ cups)
1 large onion, finely chopped (about 1 cup)
2 tablespoons olive oil
8 cups chicken broth
2 large eggs, lightly beaten
⅓ cup chopped fresh parsley, divided

½ teaspoon salt
¼ teaspoon freshly ground pepper
¼ cup freshly grated Parmesan cheese
Additional freshly ground pepper

Cook orzo according to package directions; drain and set aside.

Cook zucchini and onion in hot oil in a large skillet over medium-high heat, stirring constantly, until tender. Set aside.

Bring chicken broth to a boil in a Dutch oven. Drizzle egg into boiling broth (do not stir). Stir in orzo, zucchini mixture, 1 tablespoon parsley, salt, and pepper; cook until thoroughly heated.

To serve, ladle soup into individual soup bowls; sprinkle with remaining parsley, cheese, and additional pepper. Yield: 9 cups.

Beautiful, Bountiful Oregon
The Assistance League of Corvallis, Oregon

Hearty Lentil Soup

Smoked ham hocks permeate the broth, giving a richness to the legumes.

1 pound dried lentils
1½ pounds smoked ham hocks
4 cups beef broth
4 cups water
1 (28-ounce) can crushed
   tomatoes
1 (8-ounce) can tomato sauce
½ small cabbage, chopped
4 stalks celery, sliced
2 large onions, chopped
2 carrots, scraped and sliced
½ cup chopped fresh parsley
2 bay leaves
2 teaspoons salt
1 teaspoon dried basil
½ teaspoon pepper

Combine all ingredients in a Dutch oven; stir well. Bring to a boil; cover, reduce heat, and simmer 3 hours, stirring occasionally. Remove ham hocks; cool. Remove meat from bones; discard fat and bones. Cut meat into bite-size pieces; stir into soup. Cook over medium-high heat until heated. Discard bay leaves. Yield: 15 cups.   Cindy Blaser

Favorite Recipes
Tillamook County Dairy Women
Tillamook, Oregon

Easy Corn and Crab Soup

¼ cup butter
¼ cup all-purpose flour
2 cups chicken broth
2 cups half-and-half
1 pound fresh lump crabmeat,
   drained
1 (11-ounce) can whole kernel
   corn, drained
½ teaspoon salt
¼ teaspoon garlic powder
¼ teaspoon pepper

Melt butter in a heavy saucepan over low heat; add flour, stirring until smooth. Cook 1 minute, stirring constantly. Gradually add broth; cook over medium heat, stirring constantly, until thickened. Stir in half-and-half and remaining ingredients; cover, reduce heat, and simmer 20 minutes. Yield: 6 cups.   Pennyé L. Conner

Nun Better: Tastes and Tales from Around a Cajun Table
St. Cecilia School
Broussard, Louisiana

Mussels and Saffron Soup

10 saffron threads
3 tablespoons boiling water
8 pounds fresh mussels
2½ cups water
2 large onions, chopped
2 cloves garlic, pressed
2 tablespoons butter or
   margarine, melted
⅔ cup dry white wine

¼ cup whole wheat flour
2 cups milk
½ cup whipping cream
¼ cup chopped fresh parsley
¼ cup chopped fresh chives
1 tablespoon dry vermouth
   (optional)
Salt and pepper to taste

Combine saffron threads and boiling water in a small bowl; set aside.

Remove beards on mussels, and scrub shells with a brush. Discard opened, cracked, or heavy mussels (they're filled with sand).

Combine mussels and 2½ cups water in a Dutch oven; bring to a boil. Cover, reduce heat, and simmer 5 minutes or until mussels open, shaking pot several times. Transfer mussels to a large bowl, using a slotted spoon, and reserve broth in Dutch oven; discard any unopened mussels. Let mussels cool slightly.

Set aside 8 to 10 shells for garnish, if desired. Remove remaining mussels from shells. Discard shells; set shelled mussels aside.

Pour reserved broth through a wire-mesh strainer into a large bowl. Set broth aside.

Cook onion and garlic in butter in a large Dutch oven over medium-high heat, stirring constantly, 3 minutes or until tender. Add wine;, cook, uncovered, 10 minutes, stirring occasionally. Add flour, stirring until smooth. Cook 1 minute, stirring constantly. Gradually add reserved broth, milk, and whipping cream; cook over medium heat, stirring constantly, until bubbly. Stir in saffron. Reduce heat, and simmer, uncovered, 5 minutes. Stir in shelled mussels, parsley, chives, vermouth, if desired, and salt and pepper to taste; cook 1 minute.

To serve, ladle soup into individual bowls; garnish with reserved shells, if desired. Yield: 13 cups.   Andrea Sparenberg

Howey Cook
Howey-in-the-Hills Garden and Civic Club
Howey-in-the-Hills, Florida

Wild Rice Clam Chowder

6½ cups chicken broth
1 tablespoon fresh lemon juice
3 bay leaves
6 medium-size red potatoes, peeled and cut into ½-inch cubes
¼ cup butter or margarine
1½ cups chopped onion
6 ounces fresh mushrooms, sliced
2 (6½-ounce) cans minced clams, undrained
½ teaspoon pepper
⅓ cup all-purpose flour
1½ cups half-and-half, divided
2½ cups cooked wild rice

Combine first 3 ingredients in a Dutch oven; bring to a boil. Add potato; reduce heat, and simmer, uncovered, 10 minutes or just until potato is tender.

Meanwhile, melt butter in a skillet over medium-high heat. Add onion, and cook, stirring constantly, until tender. Add mushrooms, and cook 5 additional minutes or until mushrooms are tender. Add mushroom mixture to potato mixture. Stir in clams and pepper. Bring to a boil; reduce heat to low.

Combine flour and ½ cup half-and-half, stirring until smooth. Gradually add flour mixture to chowder, stirring constantly with a wire whisk. Cook, uncovered, over medium heat until mixture is thickened and bubbly, stirring often (do not boil). Stir in remaining 1 cup half-and-half and rice. Remove and discard bay leaves. Yield: 12 cups.

Albertina's Exceptional Recipes
Albertina's
Portland, Oregon

Sweet Potato-Corn Chowder

A tureen filled with this cozy corn chowder is just the ticket for a chilly evening's supper. It showcases sweet potatoes, leeks, and sweet red pepper warmly enhanced with bacon, thyme, and marjoram.

6 slices bacon, diced
1 medium onion, chopped
1 cup frozen whole kernel corn
½ cup chopped sweet red
　pepper
½ cup chopped leek
1 teaspoon chopped fresh
　thyme
1 teaspoon chopped fresh
　marjoram

2 sweet potatoes, peeled and
　chopped
2½ cups water
1 (14½-ounce) can chicken
　broth
2 teaspoons cornstarch
½ cup cold water
½ cup whipping cream
Salt and freshly ground pepper
　to taste

Cook bacon in a Dutch oven until crisp; remove bacon, reserving drippings in pan. Set bacon aside.

Cook onion and next 5 ingredients in drippings in Dutch oven over medium-high heat, stirring constantly, until tender. Add sweet potato, 2½ cups water, and chicken broth; cook, uncovered, 18 minutes or until sweet potato is tender.

Combine cornstarch and ½ cup cold water, stirring until smooth. Stir cornstarch mixture into soup. Bring to a boil; cook over medium heat, stirring constantly, until slightly thickened and bubbly. Reduce heat to low; add bacon, whipping cream, and salt and pepper to taste. Cook, uncovered, until thoroughly heated, stirring occasionally. Serve immediately. Yield: 8 cups.

Gwen Smith

Blue Stocking Club Forget-Me-Not Recipes
Blue Stocking Club
Bristol, Tennessee

New Wave Chili

Trendy and nourishing describe this spicy blend of beans. Raisins and cashews complete the wholesome mix.

1 (16-ounce) can kidney beans, undrained
1 (15-ounce) can garbanzo beans, undrained
1 (14.5-ounce) can whole tomatoes, undrained
¾ cup bulgur, uncooked
2 tablespoons vegetable oil
1 medium onion, coarsely chopped
3 stalks celery, coarsely chopped (about 1 cup)
1⅓ cups chopped carrot (about 3 medium)
½ cup coarsely chopped green pepper

4 cloves garlic, minced
4 to 5 tablespoons chili powder
1 tablespoon fresh lemon juice
1 tablespoon fresh lime juice
1½ teaspoons salt
1 teaspoon pepper
1 teaspoon ground cumin
1 teaspoon dried basil
2 cups vegetable juice or tomato juice (we tested with V-8)
¾ cup raw cashews
½ cup raisins

Drain kidney beans, garbanzo beans, and tomatoes, reserving liquid. Set beans aside. Coarsely chop tomatoes, and set aside.

Bring 1 cup reserved liquid to a boil in a medium saucepan. Remove from heat, and stir in bulgur. Cover and let stand.

Meanwhile, heat oil in a Dutch oven over medium-high heat until hot. Add onion and next 11 ingredients, stirring constantly, 10 minutes or until vegetables are crisp-tender. Add reserved beans, tomatoes, bulgur, and vegetable juice. Cover, reduce heat, and simmer 20 minutes, stirring occasionally. Stir in cashews and raisins, and simmer 5 additional minutes. Stir in remaining reserved liquid, and cook, uncovered, until thoroughly heated, stirring often. Yield: 9 cups.

Beyond Chicken Soup
The Jewish Home of Rochester Auxiliary
Rochester, New York

Hearty Polish Stew

Kielbasa and sauerkraut make this stew a standout. Tasty bits of apple and caraway seeds add a sweet, nutty touch. Serve this stew with a dark rye or pumpernickel bread and a rich ale to complete the experience.

1 pound lean beef stew meat
¼ cup butter or margarine, melted and divided
1 small onion, chopped (about 1 cup)
1 medium Rome apple, chopped (about 1 cup)
1 clove garlic, minced
1 (14.5-ounce) can shredded sauerkraut, rinsed and drained
1 (14.5-ounce) can diced tomatoes, drained
1 (14½-ounce) can beef broth
7 small round red potatoes, unpeeled and cut into 1-inch cubes
½ pound kielbasa, cut into ¾-inch slices
¾ teaspoon caraway seeds
¼ teaspoon pepper

Brown beef in 2 tablespoons butter in a Dutch oven over medium-high heat, stirring constantly. Stir in remaining 2 tablespoons melted butter; add onion, apple, and garlic, and cook, uncovered, over medium heat until tender, stirring often. Stir in sauerkraut and tomatoes.

Gradually stir in beef broth, deglazing pan by scraping particles that cling to bottom. Add potato and remaining ingredients. Cover and simmer 1 hour and 10 minutes or until beef is tender. Yield: 11 cups.

Our Best Home Cooking
The Polish Hill Civic Association of Pittsburgh, Pennsylvania

Gulf Fisherman's Stew

1 head fennel (about 1 pound)
2 cups chopped onion
6 large cloves garlic, minced
¼ cup olive oil
4 cups chopped fresh tomato
1 cup thinly sliced sweet red pepper
1 cup thinly sliced green pepper
4 cups chicken broth
2 cups dry white wine
½ cup chopped fresh basil
2 tablespoons chopped fresh rosemary
2 teaspoons fennel seeds
1 teaspoon ground coriander
½ teaspoon hot sauce
10 saffron threads
1 bay leaf
½ pound unpeeled large fresh shrimp
1 pound firm white fish fillets (such as snapper, black drum, flounder), cut into 1-inch pieces
1 (12-ounce) container fresh Select oysters, drained
¼ cup chopped fresh parsley
¼ cup fresh lemon juice
Salt and freshly ground pepper to taste

Rinse fennel thoroughly. Trim and discard bulb base. Trim stalks from bulb; discard stalks. Cut bulb into thin slices. Set aside 2 cups sliced fennel; reserve remaining fennel for another use.

Cook onion and garlic in oil in a Dutch oven over medium-high heat, stirring constantly, until tender. Add 2 cups fennel, tomato, sweet red pepper, and green pepper; cook 3 minutes, stirring often. Add chicken broth and next 8 ingredients; bring to a boil. Cover, reduce heat, and simmer 30 minutes, stirring occasionally.

Peel shrimp, and devein, if desired. Add shrimp, fish, and oysters to vegetable mixture; cook 4 to 5 minutes or until shrimp turn pink and oyster edges begin to curl. Stir in parsley, lemon juice, and salt and ground pepper to taste. Yield: 15 cups.

Herbal Harvest Collection
Herb Society of America, South Texas Unit
Houston, Texas

Vegetables

Roasted Garlic Mashed Potatoes, page 316

Asparagus with Basil-Mayonnaise Sauce

Crisp-tender spears of spring-green asparagus cuddle under a warm blanket of creamy sauce made with mayonnaise, tomato, basil, and lemon. Serve any leftover sauce on top of grilled fish or use as a dip for fresh vegetables.

2 pounds fresh asparagus
1 cup mayonnaise
1 tablespoon lemon juice
1 teaspoon dried basil
¼ teaspoon pepper
1 medium tomato, peeled, seeded, and finely chopped

Snap off tough ends of asparagus. Remove scales from stalks with a vegetable peeler, if desired. Cook asparagus in boiling salted water to cover 6 minutes or until crisp-tender; drain.

Combine mayonnaise and next 3 ingredients in a saucepan, stirring well. Cook over medium heat, stirring constantly, until heated. Gently stir in tomato. Serve warm over asparagus spears. Yield: 6 servings.

Sterling Service
The Dothan Service League
Dothan, Alabama

Spanish Black Beans

This black bean basic is enhanced with tomato, onion, and green pepper. Punch up their personality with cilantro, dried crushed red pepper, and cumin. Serve this mighty mix over rice for a meatless main dish, and be sure to pile on the tempting toppers of green onions, sour cream, and shredded cheese.

1 small onion, chopped
½ green pepper, diced
1 tablespoon olive oil
2 cloves garlic, pressed
2 teaspoons ground cumin
1 (19-ounce) can black beans, drained
1 (14.5-ounce) can whole tomatoes, undrained and chopped
2 tablespoons red wine vinegar
1 tablespoon lemon juice
½ teaspoon dried crushed red pepper
2 tablespoons finely chopped fresh cilantro
Toppings: sliced green onions, sour cream, shredded Cheddar cheese, shredded Monterey Jack cheese

Cook chopped onion and green pepper in oil in a heavy 2-quart saucepan over medium heat, stirring constantly, until tender. Stir in garlic and cumin. Add beans and next 4 ingredients; cover, reduce heat, and simmer 30 minutes. Sprinkle with cilantro and desired toppings. Yield: 4 servings.

Praiseworthy
The Foundation for Historic Christ Church
Irvington, Virginia

Lima Beans

Crisp bits of bacon and melted Monterey Jack liven up these limas.

1½ cups water
½ teaspoon salt
2 (10-ounce) packages frozen
   lima beans
8 slices bacon, diced
1 cup chopped onion

½ cup chopped celery
1½ cups (6 ounces) shredded
   Monterey Jack cheese
¼ teaspoon pepper
Dash of Worcestershire sauce

Combine water and salt in a large saucepan; bring to a boil. Add lima beans; cover, reduce heat, and simmer 8 to 10 minutes or until tender. Drain beans, reserving ½ cup liquid; set aside.

Cook bacon in a large skillet until crisp; remove bacon, reserving 3 tablespoons drippings in skillet. Set bacon aside.

Cook onion and celery in drippings in skillet, stirring constantly, until tender.

Combine reserved lima beans, reserved liquid, onion mixture, cheese, pepper, and Worcestershire sauce. Spoon in a lightly greased 2-quart baking dish. Sprinkle with bacon. Bake, uncovered, at 350° for 25 minutes or until heated. Yield: 6 servings.   Gayle Hara

Sharing Tasteful Memories
L.A.C.E. (Ladies Aspiring to Christian Excellence) of
First Church of the Nazarene
Longview, Texas

Chinese Pickled Beets

Beet lovers beware—you'll become addicted to this simple side dish. A unique blend of ketchup, cloves, and vanilla emboldens the ruby slices.

2 (15-ounce) cans sliced beets, undrained
⅔ cup sugar
⅔ cup white vinegar
16 whole cloves

2 tablespoons ketchup
4 teaspoons cornstarch
1 teaspoon vanilla extract
⅛ teaspoon salt

Drain beets, reserving 1 cup juice. Set beets aside.

Combine 1 cup juice, sugar, and remaining 6 ingredients in a saucepan; cook over medium-high heat, stirring constantly, 5 minutes or until sugar dissolves. Add beets; reduce heat to medium, and cook 10 minutes or until thickened. Serve warm or cover and chill. Serve with a slotted spoon. Yield: 8 servings.   Wesley R. Thompson

Past Receipts, Present Recipes
Cumberland County Historical Society
Carlisle, Pennsylvania

Broccoli Blue

Fresh broccoli benefits from a rich coating of blue cheese sauce and lots of buttery cracker crumbs.

2 pounds fresh broccoli
2 tablespoons butter
2 tablespoons all-purpose flour
1 (3-ounce) package cream cheese, softened

¾ cup crumbled blue cheese
1 (8-ounce) carton sour cream
⅓ cup crushed round buttery crackers (about 6 crackers)

Remove and discard broccoli leaves and tough ends of stalks; cut into bite-size pieces. Arrange broccoli in a steamer basket over boiling water. Cover and steam 5 minutes or until crisp-tender. Set broccoli aside, and keep warm.

Melt butter in a saucepan over low heat; add flour, stirring until smooth. Cook 1 minute, stirring constantly. Add cream cheese and blue cheese; cook, stirring constantly, until smooth. Add sour cream, and bring just to a boil. Remove from heat, and pour over broccoli;

toss gently. Place broccoli mixture into a lightly greased 1-quart baking dish; sprinkle with cracker crumbs. Bake, uncovered, at 350° for 30 minutes. Yield: 8 servings.

Treasures of the Great Midwest
The Junior League of Wyandotte and Johnson Counties
Kansas City, Kansas

Thai-Flavored Cabbage

A dash of fish sauce adds intense flavor to this savory side dish. You'll find this dark brown liquid made from ground anchovies in most Asian markets.

1 tablespoon peanut oil	1 teaspoon sugar
2 cups chopped sweet onion	2 teaspoons fresh lime juice
3 large cloves garlic, minced	8 cups thinly sliced napa
1½ tablespoons minced fresh	cabbage
ginger	2 cups thinly sliced green
6 cups coarsely chopped	onions
cabbage	⅓ cup dry roasted peanuts
1 cup chopped carrot	¼ cup chopped fresh cilantro
2 tablespoons fish sauce	Chopped fresh mint (optional)

Pour oil around top of a preheated wok, coating sides, and heat at medium-high (375°) for 2 minutes. Add sweet onion, garlic, and ginger; stir-fry 1 minute. Add chopped cabbage and next 4 ingredients; stir-fry 2 minutes or until vegetables are crisp-tender. Add napa cabbage and next 3 ingredients; stir-fry 2 minutes. Sprinkle with mint, if desired. Serve immediately. Yield: 11 servings.

Savoring San Diego: An Evolving Regional Cuisine
University of California, San Diego Medical Center Auxiliary
San Diego, California

Baked Carrots with Apples and Cranberries

1 (10-ounce) package shredded
   carrot (about 4 cups)
1 medium Granny Smith apple,
   peeled, cored, and chopped
1 cup fresh or frozen
   cranberries, thawed
½ cup apple juice
¼ cup firmly packed brown
   sugar
2 teaspoons grated orange rind
½ teaspoon ground cinnamon
½ teaspoon ground nutmeg
2 tablespoons butter or
   margarine

Combine first 8 ingredients in a medium bowl; toss well. Spoon mixture into a greased 11- x 7- x 1½-inch baking dish. Dot with butter. Cover and bake at 350° for 1 hour or until carrot is crisp-tender, stirring after 30 minutes. Yield: 4 to 6 servings.   Debbie Greeno

What's Cooking in York
York Police Explorer Post #393
York, Maine

Spicy Cauliflower

¼ cup vegetable oil
1 teaspoon mustard seeds
1 medium onion, sliced
1 (1-inch) piece fresh ginger,
   peeled and thinly sliced
1 jalapeño pepper, finely
   chopped
1 teaspoon ground turmeric
1 large cauliflower, separated
   into flowerets
1 teaspoon salt
2 teaspoons fresh lemon juice
1 tablespoon chopped fresh
   cilantro

Heat oil in a skillet over medium-high heat; add mustard seeds. Cover and cook 1 to 2 minutes until seeds stop popping. Add onion and next 3 ingredients; cook, uncovered, 3 minutes, stirring occasionally. Add cauliflower, salt, and lemon juice; cover, reduce heat, and simmer 25 minutes or until cauliflower is tender, stirring occasionally. Sprinkle with cilantro, and serve immediately. Yield: 4 to 6 servings.

Here, There & Everywhere
Volunteers in Overseas Cooperative Assistance
Washington, DC

Portobello Mushrooms Stuffed With Eggplant

Meaty portobello mushrooms play host to a vegetable medley that includes eggplant, tomato, onion, and olives. A generous sprinkling of grated Parmesan cheese unifies the Mediterranean-inspired mix.

1 medium eggplant, peeled and cut into ¾-inch cubes
1 teaspoon salt, divided
8 medium portobello mushrooms
2 tablespoons butter or margarine, melted
3 tablespoons olive oil
1 medium onion, finely chopped
1 large tomato, peeled, seeded, and chopped
12 ripe olives, pitted and sliced
3 large fresh basil leaves, chopped
1 teaspoon lemon juice
1 teaspoon minced fresh parsley
½ teaspoon freshly ground pepper
¼ teaspoon ground cumin
¼ cup grated Parmesan cheese, divided

Place eggplant in a colander; sprinkle with ½ teaspoon salt, and let drain 10 minutes.

Clean mushrooms with damp paper towels. Remove stems, and set caps aside. Trim and chop stems, and set aside.

Cook mushroom caps in butter in a _____ ver medium heat 5 minutes on each side. Remove from _____ set aside. Wipe drippings from skillet with a paper towel.

Heat oil in skillet over medium-high heat, add onion, and cook until golden, stirring often. Add eggplant and reserved mushroom stems; cook until tender, stirring often. Add tomato and next 6 ingredients; stir well. Stir in remaining ½ teaspoon salt and 3 tablespoons Parmesan cheese; cook until thoroughly heated.

Place mushroom caps in a greased 13- x 9- x 2-inch baking dish. Spoon eggplant mixture evenly into mushroom caps. Sprinkle evenly with remaining 1 tablespoon Parmesan cheese. Bake, uncovered, at 350° for 20 to 25 minutes or until thoroughly heated. Serve immediately. Yield: 8 servings.

Noteworthy Two
Ravinia Festival Association
Highland Park, Illinois

Onions Parmesan

Bring out your electric skillet to slowly and sweetly caramelize onion slices in a creamy Parmesan cheese sauce with spectacular results.

6 small sweet onions
1 tablespoon butter
½ cup freshly grated Parmesan cheese
1 cup half-and-half
2 tablespoons all-purpose flour

2 teaspoons salt
¼ teaspoon Worcestershire sauce
⅛ teaspoon freshly ground pepper
Paprika

Cook onions in boiling water to cover 1 minute; remove onions from water, and immediately plunge into ice water to stop the cooking process. Peel onions; cut into ¼-inch-thick slices.

Melt butter in a 10-inch electric skillet on low heat. Arrange half of onion slices in 3 rows in skillet; sprinkle with ¼ cup Parmesan cheese. Layer with remaining half of onions; sprinkle with remaining ¼ cup Parmesan cheese. Combine half-and-half and next 4 ingredients; stir well, and pour evenly over onions.

Cover and cook at 275° for 15 to 17 minutes or until onion is tender. Sprinkle with paprika. Serve immediately. Yield: 6 servings.

Texas Ties
The Junior League of North Harris County
Spring, Texas

Green Peas with Pine Nuts and Rosemary

½ cup chicken broth
2 (10-ounce) packages frozen English peas, thawed
3 green onions, cut into ½-inch pieces
½ teaspoon sugar

¾ cup pine nuts
3 tablespoons butter or margarine, melted
1 tablespoon chopped fresh rosemary
Salt and pepper to taste

Bring chicken broth to a boil in a medium saucepan over medium-high heat. Add peas, green onions, and sugar; cover, reduce heat, and simmer 5 minutes or until peas are tender. Drain well, and set aside.

Cook pine nuts in butter in a saucepan over medium heat, stirring constantly, 2 to 3 minutes or until golden. Add pea mixture, rosemary, and salt and pepper to taste; cook, uncovered, 2 minutes or until thoroughly heated. Yield: 8 servings.

Eat Your Dessert or You Won't Get Any Broccoli
The Sea Pines Montessori School
Hilton Head Island, South Carolina

Yellow Pepper Enchiladas with Spinach Sauce

Pair these colorful vegetable enchiladas with chicken, pork, or beef, and you'll be responsible for creating a fabulous match.

1 large sweet yellow pepper, cut into strips
1 tablespoon olive oil
1 (10¾-ounce) can cream of celery soup
1 (8-ounce) carton plain low-fat yogurt
1 (10-ounce) package frozen chopped spinach, thawed and drained

6 slices jalapeño pepper
1 clove garlic
¼ teaspoon salt
1½ cups (6 ounces) shredded Monterey Jack cheese
2 tablespoons finely chopped onion
8 (8-inch) flour tortillas

Cook pepper strips in oil in a skillet over medium heat 6 to 8 minutes or until crisp-tender, stirring often. Set aside.

Combine soup and next 5 ingredients in container of an electric blender; process until smooth, stopping once to scrape down sides. Pour half of spinach sauce in bottom of a lightly greased 13- x 9- x 2-inch pan. Set pan and remaining sauce aside.

Layer cheese, onion, and reserved pepper strips evenly down center of each tortilla. Roll up tortillas; place, seam side down, in prepared pan. Drizzle remaining sauce evenly over tortillas. Bake, uncovered, at 350° for 20 to 25 minutes or until cheese melts. Yield: 8 side-dish or 4 main-dish servings.   Mark and Adele England

Bone Appetit: A Second Helping
Operation Kindness
Carrollton, Texas

Deep-Fried Potato Balls

Bring out the ketchup, and let these fried potato balls take a dive.
They're a family-pleasing way to use up leftover spuds.

1 cup mashed potatoes
1 cup all-purpose flour
1 teaspoon baking powder
1 teaspoon salt

¼ cup plus 1 tablespoon milk
1 large egg, lightly beaten
Vegetable oil

Combine all ingredients except oil in a medium bowl; stir until blended. Pour oil to depth of 2 inches into a Dutch oven; heat to 375°. Drop batter by tablespoonfuls into hot oil. Fry about 11 to 13 minutes or until golden. Drain on paper towels. Serve immediately. Yield: 6 servings.
Anna Lasley

The Flavors of Mackinac
Mackinac Island Medical Center
Mackinac Island, Michigan

Roasted Garlic Mashed Potatoes

2 pounds baking potatoes,
   peeled and cut into 3-inch
   pieces
½ teaspoon salt
Roasted Garlic Puree
2 tablespoons unsalted butter

2 tablespoons olive oil
⅛ teaspoon ground white
   pepper
⅔ cup half-and-half
2 tablespoons chopped fresh
   parsley

Cook potato in boiling salted water to cover 15 minutes or until tender; drain. Mash potatoes in a large bowl; stir in Roasted Garlic Puree and next 3 ingredients.
Heat half-and-half in a small saucepan just until warm (do not boil). Gradually stir warm half-and-half into potato mixture to desired consistency. Remove potato mixture to a serving bowl, and sprinkle with parsley. Yield: 3 servings.

Roasted Garlic Puree

2 large heads garlic

Gently peel outer skins from garlic, and discard skins. Cut off and discard top one-fourth of each garlic head. Place garlic, cut side up, in center of a piece of heavy-duty aluminum foil; fold foil over garlic, sealing tightly. Bake at 350° for 1 hour or until garlic heads are soft. Remove from oven; let cool completely.

Remove and discard skins from garlic. Scoop out garlic pulp with a small spoon; mash pulp with spoon, and stir until smooth. Yield: about 2 tablespoons.

Palette Pleasers
St. Luke Simpson United Methodist Women
Lake Charles, Louisiana

Apricot-Glazed Sweet Potatoes

Fork-tender slices of sweet potato glisten with a glaze of apricot nectar, brown sugar, and butter. A generous topping of crunchy pecans adds toasty taste and texture appeal.

3 pounds medium-size sweet potatoes	2 tablespoons hot water
1 cup firmly packed brown sugar	¼ teaspoon salt
1 cup apricot nectar	⅛ teaspoon ground cinnamon
1½ tablespoons cornstarch	½ cup chopped pecans
	2 tablespoons butter

Cook potatoes in boiling water to cover 10 minutes. Let cool to touch; peel potatoes, and cut into ½-inch-thick slices. Arrange potato slices in a lightly greased 2-quart casserole.

Combine brown sugar and next 5 ingredients in a small saucepan, stirring with a wire whisk. Cook, uncovered, over medium heat until thickened and bubbly, stirring often. Stir in pecans and butter. Pour sauce over potato. Bake, uncovered, at 350° for 45 minutes or until potato is tender. Yield: 6 servings.   Frieda Obrist

Favorite Recipes
Tillamook County Dairy Women
Tillamook, Oregon

Confetti Spaghetti Squash

Toss in peas, carrots, and sweet red and green pepper to perk up golden strands of spaghetti squash with bright flavor notes.

1 (3- to 3½-pound) spaghetti
  squash
1 cup diced onion
1 clove garlic, minced
Butter-flavored vegetable
  cooking spray
¼ cup chicken broth
1 cup frozen English peas

½ cup scraped, diced carrot
½ cup diced sweet red pepper
½ cup diced green pepper
¼ cup minced fresh parsley
1 tablespoon olive oil
½ teaspoon salt
¼ to ½ teaspoon ground
  cumin

Place squash in a large Dutch oven; add water to cover. Bring to a boil; reduce heat, and simmer, uncovered, 1 hour or until tender. Drain; let cool slightly. Remove and discard seeds and membranes. Remove spaghetti-like strands with a fork, and set aside. Discard shells.

Cook onion and garlic in a large nonstick skillet coated with cooking spray over medium-high heat 5 minutes, stirring constantly. Stir in chicken broth. Add peas and remaining 7 ingredients; cook, uncovered, 5 minutes. Add reserved squash, and toss gently to combine; cook until thoroughly heated. Yield: 8 servings.   Anna Phillips

The Hallelujah Courses
Mayo United Methodist Church
Edgewater, Maryland

Samford University Squash Croquettes

Yellow squash give these crisp, golden croquettes moisture and sweetness. Use your favorite cornbread recipe for the crumbs or purchase a ready-made loaf at your deli or bakery to save time.

2 pounds yellow squash, sliced
1 to 2 cups cornbread crumbs
2 large eggs, beaten
½ cup finely chopped onion
¼ cup butter or margarine, melted

1 tablespoon sugar
1 teaspoon salt
1 teaspoon pepper
1 cup fine, dry breadcrumbs (store-bought)
Vegetable oil

Place squash in a medium saucepan; add water to cover. Bring to a boil; reduce heat, and simmer, uncovered, 20 minutes or until tender. Drain well.

Combine squash, cornbread crumbs, and next 6 ingredients; stir well. Shape mixture by ⅓ cupfuls into balls. Carefully dredge each ball in fine, dry breadcrumbs.

Pour oil to depth of 3 inches into a Dutch oven; heat to 375°. Fry in batches in hot oil 1 to 2 minutes or until golden. Drain and serve immediately. Yield: 8 servings.   Anna Schepker

Cougar Bites
Crestline Elementary School
Birmingham, Alabama

Acknowledgments

Each of the community cookbooks listed is represented by recipes appearing in *America's Best Recipes*. Unless otherwise noted, the copyright is held by the sponsoring organization whose mailing address is included.

7 Alarm Cuisine, East Mountain Volunteer Fire Department, Rte. 2, Box 162, Gladewater, TX 75647

25 Years of Food, Fun & Friendship, Clifton Community Woman's Club, P.O. Box 105, Clifton, VA 20124

60 Years of Serving, Assistance League of San Pedro-Palos Verdes, 1441 W. 8th St., San Pedro, CA 90732

150 Years of Good Eating, St. George Evangelical Lutheran Church, 803 W. Main St., Brighton, MI 48116-1333

700 lbs. of Marmalade, Woman's Club of Winter Park, P.O. Box 1433, 419 S. Interlachen Ave., Winter Park, FL 32790

a la Park, Park School Parent-Teachers Association, 360 E. Blithedale Ave., Mill Valley, CA 94941

Albertina's Exceptional Recipes, Albertina's, 424 N.E. 22nd Ave., Portland, OR 97232

Ambrosia, Junior Auxiliary of Vicksburg, MS, P.O. Box 86, Vicksburg, MS 39180

Apron Strings: Ties to the Southern Tradition of Cooking, Junior League of Little Rock, Inc., 3600 Cantrell Rd., Ste. 102, Little Rock, AR 72202

Ashland County Fair Centennial Cookbook 1895-1995, Ashland County Fair Association, Rte. 4, Box 216, Ashland, WI 54806

Azaleas to Zucchini, Smith County Medical Society Alliance, P.O. Box 7491, Tyler, TX 75711

Barnard 'Beary' Best Cookbook, Barnard United Methodist Youth Department, Main St., Box 86, Barnard, KS 67418

Bartlett Memorial Hospital's 25th Anniversary Cookbook, Bartlett Memorial Hospital, 3260 Hospital Dr., Juneau, AK 99801

Bearing Our Cupboard, Brain Tumor Support Group, Box 980631, Medical College of Virginia, Richmond, VA 23298

Beautiful, Bountiful Oregon, Assistance League of Corvallis, 547 N.W. 9th St., Corvallis, OR 97330

Beneath the Palms, Brownsville Junior Service League, Inc., 5062 Lakeway Dr., Brownsville, TX 78520

The Best of Mayberry, Foothills Lions Club of Mount Airy, President Wilford Lyerly, 125 Taylor St., Mount Airy, NC 27030

The Best of West, Junior Beta Club of West Jones Middle School, 254 Springhill Rd., Laurel, MS 39440

Beyond Burlap, Idaho's Famous Potato Recipes, Junior League of Boise, Inc., 5266 W. Franklin Rd., Boise, ID 83705

Beyond Chicken Soup, Jewish Home of Rochester Auxiliary, 2021 Winton Rd. S., Rochester, NY 14618

A Bite of the Best, Relief Society Church of Jesus Christ of Latter Day Saints, 3687 N. Littlerock Dr., Provo, UT 84604

Blessed Isle, Episcopal Church Women of All Saints Parish, Rte. 3, Box 464, Pawleys Island, SC 29585

Blue Stocking Club Forget-Me-Not Recipes, Blue Stocking Club, P.O. Box 1022, Bristol, TN 37621

Bone Appetit: A Second Helping, Operation Kindness, 1029 Trend Dr., Carrollton, TX 75006

Bully's Best Bites, Junior Auxiliary of Starkville, MS, Inc., P.O. Box 941, Starkville, MS 39760

Call to Post, Lexington Hearing and Speech Center, 635 Iron Works Pike, Lexington, KY 40511

Candlewood Classics, Community Service Club of New Fairfield, P.O. Box 8260, New Fairfield, CT 06812

Canton McKinley Bulldogs Pup's Pantry, McKinley Booster Club, 3490 Cardiff NW, Canton, OH 44708

A Capital Affair, Junior League of Harrisburg, Inc., 3211 N. Front St., Ste. 301, Harrisburg, PA 17110

Capital Celebrations, Junior League of Washington, 3039 M Street NW, Washington, DC 20007

Carolina Cuisine: Nothin' Could Be Finer, Junior Charity League of Marlboro County, Inc., 100 Fayetteville Ave., Bennettsville, SC 29512

Carolina Sunshine, Then & Now, Charity League of Charlotte, P.O. Box 12495, Charlotte, NC 28220

Celebrate Chicago! A Taste of Our Town, Junior League of Chicago, Inc., 1447 North Astor St., Chicago, IL 60610

Centennial Cookbook 1895-1995, Rogers Memorial Library, 9 Jobs Ln., Southampton, NY 11968

Cheyenne Frontier Days "Daddy of 'em All" Cookbook, Chuckwagon Gourmet, 3664 Foxcroft Rd., Cheyenne, WY 82001

Classic Favorites, P.E.O., Chapter SB, 1409 Rimer Dr., Moraga, CA 94556

The Club's Choice . . . A Second Helping, Fuquay-Varina Woman's Club, 612 E. Academy St., Fuquay-Varina, NC 27526

A Collection of Favorite Recipes of the Congregation and Friends of White Clay Creek Presbyterian Church, White Clay Creek Presbyterian Church, 15 Polly Drummond Hill Rd., Newark, DE 19711

Colorado Collage, Junior League of Denver, 6300 E. Yale Ave., Denver, CO 80222

Compliments of the Chef, Friends of the Library of Collier County, Inc., 650 Central Ave., Naples, FL 34102

A Cookbook, Life Education Department of the Cheshire Center of Applied Science & Technology at Keene High School, 43 Arch St., Keene, NH 03431

Cooking from the Heart, Girl Scout Troop 669, 4319 Newton St., Metairie, LA 70001

Cooking in Harmony: Opus II, Brevard Music Center, Inc., P.O. Box 592, Brevard, NC 28712

Cooking on the Wild Side, Cincinnati Zoo and Botanical Garden Volunteer Program, 3400 Vine St., Cincinnati, OH 45220-1399

Cooking with Legal Ease, Chester County Paralegal Association, P.O. Box 295, West Chester, PA 19381

Cooking with the Lioness Club of Brown Deer, Lioness Club of Brown Deer, 6650 N. 42nd St., Milwaukee, WI 53209

The Cook's Canvas, St. John's Museum of Art, 114 Orange St., Wilmington, NC 28401

Cougar Bites, Crestline Elementary School, 3785 Jackson Blvd., Birmingham, AL 35213

Country Recipes, Westmoreland United Church, 9 South Village Common, Westmoreland, NH 03467

Crossroads Cookbook, New Albany-Plain Township Historical Society, 107 E. Granville St., P.O. Box 219, New Albany, OH 43054

Culinary Classics, Hoffman Estates Medical Center Service League, 1555 N. Barrington Rd., Hoffman Estates, IL 60194

The Cumberland Cougars Are Cooking Now, Cumberland Elementary School PTA, 2801 Cumberland Rd., Lansing, MI 48906

Curtain Calls, Arts Society of the Norris Cultural Arts Center, 1040 Dunham Rd., St. Charles, IL 60174

Dancers for Doernbecher Present Recipes from the Heart, Dancers for Doernbecher, 12951 S.E. Vernie Ln., Milwaukie, OR 97222

Dawn to Dusk, A Taste of Holland, Junior Welfare League of Holland, P.O. Box 1633, Holland, MI 49422

Delta Informal Gardeners Cook, Delta Informal Gardeners, P.O. Box G, Brentwood, CA 94513

Dinner Bells for Handbells, Umatilla Presbyterian Church, 493 Kentucky Ave., P.O. Box 407, Umatilla, FL 32784

Eat Your Dessert or You Won't Get Any Broccoli, Sea Pines Montessori School, 9 Fox Grape Rd., Hilton Head Island, SC 29928

Exchanging Tastes, The Depot, 22 Prospect St., Midland Park, NJ 07432

Exclusively Corn Cookbook, Coventry Historical Society, Box 534, Coventry, CT 06238

Expressions, National League of American Pen Women, Chester County, 2300 West Chester Rd., Coatesville, PA 19320

Family Self Sufficiency International Cookbook, Central Falls Family Self Sufficiency Foundation, 30 Washington St., Central Falls, RI 02863

Favorite Recipes, Tillamook County Dairy Women, 7650 Fairview Rd., Tillamook, OR 97141

Favorite Recipes II, St. Isaac Jogues Senior Guild, St. Mary's of the Hills Catholic Church, 2675 John R. Rd., Rochester Hills, MI 48307

Fire Gals' Hot Pans Cookbook, Garrison Emergency Services Auxiliary, 203 E. Main St., P.O. Box 146, Garrison, IA 52229

First Baptist Church Centennial Cookbook, First Baptist Church, Moses at Little, P.O. Box 187, Cushing, OK 74023

Fishing for Compliments, Shedd Aquarium Society, 1200 S. Lake Shore Dr., Chicago, IL 60605

Flavor of Nashville, Home Economists in Home and Community, 713 Georgetown Dr., Nashville, TN 37205

The Flavors of Mackinac, Mackinac Island Medical Center, P.O. Box 536, Market St., Mackinac Island, MI 49757

Food Fabulous Food, Women's Board to Cooper Hospital/University Medical Center, One Cooper Plaza, Camden, NJ 08103

Food for the Soul, Campground Church Ladies, Midland/Fosterville Rd., Fosterville, TN 37160

Food for Thought, Friends of Centerville Public Library, 67 Long Pond Cir., Centerville, MA 02632

Food for Thought, Northeast Louisiana Chapter, Autism Society of America, P.O. Box 4768, Monroe, LA 71211

Foods and Flowers, Hermosa Garden Club, P.O. Box 782, Hermosa Beach, CA 90254

From ANNA's Kitchen, Adams-Normandie Neighborhood Association (ANNA), P.O. Box 15153, Los Angeles, CA 90015-0153

From Home Plate to Home Cooking, Atlanta Braves, 755 Hank Aaron Dr., Atlanta, GA 30315

Fun Cookin' Everyday, North Dakota Association for Family & Community Education, 2267 Springbrook Ct., Grand Forks, ND 58201

A Gardener Cooks, Danbury Garden Club, 21 Summit St., New Milford, CT 06776

Gracious Goodness Christmas in Charleston, Bishop England High School Endowment Fund, 203 Calhoun St., Charleston, SC 29401-3522

The Great Delights Cookbook, Genoa Serbart United Methodist Churches, 211 Main St., Genoa, CO 80818

Great Lake Effects, Junior League of Buffalo, Inc., 45 Elmwood Ave., Buffalo, NY 14201

Green Thumbs in the Kitchen, Green Thumb, Inc., 2000 N. 14th St. #800, Arlington, VA 22201

The Hallelujah Courses, Mayo United Methodist Church, 1005 Old Turkey Point Rd., Edgewater, MD 21037

Have You Heard . . . A Tasteful Medley of Memphis, Subsidium, Inc., 4711 Spottswood, Memphis, TN 38117

H.E.A.L. of Michiana Cookbook: A Collection of Health Conscious Recipes, Human Ecology Action League of Michiana, 4451 Cleveland Ave., Stevensville, MI 49127

Healthy Cooking for Kids—and You!, Children's Wish Foundation, c/o Holmes Regional Hospice, 1900 S. Dairy Rd., West Melbourne, FL 32904

Herbal Harvest Collection, Herb Society of America, South Texas Unit, P.O. Box 6515, Houston, TX 77265-6515

Here, There & Everywhere, Volunteers in Overseas Cooperative Assistance, 50 F St. NW, Ste. 1075, Washington, DC 20001

Home Cooking, Bison American Lutheran Church, HC69, Box 417D, Bison, SD 57620

Home Cooking, Sunshine City Library, P.O. Box 424, Prairie View, KS 67664

Howey Cook, Howey-in-the-Hills Garden and Civic Club, 1101 N. Tangerine Ave., Howey-in-the-Hills, FL 34737

Incredible Edibles, Missionary Temple CME Church, 1455 Golden Gate Ave., San Francisco,
  CA 94115

Just Desserts, Amsterdam Free Library, 28 Church St., Amsterdam, NY 12010

Just Peachey, Cooking Up a Cure, Catherine Peachey Fund, Inc., P.O. Box 1823, Warsaw,
  IN 46581

Ka Mea 'Ai 'Ono Loa: Delicious Foods from the Honolulu Waldorf School, Honolulu Waldorf School,
  350 Ulua St., Honolulu, HI 96821

The Kansas City Barbeque Society Cookbook, Kansas City Barbeque Society, 11514 Hickman Mills Dr.,
  Kansas City, MO 64134

Katonah Cooks!, Katonah Village Improvement Society, Katonah Village Library, Katonah,
  NY 10536

Kenwood Lutheran Church Cookbook, Kenwood Women of the Evangelical Lutheran Church in
  America, 324 W. Cleveland St., Duluth, MN 55811

Kimball Kub Grub, Kimball Elementary PTA, 5801 Griswold, Kimball, MI 48074

Kitchen Keepsakes, United Methodist Church Women, 801 N. Bell St., Beloit, KS 67420

Landmark Entertaining, Junior League of Abilene, TX, 774 Butternut St., Abilene, TX 79602

Let's Get Cooking, Monvale Health Resources Auxiliary, Country Club Rd., Monongahela,
  PA 15063

Literally Delicious!, California Literacy, Inc., 339 S. Mission Dr., San Gabriel, CA 91776-1105

Love for Others, Our Shepherd Lutheran Church, 2225 E. 14 Mile Rd., Birmingham, MI 48009

Loving Spoonfuls, Covenant House of Texas, 1111 Lovett Blvd., Houston, TX 77006

Low-Fat Favorites, Tri-Valley Haven for Women, 3663 Pacific Ave., Livermore, CA 94550

Main Line Classics II, Cooking Up a Little History, Junior Saturday Club of Wayne, P.O. Box 251,
  Wayne, PA 19087

Malibu's Cooking Again, Malibu's Cooking Again, 23852 Pacific Coast Hwy., #184, Malibu,
  CA 90265

The Many Tastes of Haverstraw Middle School, Home and Career Skills Department, Haverstraw
  Middle School, 16 Grant St., Haverstraw, NY 10927

McClellanville Coast Seafood Cookbook, McClellanville Arts Council, 733 Pinckney St., P.O. Box 594,
  McClellanville, SC 29458

Mediterranean Delights, St. Elias Orthodox Theotokos Society/Philoptochos Society St. Elias
  Orthodox Church, 915 Lynn St., New Castle, PA 16101

Memorial Hospital Associates Favorites, Memorial Hospital Activities Committee, 325 S. Belmont St.,
  York, PA 17405

Michigan Cooks, C.S. Mott Children's Hospital, 1500 E. Medical Center Dr., D5202, Ann Arbor,
  MI 48109-0718

Mississippi Reflections: A Collection of Recipes Seasoned with Memories, Hospice of Central Mississippi,
  224 S. 1st St., Brookhaven, MS 39601

Moments, Memories & Manna, Restoration Village, 2215 Little Flock Dr., Rogers, AR 72756

Morrisonville's 125th Anniversary Cookbook, Morrisonville Historical Society & Museum, c/o
  Dorothy Bullard, 611 Dey St., P.O. Box 227, Morrisonville, IL 62546-0227

Mounds of Cooking, Parkin Archeological Support Team, P.O. Box 677, Hwy. 64 E., Parkin,
  AR 72373

Music, Menus & Magnolias, Charleston Symphony Orchestra League, 14 George St., Charleston,
  SC 29401

Newport Cooks & Collects, Preservation Society of Newport County, 424 Bellevue Ave., Newport,
  RI 02840

Note Worthy Recipes, Wilson Presbyterian Church, 400 N. 4th St. and Locust, Clairton, PA 15025

Noteworthy Two, Ravinia Festival Association, 400 Iris Ln., Highland Park, IL 60035

Nothing But the Best, College of Human Environmental Sciences/University of Alabama, 100 Doster
  Hall, University Building, Tuscaloosa, AL 35487

Nun Better: Tastes and Tales from Around a Cajun Table, St. Cecilia School, 302 W. Main St.,
  Broussard, LA 70518

O Taste & Sing, St. Stephen's Episcopal Church Choir, 6004 Three Chopt Rd., Richmond, VA 23226

Our Best Home Cooking, Polish Hill Civic Association of Pittsburgh, 3060 Brereton St., Pittsburgh, PA 15219

Our Favorite Recipes, Claremont Society for the Prevention of Cruelty to Animals Serving Sullivan County, Inc., Rte. 3 Box 337, Claremont, NH 03743

Our Lady of Fatima and Immaculate Conception Parish Cookbook, Our Lady of Fatima, 75 Main St., New London, NH 03257

Our Sunrise Family Cookbook, Sunrise Drive Elementary School, 5301 E. Sunrise Dr., Tucson, AZ 85718

Owensburg Spring Festival Cookbook 1996, Owensburg Fire Department, P.O. Box 42, Owensburg, IN 47453

Palette Pleasers, St. Luke Simpson United Methodist Women, 1500 Country Club Rd., Lake Charles, LA 70605

The Parkway Palate, San Joaquin River Parkway & Conservation Trust, 1550 E. Shaw Ave., Ste. 114, Fresno, CA 93710

Party Pleasers, GFWC Philomathic Club, 1101 E. Plato Rd., Duncan, OK 73533

Past Receipts, Present Recipes, Cumberland County Historical Society, 21 N. Pitt St., Carlisle, PA 17013

The Phoenix Zoo Auxiliary Cookbook, Phoenix Zoo Auxiliary, 455 N. Galvin Pkwy., Phoenix, AZ 85008

Praiseworthy, Foundation for Historic Christ Church, P.O. Box 24, Irvington, VA 22480

Project Open Hand Cookbook, Project Open Hand Atlanta, 176 Ottley Dr., NE, Atlanta, GA 30324

Quad City Cookin', Queen of Heaven Circle of OLV Ladies Council, 4105 N. Division, Davenport, IA 52806

A Recipe Runs Through It, Sula Country Life Club, 1969 E. Fork Rd., Sula, MT 59871

Recipes & Remembrances, Frank P. Tillman Elementary PTO, 230 Quan Ave., Kirkwood, MO 63122

Recipes & Remembrances, Women of Opportunity Presbyterian Church, N. 202 Pines Rd., Spokane, WA 99206

Recipes from Our Home to Yours, Hospice of North Central Florida, 4200 N.W. 90th Blvd., Gainesville, FL 32606-3809

Recollections & Recipes, Deer Lake Writers' Workshop, 436 Deer Lake Dr., Nashville, TN 37221-2107

Renaissance of Recipes, Iao Intermediate School Renaissance Ke 'ala hou, 1910 Kaohu St., Wailuku, HI 96793

Rotary Wheel of Recipes, Rotary Club of Cooperstown, New York, 106 Pioneer St., Cooperstown, NY 13326

Sampler Cookbook, Clarence Log Cabin Quilters, 4895 Kraus Rd., Clarence, NY 14031

Savoring Cape Cod, Massachusetts Audubon Society/Wellfleet Bay Wildlife Sanctuary, P.O. Box 236, 291 State Hwy. Rte. 6, South Wellfleet, MA 02663

Savoring San Diego: An Evolving Regional Cuisine, University of California, San Diego Medical Center Auxiliary, UCSD Medical Center Auxiliary, 200 W. Arbor Dr., #8982, San Diego, CA 92103-8982

Savour St. Louis, Barnes-Jewish Hospital Auxiliary Plaza Chapter, One Barnes-Jewish Hospital Plaza, St. Louis, MO 63110

Seasoned with Love, United Methodist Women of United Methodist Church of Sepulveda, 15435 Rayen St., North Hills, CA 91343-5119

Seasonings Change, Ohio State University Women's Club, 3894 Chevington Rd., Columbus, OH 43220-4719

Seasoning the Fox Valley, Public Action to Deliver Shelter Ministry at Hesed House, 659 River St., Aurora, IL 60506

Second Helpings, Deerfoot Community Bible Church, 5245 Old Springville Rd., Pinson, AL 35126

Shalom on the Range, Shalom Park, 14800 E. Belleview Dr., Aurora, CO 80015

Shared Treasures, First Baptist Church, 201 St. John, Monroe, LA 71201

Sharing Tasteful Memories, L.A.C.E. (Ladies Aspiring to Christian Excellence) of First Church of the Nazarene, 2601 H.G. Mosley Blvd., Longview, TX 75605

Simply Cape Cod, Sandwich Junior Women's Club, P.O. Box 757, Sandwich, MA 02563

A Slice of Paradise, Junior League of The Palm Beaches, 470 Columbia Dr., Bldg. F, West Palm Beach, FL 33409

Somethin' to Smile About, St. Martin, Iberia, Lafayette Community Action Agency, 501 St. John St., Lafayette, LA 70501

Southern Settings, Decatur General Foundation, 1201 7th St., SE, Decatur, AL 35601

Souvenirs of Mount Dora, Florida, GFWC Mount Dora Area Junior Woman's Club, P.O. Box 362, Mount Dora, FL 32756

Special Selections of Ocala, Ocala Royal Dames for Cancer Research, Inc., P.O. Box 6163, Ocala, FL 34478

Specialties of the House, Ronald McDonald House, 333 Westmoreland Dr., Rochester, NY 14620

St. Andrew's Foods for the Multitudes and Smaller Groups, St. Andrew's Episcopal Church, 373 E. Carr Ave., P.O. Box 507, Cripple Creek, CO 80813

St. Ansgar Heritage Cookbook, St. Ansgar Heritage Association, P.O. Box 214, St. Ansgar, IA 50472

Star-Spangled Recipes, American Legion Auxiliary, Department of West Virginia, 109 E. Shaver St., Belmont, OH 43718-0104

Stepping Back to Old Butler, Butler Ruritan Club, P.O. Box 217, Butler, TN 37640-0026

Sterling Service, Dothan Service League, 460 W. Main St., Ste. 3, Dothan, AL 36301

Stop and Smell the Rosemary: Recipes and Traditions to Remember, Junior League of Houston, Inc., 1811 Briar Oaks Ln., Houston, TX 77027

Swap Around Recipes, Delmarva Square Dance Federation, 28165 Bishops Ct., Salisbury, MD 21801-0800

Sweet Home Alabama, Junior League of Huntsville, P.O. Box 2797, Huntsville, AL 35804

Take the Tour, St. Paul's Episcopal Church Women, 101 W. Gale St., Edenton, NC 27932

A Taste of Gem Valley Country Living, North Gem Valley Development Corporation, 2002 Lund Rd., Bancroft, ID 83217-0040

A Taste of Greene, Playground Committee, 417 N. 4th St., Greene, IA 50636

A Taste of Leavenworth, Washington State Autumn Leaf Festival Association, 12324 Bergstrasse, Leavenworth, WA 98826

A Taste of the Good Life from the Heart of Tennessee, Saint Thomas Heart Institute, 4220 Harding Rd., Nashville, TN 37205

Taste of the Territory, The Flair and Flavor of Oklahoma, Service League of Bartlesville, c/o Aggie Olivier, 2200 Stonewall Dr., Bartlesville, OK 74006

Tasty Temptations, Our Lady of the Mountains Church, 1425 Yagui St., Sierra Vista, AZ 85635

Texas Sampler, Junior League of Richardson, 1131 Rockingham, Ste. 1121, Richardson, TX 75080

Texas Ties, Junior League of North Harris County, Inc., 5555 Fellowship Ln., Spring, TX 77379

Treasured Recipes, Chaparral Home Extension, 637 Sunny Sands, Chaparral, NM 88021

Treasures of the Great Midwest, Junior League of Wyandotte and Johnson Counties, 509 Armstrong, Kansas City, KS 66101

Tuvia's Tasty Treats, Tuvia School of Temple Menorah, 1101 Camino Real, Redondo Beach, CA 90266

Under the Canopy, GFWC Tallahassee Junior Woman's Club, P.O. Box 944, Tallahassee, FL 32302

United Methodist Church Cookbook, Cairo United Methodist Church Women, 508 W. Medina, Cairo, NE 68824

Vermont Children's Aid Society Cookbook, Vermont Children's Aid Society, 79 Weaver St., Winooski, VT 05404

Waiting to Inhale, Pacific Coast Mothers Club, P.O. Box 1775, Huntington Beach, CA 92647

West Virginia DAR at Work for Our Schools, School Committee, West Virginia State Society
   Daughters of the American Revolution, Rte. 1, Box 710-T, Peterstown, WV 24963
What's Cooking in Our Family?, Temple Beth-El, 70 Orchard Ave., Providence, RI 02906
What's Cooking in York, York Police Explorer Post #393, 41 Main St., York, ME 03909
With Love from the Shepherd's Center of North Little Rock, Shepherd's Center of North Little Rock,
   P.O. Box 1524, North Little Rock, AR 72115
Women Who Can Dish It Out, Junior League of Springfield, Missouri, Inc., 2574 E. Bennett,
   Springfield, MO 65804
Word of Mouth, Friends of the Humane Society of Knox County, Dexter Road Extension, P.O. Box
   1294, Rockland, ME 04841

Community Cookbook Awards

The editors salute the winners of the 1998 Tabasco® Community Cookbook Awards competition
sponsored by the MeIlhenny Company, Avery Island, Louisiana.

- **First Place Winner:** *Out of the Ordinary*, Hingham Historical Society, Hingham, MA
- **Second Place Winner:** *Southern . . . On Occasion*, Junior League of Cobb-Marietta, Inc.,
  Marietta, GA
- **Third Place Winner:** *A Taste of Tradition*, Temple Emanu-El-Kulanu, Providence, RI
- **New England:** *Perennial Palette*, Southborough Gardeners, Southborough, MA
- **Mid-Atlantic:** *International Home Cooking*, United Nations International School Parents'
  Association, New York, NY
- **South:** *'Pon Top Edisto*, Trinity Episcopal Church, Edisto Island, SC
- **Midwest:** *I'll Cook When Pigs Fly*, Junior League of Cincinnati, OH
- **Southwest:** *Savoring the Southwest Again*, Roswell Symphony Guild, Roswell, NM
- **West:** *The Tastes and Tales of Moiliili*, Moiliili Community Center, Honolulu, HI
- **Special Mention:** *Cooking and Memories of Old Bourne*, Bourne Society for Historical
  Preservation, Cataumet, MA
- **Special Mention:** *1860's Foods: Union, Confederate & on the Frontier*, North Collins
  Historical Society, North Collins, NY
- **Walter S. McIlhenny Hall of Fame 1998:** *Cane River Cuisine*, Service League of
  Natchitoches, LA
- **Walter S. McIlhenny Hall of Fame 1998:** *Huntsville Heritage Cookbook*, Junior League of
  Huntsville, AL

For information on the Tabasco Community Cookbook Awards or for an awards entry form send
a self-addressed stamped #10 (legal size) envelope to
   Tabasco Community Cookbook Awards
   % Hunter & Associates, Inc.
   41 Madison Ave.
   New York, NY 10010-2202

For a free booklet about producing a community cookbook send a self-addressed stamped #10
(legal size) envelope to
   Compiling Culinary History
   % Hunter & Associates, Inc.
   41 Madison Ave.
   New York, NY 10010-2202

Index